FROM GAZA TO
JERUSALEM

FROM GAZA TO JERUSALEM

THE CAMPAIGN FOR SOUTHERN PALESTINE 1917

STUART HADAWAY

For Capt. & Mrs. Drakley

Cover illustrations: Front, top: Camoflaged Artillery. (Author's collection) *Front, bottom:* 3rd Cavalry Division Ride out of Beersheba. (Author's collection)

First published 2015
This edition first published 2023

The History Press
97 St George's Place, Cheltenham,
Gloucestershire, GL50 3QB
www.thehistorypress.co.uk

© Stuart Hadaway, 2015, 2023

The right of Stuart Hadaway to be identified as the Author
of this work has been asserted in accordance with the
Copyright, Designs and Patents Act 1988.

British Library Cataloguing in Publication Data.
A catalogue record for this book is available from the British Library.

ISBN 978 1 80399 259 4

Typesetting and origination by The History Press
Printed and bound in Great Britain by TJ Books Limited, Padstow, Cornwall.

MIX
Paper from
responsible sources
FSC® C013056

Trees for LYfe

CONTENTS

NOTE ON NAMES, QUOTES, TERMINOLOGY AND FOOT/END NOTES

This book principally concerns two empires, each of which contained numerous nationalities and ethnic groups. As a rule, I have kept to the terms 'Ottoman' and 'British' to refer to the political entities of the opposing forces. The forces of the British Empire and their allies in Egypt are generally referred to as 'the British', although they also included (among others) Australians, New Zealanders and Indians. Where particular nationalities were the majority of the forces involved, due credit has been given. The Ottoman Army mainly consisted of Turkish troops from Anatolia, although it also included Arab and Bedouin forces. Again, the term 'Ottoman' has been used as a cover-all, with particular sub-contingents credited where appropriate.

A certain amount of liberty has been taken with Arab or Ottoman names, be they places or people. For places, I have largely stuck to the names used at the time (e.g. Constantinople instead of Istanbul, Gaza for 'Azza, and Jerusalem for Yerushalayim) or the most common spelling. Arabic names get recorded in an entertainingly varied number of ways in Western sources, but I have taken the most common and, except in direct quotes, gone with that. For the names of persons, given the difficulties of anglicising Arab or Ottoman words, I have used my own judgement on which is the most acceptable translation.

Generally, I have left all quotes alone, except, in a few places, clarifying the punctuation where it is unclear.

It should also be noted that some of the words used in quotes are very much 'of their time' when it comes to opinions regarding the locals in Egypt or Arabs. These have been left in as reflecting the honest views of those present, even if they are utterly unacceptable today.

I have used both foot notes and end notes. As a rule, foot notes (at the bottom of the page) give additional information that is directly relevant to the matter at hand, but would clog up the text too much, e.g. the units that constituted various columns or forces. Generally I only do this for temporary formations put together for a particular action or campaign, and for the composition of permanent formations I recommend that you consult the Orders of Battles in the Appendices. End notes are mostly references, citing where certain information came from or recommending where you can find out more.

ACKNOWLEDGEMENTS

I would like to thank many people for their help while researching and writing this book. On the home front, I'd particularly like to acknowledge my debt to Nina for her constant support, understanding, advice and patience, and to my parents for their support. A special thank you goes to Marnie for her help on SW duties.

More professionally, as always David Buttery has been a great help, and I'd especially like to thank him for his outstanding map-reading abilities, for riding shotgun for me and for allowing me the use of some of his photographs. My interest in this campaign was first sparked many years ago while working for the Museum of the Worcestershire Soldier (to which I recommend all readers as being well worth a visit), and I'd like to thank Colonel Stamford Cartwright MBE for his (and his regiment's) many kindnesses and support then and since. My bibliography would have been considerably thinner without the help of Ian Rushforth, and the staff of the Prince Consort's Library at Aldershot, and I owe them all my thanks. And, as ever, the staff at the Imperial War Museum have been very helpful.

I owe a great debt to Yakov Kasher for sharing his knowledge of Israel with me, and also to Dr Adam Ackerman on that score.

Special thanks also go to Mohammed Odeh, the CWGC's Head Gardener in Jerusalem for his assistance. *Toda raba* to them all.

For the production of this work, I'd like to thank all of the staff at The History Press, particularly Jo de Vries and Andrew Latimer. I'd also like to thank the Trustees of the QOWH for their permission to reproduce some of the illustrations, and Lee Barton for his technical assistance with scanning.

Map 1: The Eastern Mediterranean Theatre 1914–1918

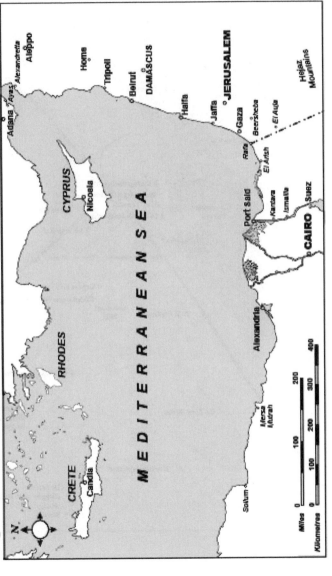

Map 2: Gaza

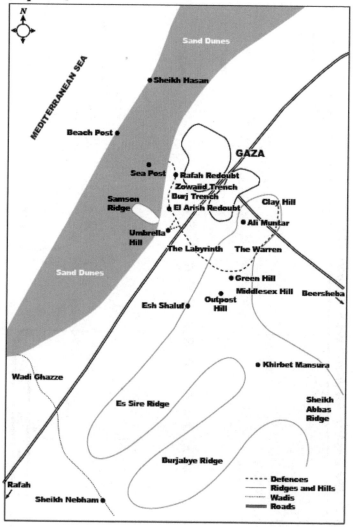

N

MEDITERRANEAN SEA

Sand Dunes

● Sheikh Hasan

Beach Post ●

GAZA

●
Sea Post

● Rafah Redoubt
Zowaiid Trench
Burj Trench
El Arish Redoubt

Samson
Ridge

Clay Hill

● Ali Muntar

Umbrella
Hill

The Labyrinth   The Warren

Sand Dunes

● Green Hill

Middlesex Hill
Outpost
Hill

Beersheba →

Esh Shaluf ●

● Khirbet Mansura

Wadi Ghazze

Sheikh
Abbas
Ridge

Es Sire Ridge

Burjabye Ridge

- - - - - **Defences**
———— **Ridges and Hills**
········· **Wadis**
═════ **Roads**

Rafah →

Sheikh Nebham ●

Map 3: The Western Desert

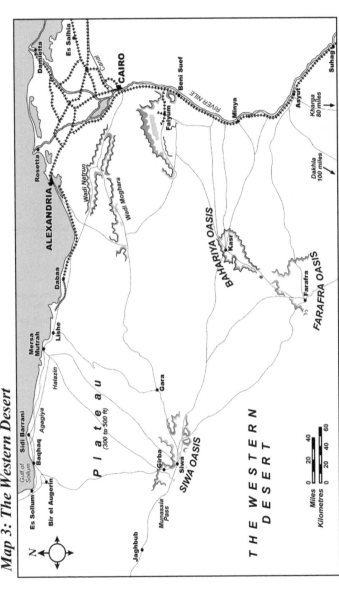

Map 4: Gaza – Beersheba defensive line

Map 5: Jerusalem

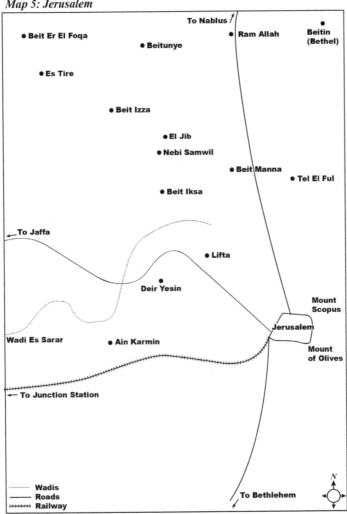

Map 6: Palestine 1917

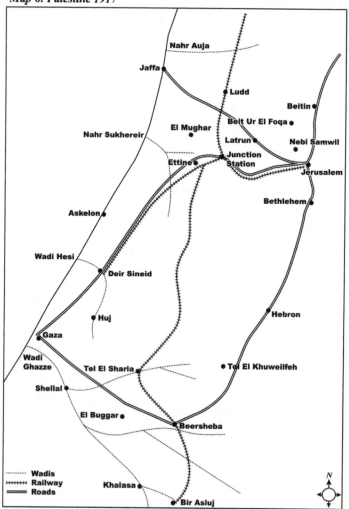

Nahr Auja

Jaffa

Ludd

Beitin

Beit Ur El Foqa

El Mughar

Latrun

Nahr Sukhereir

Nebi Samwil

Ettine

Junction Station

Jerusalem

Bethlehem

Askelon

Wadi Hesi

Deir Sineid

Huj

Hebron

Gaza

Wadi Ghazze

Tel El Sharia

Tel El Khuweilfeh

Shellal

El Buggar

Beersheba

Wadis
Railway
Roads

N

Khalasa

Bir Asluj

PROLOGUE: JERUSALEM, 9 DECEMBER 1917

HUSSEIN BEY AL-HUSSEINI, Mayor of Jerusalem, was not having an easy morning.

In fact, it had been a difficult few years, as the outbreak of the Great War brought many changes to his city, and indeed his own temporary removal from office. Troops had flooded in from across the Ottoman Empire, along with the traders, camp-followers and prostitutes who inevitably arrived to provide for them. Over the ensuing three years more change had come. Political freedoms were suppressed and a culture of fear developed. Food shortages grew, partly due to the needs of the army who simply took what they needed from local farmers and merchants, and partly due to a devastating locust plague in 1915. The army's insatiable need for wood – for building and as fuel for not only their troops but also their railways – exacerbated the problems as orchards and forests were chopped down with little thought for those who depended on them for food or a living. By late 1917 famine was a very real threat. Many starving women, their men away in the army (who barely paid enough for soldiers to supplement their own poor rations up to subsistence levels) or even killed in the fighting, were forced to turn to prostitution to make a living.

The civil population decreased, from around 85,000 to around 55,000. Muslim men were conscripted into the fighting forces, and Christians and Jews were pressed into labour battalions. Thousands more Jews had been evicted from the city, and even the country, by the Ottoman Governor of Greater Syria, Ahmed Djemal Pasha. Soon to be known as The Slaughterman, Djemal ruthlessly suppressed any opposition to the previously largely benign Ottoman Empire, commandeered Christian sites for military use, established a secret police, and hanged dissenters or those suspected of being spies. While the populace suffered, the upper classes (including Husseini) embarked on a hedonistic cycle. They, and their mistresses and other ladies of ill repute, were led by the playboy tyrant Djemal through seemingly endless drunken parties.

The more sober or religious elements of the population worried endlessly about the spiritual and moral well-being of the city, and the seeming breakdown in social order.

For the last few weeks, the situation had become increasingly tense. Starting on 31 October 1917 the British, on their third attempt, had finally broken through the Ottoman front lines in southern Palestine, strung between Gaza and Beersheba. By 24 November the British had reached Nabi Samwil, the mosque that marks the burial place of the Prophet Samuel and which is clearly visible from Jerusalem on the western horizon. An Ottoman counter-attack over the next week was repulsed, while the British paused to rest, bring up supplies and reorganise their lines. When the offensive was restarted on 8 December it was quickly obvious that the Ottoman position in Jerusalem was untenable. The 53rd (Welsh) Division was attacking from the south and south-west, but the main threat came from the 60th (2/2nd London) Division in the west and the 74th (Yeomanry) Division (infantry, despite its name) to the north-west. Both of these latter divisions were positioned to sweep around the north of the city, and cut the Ottoman and German troops in Jerusalem off from the rest of their army. As the fighting again edged nearer the big question was whether, despite the obvious hopelessness of the situation, Jerusalem itself would be defended.

Djemal Pasha had moved his headquarters to Damascus during the summer. He left Jerusalem in the charge of Governor Izzat Bey, although principal military command lay with the German Colonel Franz von Papen, part of Field Marshal Erich von Falkenhayn's Asiakorps. Falkenhayn had been relegated to commanding Germany's contribution to the Palestine campaign after his failure to take the French city of Verdun, and seemed determined not to abandon this city without a fight. The prospect of the war entering the streets of Jerusalem, complete with modern artillery and house-to-house fighting, left Husseini and von Papen deeply concerned.

However, Falkenhayn had already withdrawn his headquarters to Nablus, where he was unable to closely supervise their actions, and they used this loose rein to the fullest extent. On the evening of 8 December, Ottoman and German troops began a steady withdrawal from the city, forming a new defensive line in the mountains to the north. Izzat Bey smashed his communications equipment in the Post Office building, and then borrowed two horses and a carriage from the American Colony and joined the retreat himself in the early hours of 9 December. He was among the last to leave the city itself, although small Ottoman forces remained to the east of the city on the Mount of Olives and Mount Scopus until they were pushed off the next day.

The city was now open for an uncontested occupation by the advancing British, but the problem was how to let them know this before an attack was begun. Izzat Bey had left at 3 a.m., and Husseini and a small party of officials departed the city soon after, heading west. To mark their intentions, they carried a white flag made from a bed sheet borrowed from the ever-obliging American Colony. They intended to find the British advance troops and announce the surrender of the city. It was a simple plan that would prove bizarrely difficult to carry out.

Their first contact with the British Army occurred at around 5 a.m., in the form of Privates Albert Church and R.W.J. Andrews. These two men were cooks from the 2/20th Battalion of the London Regiment, out searching for fresh water, and if possible fresh eggs.

The two privates were offered the surrender of Jerusalem, the Holy City of the world's three great religions, the seat of civilisations, the prize of the great empires for millennia, the dream of the Christian West and the hope of the dispersed Tribes of Israel, the future site of the Day of Judgement, and the principal (for propaganda purposes at least) objective of the current campaign. These two men were offered the chance to succeed where even Richard the Lionheart had failed, 725 years before.

Becoming rather overwhelmed at the prospect, the two cooks made hasty tracks back towards their own lines, leaving the mayor and his party to continue their search.

Shortly before 8 a.m., the wandering Jerusalemites were halted at an outpost of the 2/19th London Regiment, by Sergeants Fred Hurcomb and James Sedgewick. Again, the British soldiers proved unwilling to do anything as major as accepting the surrender of an entire city, although they did agree to have their photographs taken with the mayor. They then pointed Husseini and his party towards the rear.

Next, just before 9 a.m., the now surely exasperated party encountered Majors W. Beck and F.R. Barry of the 60th Division artillery staff, out making a reconnaissance, who yet again refused the surrender but promised to inform their headquarters. Minutes after the two majors departed to do so, Lieutenant Colonel H. Bayley (commanding officer of the 303rd Brigade, Royal Field Artillery) appeared on the scene with some of his officers. He at last agreed to escort the mayor to higher authority. At the same time he despatched Major E.M.D.H. Cooke, with an orderly and an Arab policemen, to the city to take possession of the Post Office.

Bayley passed Husseini on to Brigadier General C.F. Watson, commander of 180th Brigade, at around 11 a.m. Watson sent word to army headquarters, and at noon Major General John Shea, commanding officer of 60th Division, arrived with authority from the commander of the British forces, General Sir Edmund Allenby, to accept the surrender.

On the fifth attempt, Husseini had finally managed to surrender his city.

The 'liberation' of the city was even less of a thunderclap than the surrender had been. In the city, Major Cooke had been greeted by ecstatic crowds, whom he forced his way through to find the Post Office, an important hub of communications in the city. While standing outside, a party of over fifty Ottoman troops marched past in good order, heading north to join their own forces and completely ignoring the British officer and his two companions. Others paid much more attention, and over the two hours he stood there 'he suffered from the attentions, more especially of the female portion, of the thankful and rejoicing crowd'.[1]

One member of that crowd was an Orthodox Christian Arab, oud-player, sometime civil servant and (briefly) member of the Ottoman Navy named Wasif Jawhariyyeh. He would later turn against the British as a 'curse on our dear country', but for now he and his family and community celebrated the:

> British occupation that freed the Arab people from the despotic Turks. We were all nurturing great hopes for a better future, particularly after what we had been through – the miseries of war, famine, disease, epidemics, and typhus that spread throughout the country, and we thank the Lord who saved all our young men from the damned military service.[2]

> As for me (age twenty), I was dancing in the streets with
> my friends and raising toasts to Britain and the occupation
> … for the joy and ecstasy of victory that we felt had been
> extreme, and we had drunk excessively as we celebrated.[3]

In the late morning, General Watson and Colonel Bayley arrived
to assess the situation, bringing reinforcements in the form of
an artillery sergeant and six gunners. A short while afterwards,
a mounted patrol from the 2nd County of London Yeomanry
(Westminster Dragoons) nosed their way into the city from the
south; they were scouting for the 53rd (Welsh) Division, which
had just occupied Bethlehem, a few miles away. Next in the
drip of units was an infantry company from the 2/17th London
Regiment. There were now sufficient numbers to detail men
also to guard the Jaffa Gate and some of the hospitals in the city.

At noon General Shea appeared to announce that the surrender
had been accepted, to much rejoicing among the crowds who had
gathered to watch the trickle of British units enter the city. This
trickle now sped up a little, the 2/18th (London Irish) Battalion of
the London Regiment marching in, followed by the 301st Brigade,
Royal Field Artillery. Further guards could now be placed on the
gates of the city and the important points within, including the
various religious sites and shrines. Islamic sites were guarded by
Christian troops for only as long as it took to bring Muslim Indian
units up from the rest of the army. Dusk brought the more glam-
orous appearance of the 10th Regiment Australian Light Horse,
arriving en masse with the emu-feather plumes in their hats toss-
ing as they rode. They had been detached from their own division
weeks ago and kept in the Judean Mountains close to the front just
so as to be on hand and represent Australia on this day. Although
the symbolism and impact of the moment was not lost on the
Australians, so late in the day other matters all came to mind:

> It seemed we had some difficulty in finding a place to stop for
> the night, but eventually the Turkish Cavalry barracks were

taken over. We were still wet and cold, but were able to get a
hot cup of tea with a tin of bully beef and biscuits.[4]

As the city of Jerusalem was secured within, so were the exterior
threats pushed back. Having taken Bethlehem, the 53rd (Welsh)
Division turned to the north. The 60th (2/2nd London)
Division swept either side of the city, and its 181st Brigade
pushed the Ottoman rearguard off the Mount of Olives and
Mount Scopus. The 74th (Yeomanry) Division kept the pressure
on to the north-east, keeping hard on the heels of the retreating
Ottomans. Within a day or two, the front lines had passed safely
into the mountains to the north, and out of artillery range of
the city.

The grand entry into Jerusalem by General Allenby finally
occurred on 11 December; although a somewhat grander event
than the shambling surrender two days before, the entry was
kept muted. In 1898 the German Kaiser, Wilhelm II, had entered
Jerusalem dressed in a white uniform of his own devising, followed by Prussian Hussars carrying medieval-style banners
and Ottoman lancers in full regalia. His full entourage – over
800 people not including his military escorts – and their supporting logistics for his tour of Palestine had needed the
expertise of Thomas Cook's travel company to organise them.
So grand was the cavalcade that a section had to be knocked out
of the city walls, just to the side of the Jaffa Gate, to let them
in. The Kaiser had ridden in splendour and glory. By contrast,
at the urging of General Sir William Robertson, the Chief of
the Imperial General Staff, and the Foreign Office, Allenby dismounted outside the Jaffa Gate and entered through the original
gate on foot.[5] In deliberate contrast to the colourful entourage
of the Crusader-obsessed Wilhelm, Allenby wanted to be seen
as coming in humility and as a liberator rather than a conqueror.

As he entered the city, Allenby was flanked by commanders of
the small French and Italian contingents with his army and followed by some of his senior officers, the political representatives

of his allies, and various staff officers, including a dishevelled Major T.E. Lawrence, freshly returned from Arabia and wearing a uniform made up of whatever items he could borrow. In the square just inside the gate, Allenby was met by a parade of troops drawn from the four home nations, together with Australia, New Zealand, India, France and Italy. Rounding the corner, Allenby and his staff mounted the steps to the gate of the Citadel, to be met by the civil and religious leaders of the city. Husseini formally handed over the keys to the city.* A proclamation was read out announcing British occupation of the city, the implementation of Martial Law, and a promise to protect the livelihoods of the inhabitants and the sanctity of all the holy sites. The same message was then read out in French, Arabic, Hebrew, Greek, Russian and Italian. This task completed, Allenby led his party back through the Jaffa Gate, leaving the city in the hands of Brigadier General William Borton, the new Military Governor and now known to his two cousins, both serving with the EEF, as 'Pontius Pilot II', to assess the population's immediate needs. According to the Official History:

> The whole ceremony was simple and dignified. The onlook-
> ers were obviously content with the turn of events, but there
> was no exuberant enthusiasm. No flags were flown.[6]

The ceremony was of course as much a political and diplomatic event as a military one. Throughout, the British had been keen to avoid any impression of being conquerors, and in the official statements and proclamations great care had been taken to avoid the term 'crusade'.

Even while efforts were made to play it down locally, the shadow of the Crusades fell heavily across this campaign at the time and ever since. Many commentators drew comparisons

---

* At the time of writing, these keys reside in the Museum of the Royal West Kent Regiment in Maidstone. Presumably, the locks have been changed since 1917.

both in Palestine and back in Britain. The press jumped on the idea of Allenby succeeding where Richard the Lionheart had failed, and popular newspapers such as *Punch* had a field day with cartoons on that subject. This was in fact encouraged; Lloyd George had been very conscious of the symbolism of Jerusalem ever since ordering its capture back in the spring. In a year that had seen privations caused by an increasing submarine blockade at home, the withdrawal of Russia from the war, and a continuing litany of bloody failures in France and Belgium, seizing Jerusalem did not just offer a rare victory. To many it was confirmation that God was on their side in this war between the righteous Entente powers, who had entered the war to defend against German aggression, and (as they saw it) the barbarous alliance between the German 'Huns' and the Muslim Ottomans.

A question remains as to how much of this 'spirit of the Crusader', or 'spirit of a pilgrim', was felt by the average soldier. Certainly, religious references appear in the letters and diaries of many of the soldiers who fought in Palestine, usually relating to the stories of the places they were passing through. However, much of the crusading imagery doesn't appear until the publication of memoirs and accounts of the campaign in the post-war period. There is a strong argument that it was done because by then it was expected by the public, who had been heavily subjected to such sentiments in the press at home.[7] After all, those same letters and diaries also tend to dwell on the historical sites around them – the paths of pharaohs, Alexander the Great and even Napoleon. If this is to a lesser extent than allusions to biblical tales or the Crusades, it is mostly because there is so much more of the latter to see. However, no one claims that the frequent references to historical events means that the average soldier entered Palestine in the 'spirit of an historian'. Over all, it is perhaps fairer to say that biblical stories in particular form such a strong element in soldiers' letters because they create a familiar framework (for both the soldiers and their families) for their movements and experiences in an otherwise distant, strange and alien land. Or an even more pragmatic answer would be that without such interest, not only the letters home from the army in southern Palestine but also the lives of the soldiers, living as they did in a largely empty desert, would be rather dull.

And, clearly, not everyone felt a great surge of religious feeling. Gunner Thomas Edgerton of the 301st Brigade, Royal Field Artillery, was among the first soldiers to enter the city on the night of 9 December:

> I am afraid not many of us felt like gallant Christian soldiers after wresting Jerusalem from the Infidel after thousands of years. The spirit of the Crusaders was conspicuous by its absence. It was dark when we went through, and teeming down with rain. The fighting had been bitter and many of our friends were no longer with us. What we could see was not very impressive. Narrow streets and the smell none too sweet. The progress that night was very slow and the rain was very cold.[8]

Edgerton was not alone in his feelings. The phrase 'land of milk and honey' appears frequently in letters and memoirs, and is almost always used ironically or sarcastically. The greenery of southern Israel as we see it today is the result of over half a century of careful land reclamation and impressive irrigation technology. In 1917, the harsh gravelly desert stretched all the way up to the foot of the Judean Mountains, interspersed only sparingly with small farms, orchards and settlements that attempted to scratch a living in the arid dust. While water, wildlife and people were more abundant than they had been in the Sinai Desert, this was still a parched and inhospitable land for most of the year. The exception was during the rainy season, over the winter months (roughly November to February). During this time, the land was susceptible to flash-floods, wadis became positively dangerous, and the coastal regions tended to turn into temporary marshland. Worse, especially for the troops now fighting in the high Judean Mountains, it became bitterly cold.

For men who were still equipped and acclimatised for desert warfare, December 1917 was a grim period. The fighting did not end with the fall of Jerusalem. Even as the supply situation became more acute, with convoys struggling to keep up with the army, especially on narrow and muddy mountain tracks, several small operations were mounted to push the Ottoman forces back further from Jerusalem. An Ottoman counter-attack towards the city followed in the last days of the month, although it was successfully stopped and thrown back, before both sides fell into exhausted inactivity. Meanwhile, on the coastal plain to the north-west, a final effort was made to push the Ottoman forces further north to secure the port of Jaffa as a new supply base for the British. Strategically speaking, this port was the real prize of the offensive. Although steeped in cultural and religious significance, Jerusalem had very little military importance; it was the shortening of the supply lines that was the most valuable achievement.

On 30 December 1917, the arguably most successful British offensive of the war to date finally ran out of steam and came to a halt, having advanced over 80km (50 miles) in two months, killing, wounding or capturing some 28,000 Ottoman troops, and capturing large numbers of guns and amounts of stores. In return, the army had suffered around 5,000 men killed and 18,000 wounded or missing, and tens of thousands of sick. After a very bad start, the 1917 campaign had ended spectacularly.

1

TO THE BORDERS OF
PALESTINE, 1882-1916

AT THE OPENING of 1917, the British Army in Egypt was geographically more or less exactly where it had been at the start of the war: on the far eastern edge of the Sinai Desert, on the border between Egypt and Ottoman-held Palestine. On the outbreak of war in 1914 the British had withdrawn from the border, back to a defensive line based on the Suez Canal, and had spent most of 1916 regaining that lost ground. But if the army was now back in the same physical position, their material and political positions were radically different.

Britain had been sporadically involved in the internal affairs of Egypt for over a hundred years, protecting what was the quickest and most direct route between the home country and India. However, they did not take up permanent residence until the 1870s when Egypt, crippled by international debt, was declared bankrupt. The European Great Powers, including Britain, stepped in and took control of the country's finances. Resentment over this grew in Egypt until a military-led revolt seized control of Egypt in 1881. An Anglo-French fleet assembled to restore control, but the French element subsequently pulled out at the last moment. It was left to Britain to effectively invade Egypt and, by the autumn of 1882, take control of the country.

It was not quite as clear cut as that, however. Although a British Agency, under a Consul-General, controlled all finances, and slowly British procedures and staff crept into most government departments, Egypt technically remained under the rule of the *Khedive*, and a part of the Ottoman Empire. The Ottomans, facing their own internal and external threats and wars over the next thirty years, paid little attention to the problem, although attempts were made to decrease Egypt's boundaries (ones which the British led the way in deflecting, even to the extent of threatening war with Constantinople). Within Egypt opinion was divided about the British presence, and the effects that they had on public and private life at different levels of society.

In 1912 a new British Consul General was appointed, Field Marshal The Right Honourable The Viscount Kitchener, who had served extensively in the country in the 1880s and 1890s, leading campaigns to secure Egyptian control over the Sudan. Kitchener was on leave in England when the crisis of July 1914 broke. Although he attempted to return to Egypt, he was instead appointed Secretary of State for War, and authority in Egypt fell to his senior subordinate, Sir Milne Cheetham.

The outbreak of war in Europe led to two major and interconnected concerns about Egypt. Firstly, how would the Ottomans react, and secondly, how would the Egyptians?

It looked very likely that the Ottoman Empire would ally itself to Germany (and indeed the two had signed a secret treaty on 2 August 1914), and the possibility was that the Ottomans would take action to regain Egypt. This could take the form of a conventional attack, but the most feared option was the use of a religious uprising. The nominal head of the Ottoman Empire was also the *Caliph*, the symbolic head of Islam. Britain was deeply concerned that the *Caliph* would use his position to call for a *jihad*, a holy war, against them and the French. This could not only lead to uprisings in Egypt and the Sudan, but across numerous other African and Asian colonies, and, worst of all, perhaps even India. An equal possibility, although not as feared, would be that the nationalists in Egypt would take advantage of the international crisis to start their own rebellion, with or without outside support. These two fears meant that the Egyptians had to be handled very carefully.

After all Egypt, or at least the canal that ran through it, was a crucial strategic asset for the British and their French partners in the *Entente Cordiale*. Even in peacetime massive amounts of the raw materials that fed the British economy came through the Suez Canal. In wartime these imports would be absolutely vital, and would likely increase dramatically. While cargoes from the Far East could go via South Africa instead (as, indeed, many would from late 1916 due to the submarine threat in the Mediterranean) this would add time delays to each voyage. With shipping tonnage at a premium, the faster a ship could deliver a cargo and steam off to collect another, the better. And of course the cargoes were not just raw materials for the British war machine, but also men for her armies. Particularly in the early months of the war, the tens of thousands of trained troops despatched from India and the recalled British garrisons from around the world would prove crucial in stemming the German advance in France. Later, India, New Zealand and Australia would provide a steady stream of invaluable reinforcements for the Western Front.

Protecting the canal from local or outside threats was paramount, but there was little idea on how to do so. The Foreign Office had considered the issue as recently as 1913, and then effectively given up due to the complexities involved. An outright annexation of the country could spark the feared internal revolt, possibly spreading elsewhere, tying down valuable troops and threatening the canal. On the other hand, the status quo was also unacceptable. Officially, the *Khedive* controlled all matters to do with law and order, and also commerce. The British would not be able to legally do anything to round up spies or saboteurs, or stop the Egyptians trading with Britain's enemies. Technically, although it was unlikely, they would not even be able to stop German or Ottoman shipping, even warships, using the canal. The final conclusion was that the 'man on the spot' would have to make a judgement call when the time came.

When that time did come, the 'men on the spot' were Sir Milne Cheetham and the Egyptian President of the Council of Ministers, Hussein Rushdi Pasha. Thankfully for them the *Khedive*, Abbas Hilmi, who was notoriously anti-British and lost few opportunities to cause them difficulties, was out of the country at the time and staying in Constantinople. Cheetham and Pasha were both able to keep a level head and calm control of the situation. Their final decision was to issue on 5 August 1914, the day after Britain declared war on Germany, a 'document which committed Egypt virtually to a declaration of war against the [British] King's enemies.'[9] In it, several war-time measures were detailed, such as forbidding Egyptian citizens from trading with Britain's enemies or giving them loans. These would realistically have only limited impact on the country while at the same time making it publically clear that they were supporting Britain.

There was a general lack of response to the document. Apart from the usual market fluctuations to be expected when a major war breaks out, there was little response in Egypt. The British held their breath, waiting for the nationalist or Islamic backlash, but it did not come. The Ottomans did not immediately attack, declare a *jihad* or indeed take any action at all, and it was not until three months later that the hiatus was broken. The Ottomans resisted German pressure to join the war for as long as possible, but finally had to relent. On 2 November 1914 Ottoman warships, crewed and commanded by German sailors, and acting under pressure from Germany, bombarded Russian military targets in the Black Sea, and brought the Ottoman Empire into the war.

In Egypt, the open state of war led to a declaration of Martial Law. The British military commander in the country,

Lieutenant General Sir John Maxwell, took charge of all matters pertaining to the defence of Egypt. The immediate results of this included the abandoning of the Sinai Desert as being indefensible with the resources available, and the use of the Royal Navy to sweep German, Austrian and other enemy shipping out of the Suez Canal, in contravention of international law. Indeed, the Royal and French Navies began to impose their control on the whole of the eastern Mediterranean, snapping up enemy merchant vessels, and patrolling (including the innovative use of seaplanes) and raiding the Syrian and Palestinian coasts. On 18 December 1914 the de facto British control of Egypt was formalised by the declaration that the country was now a Protectorate. Again, internal Egyptian response was muted; even the declaration of *jihad* by the *Caliph* in November had failed to cause any mass stirrings. Despite this, the spectre of an Islamic uprising would remain a serious concern for the British authorities throughout the war.

The regular British Army contingent in Egypt was badly needed in France, so alternative arrangements were made. The Egyptian Army was not entirely trusted, and besides was largely tied up in garrisons in the Sudan, so outside assistance was needed. Several divisions of Indian troops passed through the Suez Canal in early September on their own way to France, and the 9th (Sihind) Brigade and 3rd Mountain Artillery Brigade were landed in Egypt to bolster the garrison. By the end of the month British troops began arriving in the form of East Lancashire Division (Territorial Forces), soon to be renumbered as the 42nd (East Lancs) Division. These were part-time soldiers, whose training was not good enough to allow them to face the Germans in Europe. Instead, they came to Egypt to complete their training while also guarding the canal. As they arrived, British regular units departed, leaving just one brigade of fully trained troops to guard the whole of Egypt.

In November more Indian troops arrived, although many were Imperial Service Troops; raised, trained and equipped by local Indian rulers, and below par compared to their regular Indian Army comrades. More reinforcements arrived in early December in the form of the volunteers of the Australian and New Zealand Army Corps (ANZAC). Although great in number and enthusiasm, their training had hardly begun before they had been put on the ships to Egypt. However, although almost all of the forces in Egypt needed significant amounts of training, there were now at least sufficient numbers to create an illusion of safety.

The illusion was tested in early February 1915, when the Ottoman forces in Palestine crossed the Sinai Desert and attacked the Suez Canal defences. Led by the military governor of Greater Syria (the Ottoman province that included Palestine), Djemal Pasha, the Ottoman troops left the garrison town of Beersheba in mid January. Despite taking precautions, such as travelling by routes far inland, they were quickly spotted by British and French seaplanes launched from warships off-shore, and later by Royal Flying Corps aeroplanes operating from Egypt. The first wave of the attack, drawn mostly from the 25th (OT) Infantry Division, with cavalry, artillery and Arab cameliers in support, struck at several points along the canal on the night of 2/3 February. The main attacks fell around Tussum, at the southern end of Lake Timsah, while smaller diversionary attacks were made in the north and south.

The defences of the canal had been built mostly on the western bank, using the canal itself as a physical barrier. The wisdom of this had been questioned, but during this first attack the strategy paid off. Indian troops entrenched behind the canal were able to rake the Ottoman troops as they attempted to cross, while Entente warships on the canal provided heavy artillery support. Despite taking heavy casualties, the Ottomans persevered until the early afternoon of 3 February before Djemal Pasha called a retreat. His second wave, the 10th (OT) Infantry Division was still fresh and unused, but most of the Ottoman boats had been destroyed and the element of surprise was lost.

Leaving small rearguard units behind, the Ottomans withdrew to Beersheba.

It had been a valiant attempt, especially given the chaotic state of Ottoman Army logistics. To bring a force of over 20,000 men across the Sinai Desert had been a creditable feat, and the British were loath to make any kind of pursuit. The Indian troops, bolstered by Egyptian artillery, had held the line well, but they were still the only fully combat ready troops in the country. The Australians, New Zealanders and British Territorials were making great progress in their training, but to commit them against unknown numbers in a desert environment would not have been wise. Equally, not enough pack animals were available to carry the supplies needed for any sizable force to operate in the desert. Although the decision not to pursue the defeated Ottomans would be questioned by many, it was undoubtedly the correct one.

For the rest of 1915, British attention in the eastern Mediterranean was focused on the ill-fated campaign in the Dardanelles. Egypt was stripped of most of its British and ANZAC troops to fight in the campaign as part of the Mediterranean Expeditionary Force (MEF). It also became the base of operations for the MEF, with supplies (including fresh water) being gathered in and despatched from Egypt, along with reinforcement troops. The country also mobilised a massive effort to supply medical care to the wounded and sick pouring out of Gallipoli, of whom the latter were the majority. Apart from army hospitals, state and private hospitals were fully or partly turned over for military use, while others were set up by well-meaning civilians or the Red Cross or Red Crescent Societies. By the end of 1915, there were 18,000 hospital beds being used by the army in Egypt, as well as 17,000 spaces in convalescent homes.

The operations of the MEF left the defences of the Suez Canal once again perilously thin. Thankfully, the campaign in the Dardanelles had a similarly draining effect on the Ottoman forces in the eastern Mediterranean, and no troops could be spared to take advantage of the British weakness on the Sinai front. It was another matter on the other, western border of Egypt, though. Ottoman and German agents encouraged an invasion of the Western Desert by the Senussi, a religious sect based in Libya. For a relatively small outlay in equipment, gold and instructors, the Ottomans and Germans provoked increasing hostility between the Senussi and the Anglo-Egyptian authorities, neither of whom were keen to fight each other. In November 1915 the actions of a German submarine forced the Senussi's hand by passing over to them captured British sailors, and then bombarding the Egyptian Coast Guard station at Sollum. A Senussi invasion of the Western Desert along the Mediterranean coast followed.

The initial British response was to pull back into Egypt while suitable forces were gathered. Few troops could be spared from outside the country, while only a few small garrisons and depots remained in Egypt. A scratch force was thrown together, but fared badly in the first few engagements against the Senussi, who were born and bred desert fighters. Only in late December did the British manage to stop the Senussi advance, and it was not until mid February that they were able to begin recapturing lost ground. By then the campaign in the Dardanelles had been declared a lost cause, and the troops withdrawn to Egypt. The returning troops began to retrain and be re-equipped. They were designated the Imperial Strategic Reserve, and marked as being available for sending anywhere in the world where they may be needed. Some of them were immediately sent against the Senussi, fighting back along the coast to Sollum, and also beginning to evict Senussi garrisons from several of the oases far in land and deep inside the Western Desert. By the end of March 1916 the coastal campaign was over, although minor operations continued in conjunction with Italian forces in Libya. Further south, most of the oases were cleared by the end of 1916, although a large garrison remained at Siwa.

With the drain of the Gallipoli campaign removed, and the threat to the western half of the country dealt with, thoughts again turned to the Sinai Desert. In fact, General Maxwell had been making what preparations he could even while the fighting in the Dardanelles continued. He had updated much of the road and rail network in Egypt, significantly expanding both in the Canal Zone. Should the army wish to advance in any numbers into the Sinai, logistics would be a crucial consideration and the new infrastructure would be invaluable. Likewise a start, albeit a small one, was made in gathering camels as well as herders and Egyptian labourers to support the army. It was not until the spring of 1916 that any serious efforts could be made, though, and first a certain amount of work was needed to get the army's house in order.

During the Dardanelles campaign, the organisation of the army in Egypt had become increasingly fractured and confused, with different organisations having responsibility for different areas of the country, or different functions regardless of area. The situation had reached the state where many senior officers were themselves unclear as to who they answered to, and an effort was made to simplify the command structure. The final upshot of the reorganisations was Maxwell's replacement in March 1916 by Lieutenant General Sir Archibald Murray, former commander of the MEF, and now commander of the newly created Egyptian Expeditionary Force (EEF). Not that the army was in any fit state to go on any expeditions.

Although limited patrols and sweeps were made into the Sinai Desert, where an Ottoman force under the command of the German Colonel Friedrich Freiherr Kress von Kressenstein was active in monitoring and probing the Suez Canal defences, large-scale manoeuvres were still out of the question. To rectify this, the railway network now began to be expanded into the Sinai, stretching out from Kantara towards the cluster of wells and oases at Katia. In April, Kress von Kressenstein led a large Ottoman force against the works at Katia, with the intention of then establishing positions that would directly threaten the Suez Canal. His force surprised the British garrison, and in a stiff fight the three yeomanry cavalry regiments of the 5th Mounted Brigade suffered heavy casualties before being forced to withdraw. The Ottomans had also received a bloody nose, though, and themselves withdrew to await reinforcements. Murray took advantage of the respite to push the railway out further, towards the wells at Romani, along with a pipeline to pump fresh water out to the army in the desert.

At Romani, the British dug in. The exact size of the EEF was still in flux, with its status as the Imperial Strategic Reserve seeing ten of the fourteen infantry divisions withdrawn from Gallipoli being sent elsewhere by June 1916. The four that remained were considered weak, although the army was at least strong in cavalry; principally (in numbers) the Australian Light Horse (ALH), with smaller numbers of British yeomanry units and New Zealand Mounted Rifles (NZMR). The actual troop numbers available was something of a moot point, however, as the available wells, supplemented by supplies brought up on the railway and by the fledgling water pipeline, could only maintain a force of two infantry divisions and the equivalent of two cavalry divisions by July 1916.

In July, the Ottomans began a second, larger attack across the Sinai Desert. They closed with the British forces at Romani in early August 1916. The British enjoyed a slight numerical advantage – about 14,000 men to the Ottomans' 12,000 – although only one of the two British infantry divisions had as yet arrived. The 52nd (Lowland) Division had established well-dug-in positions east of Romani, while the 42nd Division was still moving up, and its first two brigades would only arrive as the battle raged. The British expected the Ottomans to swing to the south of their line, and the Australian and New Zealand (A&NZ) Mounted Division was deployed in that area to intercept and delay the enemy. As part of the plan, the Australians and New Zealanders were not allowed to prepare any defensive positions, so that the Ottomans would not be able to spot the trap they were walking in to. The A&NZ Mounted Division would then retreat slowly in front of the enemy, withdrawing to the north towards Romani. Once the Ottomans were adequately worn down, fresh cavalry and infantry units (from the 42nd Division) would strike their exposed flank and destroy them.

It was in many ways a risky plan, but it is also notable as being one of the few battles in history that has gone almost exactly according to plan. The Ottomans attacked straight into the Light Horse positions south of Romani on the night of 3/4 August. The Australians performed magnificently in fighting over-whelming odds in the dark, while also conducting an orderly and controlled retreat. It was a close-run thing in many places, but the line held, and the following afternoon the counter-attack rolled up the Ottoman line and forced them into a general retreat. This time, a pursuit was mounted, although it met with mixed success. Unacclimatised to desert operations, several infantry brigades were forced to give up their marches after only a few miles, while Ottoman rearguard positions resisted with a stubborn fierceness. While several were overcome by cavalry attacks, more successfully held before retiring in good order in their own time. Still, by September the Ottomans were pinned back against the eastern side of the Sinai Desert.

There followed a short pause as the British caught up with themselves. The railway and pipeline continued to advance, and the units in the Sinai and on the Suez Canal were separated out from the EEF and redesignated as the Eastern Frontier Force, or more commonly simply Eastern Force (EF), under the command of Lieutenant General Sir Charles Dobell. The forces at the sharp end of the advance towards Palestine – the A&NZ Mounted Division, 5th Mounted Brigade, 42nd Division and 52nd Division – were formed into the Desert Column under Lieutenant General Sir Philip Chetwode.

In December the advance was resumed, clearing out the remaining Ottoman garrisons on the Egyptian side of the border.

The town of El Arish, 3.2km (2 miles) inland and on the Wadi El Arish, was captured without resistance on 21 December 1916, giving the British access to water sources in the Wadi and an appropriate area to build a dock, to bring up supplies and men by sea. Two further strongholds had to be taken by force – El Magdhaba on 23 December 1916 and El Magruntein (just outside Rafah) on 9 January 1917. In both cases, strong cavalry forces marched to the sites overnight, surrounded them, and then attacked in the morning. In both cases, the fighting lasted all day and nearly ended in disaster.

While the cavalry were invaluable for operations in this kind of country – able to cover large distances quickly and attack without warning – they had two severe drawbacks that came into play in both attacks. Firstly, cavalry units were weak. By the First World War only the British cavalry still carried swords, and even they, like the Australians and New Zealanders, were actually trained to fight as mounted riflemen rather than cavalry-men. The principal doctrine was that the cavalry would ride into battle, and then dismount and fight on foot. Cavalry regiments were already half the size of the comparable infantry tactical unit, the battalion. On top of this, when they dismounted to fight one in four of the men would lead the horses of the other three to the rear, further weakening their fighting strength. This all meant that although cavalry could have a considerable effect, especially in speed and surprise, they were considerably weaker than infantry in a straight fire-fight. When it came to assault-ing well-dug-in and well-prepared defensive positions like those at El Magdhaba and El Magruntein, at which the Ottomans excelled, they struggled to put sufficient firepower into a small enough area to overwhelm the defences.

The second disadvantage was water. Horses are thirsty crea-tures, and in both battles the need to water the horses within a set time limit was a paramount consideration. Most of the army's horses were already in fairly fragile physical condition from months spent living in the desert with not enough water or fresh fodder. While they could operate for twenty-four or even thirty-six hours without water, this would leave them weak. Much longer than that, and the health problems could become both serious and permanent, and possibly even fatal. An increased sickness or death rate among the horses would greatly decrease the strength and effectiveness of the army's main offensive and scouting arm, with serious repercussions for the continuation of the campaign.

In both of the attacks on the Egyptian border the senior commanders would be preoccupied by this concern. In both cases the commanders would call off the attack in the late afternoon, only to have their orders ignored and a last, desperate charge mounted by one of their subordinate units. In each case the final charges were successful, although it was close both times. The preoccupation with water for the horses would continue to be a major issue in the 1917 campaigns.

While the army was still operating largely in desert conditions, at least the general environment was improving slightly. The temperature had dropped at the end of December, and the cold spell lasted into February. Sergeant Garry Clunie of the Wellington Mounted Rifles wrote home that:

> It seems quite strange to think that in this country where we have always growled about the heat that it should be so cold as it is now. Ever since Christmas it has blew and rained off and on in heavy showers and has been as cold as charity but even so it is far better this way than to have the heat and flies of summer.[10]

Of course, the temperature was purely relative, and seemed cold only to the men who had been in the Sinai over the summer. One officer in the 5th Highland Light Infantry later recorded how:

> It is a curious commentary on the complaints on the cold that we have just voiced, that the men of a new draft reached el

Arish, running with sweat and vowing they had never been
so hot in their lives, in spite of being in shirt sleeves, while the
rest of us wore our tunics, and were hardly even thirsty.[11]

Unlike the endless desert of the Sinai, here there was vegetation
and (relatively) abundant animal life, and landmarks and sights to
brighten 'a life of dreary monotony on a dead land'.[12] Although
still thin and patchy, vegetation grew on the Palestine side of
the border; grass, and even crops of barley, interspersed with
fruit trees and cactus hedges. The change could be a sudden one,
even dramatic. Corporal Victor Godrich of the Queen's Own
Worcestershire Hussars (Yeomanry) (QOWH) found that:

> We all knew by our maps that we were crossing into the Holy
> Land, but we hardly expected such a transformation that
> shortly met our gaze. We had been trekking quietly along for
> some miles and climbed a high ridge. When we topped the
> ridge the view that met us took our breath away.
>
> Down in the valley laid [sic.] a village of white houses sur-
> rounded by thousands of trees in bloom, beyond those miles
> of barley. Everyone was astounded.[13]

While hardly the 'land of milk and honey' promised in the
Bible (and which promise many diarists and letter-writers
alluded to with irony), it was still a salve to the spirits and the
eye, although the lighter, soil-like sand in the coastal regions
had certain drawbacks:

> The effect of this change was immediate, and [even] the least
> poetical and imaginative among us felt a thrill of joy in the
> relief from the desolation of eternal sand … Unfortunately
> the dust storms were even worse here than among the heavier
> sand and the place swarmed with centipedes, scorpions and
> other undesirables. But we were not in the mood to be critical
> when we retired to rest beneath the stars, with the fresh smell

of living flowers in our nostrils, or woke at dawn to hear little crested larks.[14]

There was also a return to having real human contact with settled villages. For some, this reminder of a world outside the small units which had been their isolated homes in the desert for months also served to boost morale. For them, it was 'a real pleasure to see human beings living their ordinary lives, catching fish and watering crops in unmilitary and restful unconcern.'[15] For others, the interaction with the local population was less pleasant. A few days after the army occupied Khan Yunis, Brigadier General Sir Guy Dawnay, Dobell's Chief of Staff, visited the village to inspect the two important wells, and assess the level of damage done to them by the retreating Ottomans. He had mixed feelings about the village itself, admiring the remains of a fourteenth-century Caravansary (fortified resting stop for caravans, often mistaken in letters and journals for a Crusader castle), but being less than impressed with the main village:

> Nearby [was] the shopping quarter of town; two or three narrow streets, only a few score yards long with open mud-brick 'shops', like small boxes lying open on their ends. The wares seemed to be mainly agricultural; vegetables, oranges (fine Jaffa ones), eggs, poultry, lambs; and odds-and-ends shops (common to villages in all countries); and the local industries, such as the blacksmith. The streets were full of men; Syrians with faces like Christ; Arabs; Jews; mongrels who might have been part Greek, part Egyptian; black Nubians. A few shrouded women, faces concealed by their cloaks; and numbers of children. All very dirty, but showing no signs of want particularly. The whole place full of atrocious smells![16]

Dawnay also visited the sites of the actions at El Magdhaba and El Magruntein, to inspect the Ottoman defences. At El

Magruntein he found 'a splendidly selected position on a small
rise in a gently rolling, grassy plain; absolute "glacis" slopes all
round – not a mouse could move up to attack it without being
seen from ever so far.' At El Magdhaba, the Ottoman 'works
around the place were the most cunningly sited I have ever seen.
You can't see them at all till you absolutely walk into them. Our
artillery could never pick them up.'[17] Unfortunately, neither he
nor any of the other senior staff seem to have drawn any lasting conclusions from these examples of Ottoman excellence at
building prepared defences, with serious consequences later outside Gaza.

2

FIRST BATTLE OF GAZA: OPENING MOVES

WITH THE LAST Ottoman garrisons on the Egyptian side of the border captured, the question remained as to what the objectives of the 1917 campaigns would actually be. On the Palestine side of the border were now two large garrison towns – Gaza and Beersheba – and various small forces in between. Any advance into Palestine would need to go through or past these. Gaza stood on high ground 3.2km (2 miles) in from the sea about 32km (20 miles) north of the Egyptian border, and dominated the coastal route into Palestine. The word 'Gaza' means 'fortress', and this one had stood since biblical times. Every army that had passed between Egypt and Palestine for thousands of years – pharaohs, Alexander the Great, Saladin, even Napoleon – had all been forced to take the city in order to pass safely. To bypass it would mean cutting deep inland, away from the support afforded by the Royal Navy off the coast, and leaving a significant enemy garrison standing next to the army's supply lines. Beersheba, which also harked back to biblical times as the site of the Wells of Abraham, stood about 40km (25 miles) to the south-east of Gaza. It had good rail connections heading north and south, and would give ready access to the interior of Palestine. Murray also expressed the hope that the seizure of Beersheba would allow direct attacks to be made against the

Hedjaz railway, which ran down into Arabia where a rebellion was breaking out among the tribesmen. As well as encouraging the existing revolt, he also hoped that taking Beersheba would spark a new and similar uprising in Palestine.[18] But getting there would be difficult. It meant a long trek across waterless desert, and would still leave the Gaza garrison to the British rear.

The further actions of the Eastern Force (EF) were not just a tactical decision, but also a strategic one to be taken at the highest of levels. In December 1916 David Lloyd George had become Prime Minister. He was a convinced 'Easterner'; one who believed that the war could not be won by the mass, bloody battles on the Western Front, but instead by attacking Germany's allies further east. However, his senior military commander, the Chief of the Imperial General Staff, General Sir William Robertson, was a firm 'Westerner'; one who believed that the war could only be won by defeating the Germans head-on in France and Belgium. The future of the army in Egypt became the focus of a tug-of-war between the opposing views. While Lloyd George encouraged Murray to advance, Robertson encouraged caution. Murray had asked in mid December 1916 for a further two infantry divisions to be sent to him, to sustain active operations through the winter and spring months. Lloyd George, eager for any victory to buoy up flagging morale at home, was keen, but resources were limited and already offensives were being planned for the spring in Mesopotamia, Macedonia, and across the Western Front. Instead, Robertson reminded Murray that, while he was to maintain the offensive where possible, his core task was to defend Egypt and that, in his view, Murray had more than adequate strength for this already.[19]

In mid January 1917, Murray's request was formally declined. On 11 January Murray was not only informed that any major action in Palestine would have to be suspended until the following winter (although he should continue to make limited local attacks), he was now to relinquish one of his divisions to send to France. Murray chose the 42nd Division, which he considered to be his best, and which began leaving Egypt in February.[20] In partial compensation, Robertson gave permission for a new infantry division to be raised in Egypt, based upon three yeomanry brigades that still not been remounted since their withdrawal from the Dardanelles a year earlier. The 2nd Dismounted Brigade became the 229th Infantry Brigade, the 3rd Dismounted became the 230th Infantry, and the 4th Dismounted the 231st Infantry Brigade. Together, they formed the 74th (Yeomanry) Division, although they remained lacking in artillery and other support troops for a considerable period.[21]

At the same time, the cavalry of the EF was reorganised. The A&NZ Mounted Division, under Major General Harry Chauvel, now consisted of the 1st and 2nd ALH Brigades, the NZMR Brigade and the 22nd Mounted Brigade. The 3rd and 4th ALH Brigades and the 5th and 6th Mounted Brigades now formed a new unit, the Imperial Mounted Division, under the command of Major General Henry Hodgson. This move greatly simplified the command structure of the cavalry, which up to then had included several independent brigades, but it also caused a stir among some of the Australian units, who would have preferred to have been grouped together as a single division.[22]

While these discussions and reorganisations took place, the EF continued to probe the Ottoman positions, and to prepare for further operations. Construction of the railway and pipeline continued, the former reaching Rafah, about 32km (20 miles) south of Gaza, by 21 March, and the latter following shortly behind.[23] Meanwhile, the remaining Ottoman garrisons south of Gaza had been withdrawn. The village of Khan Yunis, which contained important wells, was found to have been abandoned on 28 February and was occupied by the Desert Column. Further east the Ottomans had been developing a significant strongpoint around the wells and springs at Shellal (Besor Park), on the Wadi Ghazze. However, the position was judged too exposed by the Ottomans, who were mindful of the ability of the British cavalry to strike at such isolated garrisons.[24] On

5 March patrols from the Royal Flying Corps reported that the
garrison was being withdrawn, and this too was occupied without resistance.[25]

The Ottoman line now ran from Gaza south-east to Tel Esh
Sharia, where the 16th (OT) Infantry Division was based, and
then on further south-east to Beersheba. Despite the lack of
practical support from London, Murray was determined to press
ahead with localised attacks into Palestine, starting with seizing
Gaza as a gateway into southern Palestine. Moving the army into
position was a drawn-out process. Troops moved mostly at night
and then took cover during the day to be hidden from German
aeroplanes. Although the RFC enjoyed a numerical advantage,
the far fewer aircraft available to the Germans were newer and
of a considerably higher performance, and little could be done
practically to stop them roaming over the British lines at will.

In return, the British took advantage of the small num-
bers of enemy aeroplanes to raid into Ottoman territory. On
20 March 1917 a flight from No. 1 Squadron, Australian Flying
Corps, was detailed to bomb the railway over the Wadi Hesi.
Two bomb-carrying BE2cs, flown by Captain D.W. Rutherford
and Lieutenant Drummond, were escorted by two Martynside
G.100s, flown by Lieutenant L. Ellis and Lieutenant Frank
McNamara. Although officially escorts, the Martynsides each
had a few bombs on board. On arriving over the target, the two
BE2cs dropped their bombs first, with Lieutenant Ellis following suit. McNamara dropped his last, flying low over a train to
do so. Too low, in fact, as shrapnel from the explosions tore into
his own aircraft, and his right buttock. As he turned for home, he
spotted a BE2c on the ground, and, despite his wound, made the
swift decision to land and pick up the pilot, Captain Rutherford.
He landed successfully, but on take-off his wound began to
tell. As his right leg weakened, the aircraft swung to one side,
hit rough ground and the undercarriage tore off. Rutherford
and McNamara clambered out of the wreckage, and, pausing
only to set fire to the Martynside, ran and hobbled back to the

BE2c. By now, Ottoman cavalrymen were closing in rapidly on the pair, but McNamara scrambled into the cockpit while Rutherford started the engine. With McNamara at the controls, they somehow coaxed the damaged aircraft into the air, even as the Ottoman horsemen raced along beside them. During the 70-mile flight to the nearest British airfield, McNamara could only keep himself conscious by sticking his head out the cockpit into the slipstream, and on landing he collapsed from loss of blood. For his actions, he received the first Victoria Cross of the Palestine campaign.[26]

Meanwhile, the army closed on Gaza. Units had to move by stages dictated by the available water sources, and in numbers that would not over-tax that supply. Under these circumstances, it took six days to move the army into place. By midnight on 25 March 1917 the troops were concentrated at the closest points they could without being discovered by the enemy.

At Deir el Belah, about 13km (8 miles) south-west of Gaza, stood the Desert Column under Chetwode. His two mounted divisions were both reduced to three brigades for the operation – the A&NZ Mounted Division lost the 1st ALH Brigade and the Imperial Mounted Division lost the 4th ALH Brigade. Having also lost the 42nd Division to France, for this battle the 53rd (Welsh) Division, under Major General A.G. Dallas, were attached to his command. The rest of the Eastern Force was spread out around them. The 52nd (Lowland) Division was at Khan Yunis 8km (5 miles) further south-west, as a general reserve. The 54th (East Anglian) Division stood 3.2 km (2 miles) east of the Desert Column at In Seirate, and the Imperial Camel Corps at Abasan el Kebir, 8km (5 miles) south-east of Khan Yunis.[27] Both of these formations would move east for the battle, protecting the army's inland flank.

The Desert Column was to bear the brunt of the fighting. The A&NZ Mounted Division and the Imperial Mounted Division were to cross the Wadi Ghazze to the east, and head north to cast a protective cordon around the city. Their task was two-fold.

Firstly, they were to prevent the garrison of Gaza, judged to be about 2,000 men, from escaping. Throughout the planning for the battle, the overriding assumption by most of the senior officers, based on Ottoman actions over the past eight months in the Sinai and just across the border, was that the garrison would not stand and fight, but would rather withdraw after a token resistance.[28] Murray wanted the garrison of Gaza eliminated from the Ottoman order of battle, and so to prevent any such running, the A&NZ Mounted Division was to cut them off to the north and north-east, and the Imperial Mounted Division to the north-east and east. Their second task would be to prevent Ottoman reinforcements from entering the city from those directions. The Imperial Camel Corps (ICC), acting under the direct command of Dobell instead of under Chetwode, would operate to the south of the Imperial Mounted Division, cutting off the routes to or from Beersheba, and completing the encirclement. The two divisions and the ICC together would amount to some 11,000 men, although only around 6,000 of them would be capable of fighting in the firing line.[29] This was a lower proportion than usual; the mounted troops would have to operate for several days away from their camps and so took large numbers of pack animals along to carry rations, ammunition and small supplies of water. The extra handlers needed to lead these animals would not be able to fight. Crucially, it was not expected that the two divisions of horsemen would be able to find sufficient water to meet their needs during the day, and this assumption placed a clear deadline on the action.[30]

The actual assault on Gaza was to be carried out by 12,000 infantry, mostly of the 53rd (Welsh) Division – the 158th, 159th and 160th Brigades, plus the 161st Brigade attached from 54th Division. Their attack would come at Gaza from the south-east, running along two ridge lines to converge just outside the city.

Along the coast runs a strip of sand dunes, at times several miles wide. In the area directly south-west of Gaza they run to about 3.2km (2 miles) inland, until reaching a low ridge along which the main Rafah–Gaza road runs. This ridge was low enough to have little tactical or strategic significance for the coming battle, although on the seaward side a mixed detachment under Lieutenant Colonel N. Money DSO was placed to cut off any attempts of the Ottomans to escape or counter-attack along the beach.* Just to the east of the main road a higher ridge runs from Khirbet el Sire north to the eastern edge of Gaza. Here, it terminates in a hill topped by a mosque. Known as Ali Muntar, this hill rises about 91m (300ft) over Gaza, and was about 800m (half a mile) from the edge of the city in 1917. Just south of it on the ridge, known as Es Sire Ridge, stands Green Hill. Just to the north of Ali Muntar, but separate from it, stood Clay Hill. Together, the two hills covered the approaches to Ali Muntar, while Ali Muntar dominated Gaza. Although the exact strengths and locations of any defences were not know, it was expected that these would be the crux of the Ottoman positions.

To the east of Es Sire Ridge runs a broad valley, on the other side of which (and parallel to Es Sire Ridge) ran Burjabye Ridge. About 4.8km (3 miles) south-east of Gaza this ridge terminates in a plateau at Khirbet Mansura. This provided a good platform for any artillery supporting an attack on Ali Muntar. To the east of these at the head of another ridge is another plateau, Sheikh Abbas. From this latter position a good view over the surrounding area can be obtained, and it was here that 54th (East Anglian) Division was to stand ready to support either the attacking infantry or the defending cavalry.

For most of their length, the areas along and between the ridges of Es Sire and Burjabye was almost devoid of cover, apart from the frequent, steep-sided and deep but generally narrow nullahs (dried stream beds) that ran down their sides. There was

---

* This consisted of the 2/4th Royal West Kents ('The Dirty Half Hundreds'), the Royal Gloucestershire Hussars, and the 15th Heavy Battery Royal Garrison Artillery.

some crop growth, but this was quickly trampled. Closer to the city, a serious obstacle arose in the shape of cactus hedges. These grew all around the edges of the city, but were particularly dense in the south, just beyond Green Hill in an area known as 'The Labyrinth'. They were used, as they still are today, to mark the boundaries of fields and orchards. They grew to a considerable height, and could be 1.2 to 1.5m (4 or 5ft) thick. They were flexible enough for shell fire to have little serious effect, and the only way for the attackers to get through them would be by hacking at them with bayonets; even then, the soldier was likely to only be faced with another hedge a few metres further on. While slowing down the attackers, these hedges also provided excellent cover and protection for the defenders. The slopes running up to the three key hills, though, were clear of cacti. Indeed, they were almost devoid of any cover at all.

The attack started in the early hours of 26 March. Different units began at different times, depending on how far they had to travel. The 53rd (Welsh) Division began at 1 a.m., despite having already marched 11km (7 miles) earlier in the evening. They now faced another 6.5km (4 miles) to reach the Wadi Ghazze, which they were to cross by 4 a.m. From there, it would be 4.8 more kilometres (3 miles) to Esh Sheluf on Es Sire Ridge and Mansura on Burjabye Ridge, which were to be the start points for the actual assault.[31] The cavalry moved out slightly later.

At 4 a.m., as dawn began to break, a fog started to roll in off the sea. By 5 a.m. it had thickened to a point where visibility was in places just 20m (21yds); difficult conditions for navigating unfamiliar territory that is lacking in landmarks at the best of times. And it was unfamiliar territory. So as to maintain the element of surprise, little reconnaissance had been done of this area, and even less of the defences themselves. The officer commanding 53rd (Welsh) Division had only personally visited the area just north of the wadi, and had not ventured to where the battle itself would be fought.[32] On the eve of the battle he approached the area again with his senior commanders, although only as far as the wadi. While doing so, they made careful notes and recorded compass bearings to enable them to find their way to their crossing points in the dark, but on returning to the divisional camp were told that they would instead follow routes marked by the Royal Engineers. It was now too late for them to familiarise themselves with these in daylight.[33]

Opinion is divided on how much of a problem the fog was. It certainly slowed the progress of some of the units and formations involved, although comparing unit records shows that the fog was patchy and lifted at different times in different places. In particular, the infantry suffered more than the cavalry, and it was the latter's greater experience in riding across unfamiliar country that probably helped here. The level of impediment to the movements of the infantry also varied. Some of the first units to cross the Wadi Ghazze were fine; the 160th Brigade of the 53rd (Welsh) Division were across the Wadi and in position by 5 a.m., before the fog closed in. Behind them, the 158th Brigade found that the tapes the Royal Engineers had laid to mark the path had been removed (by the Australians, they assumed, although this is probably a case of a 'give a dog a bad name', or rather 'a digger an undisciplined reputation'), and were over an hour late in reaching their starting point.[34] Even today, with Gaza and the surrounding area heavily settled, and roads and power-lines criss-crossing the whole area, it is easy to become lost or disorientated without clear sight of landmarks or buildings. While a compass is useful, it does not take too many diversions to avoid nullahs to throw out any hopes of keeping to a straight line.

But it was not so much the delay in getting troops into position, but the delays that the fog caused in allowing the higher command to establish themselves that really caused the problems. Brigades and divisions had problems keeping contact with each other, but perhaps most importantly it blocked the Ottoman positions from sight. The plans for the attack had been left deliberately vague, waiting for close observation of the enemy positions to be carried out at dawn before detailed orders could be drawn up. And, once they had been drawn up, the next problem would be issuing them and establishing proper communications around the battlefield despite the fog.

Communications were the glue that held the army together, carrying information and orders up and down the chain of command, but also allowing effective coordination between units that were fighting side by side, and between the infantry making the attack and the artillery who were supporting them. In 1917, the communications technology available on battlefields was lagging behind the advances in weaponry and tactics. Battlefields now stretched over many kilometres, making it beyond the ability of a single commanding general to monitor the field and issue orders in person. To have any real chance of controlling his forces, a divisional or corps commander had to stand well back from the battlefield (something for which First World War commanders are often unfairly criticised) and rely on a communications network to bring reports in and send orders out. These commanders and their HQs had to be static, too; the commander had to stay where his subordinates, and indeed superiors, could find him, without them wasting time and effort searching the battlefield for their errant general. When General Dallas went forward to reconnoitre soon after dawn, Chetwode found himself unable to contact one of his senior commanders for a considerable period, much to his frustration.[35]

Wireless and telephone sets were available, but they were cumbersome, unreliable and fragile. In the case of the 1st Battle of Gaza, it was additionally found that the Ottoman wireless equipment in Gaza put out a signal strong enough to swamp the British transmissions, making their wireless sets useless.[36] Telephones were more reliable, as long as the wires were not cut by a shell or a wheel passing over them. They were used not only between units and headquarters, but also between artillery batteries and their forward observers. However, shortages of cable made themselves felt, especially as batteries changed position and had to lay extra lines to the new site, or as the infantry advanced. Many of the observers found themselves having increasing difficulties in staying in touch with the guns they were supposed to be directing, with the result that the infantry did not get the support they needed.[37]

Apart from these dubious electronic means, all other communications methods available relied upon the ability to see. Scouts (mostly the cavalry), runners and staff officers were still a major part of this system, seeing the situation for themselves and then reporting their findings to HQ. This limited the speed of information to that of a horse or motorcycle. Aeroplanes could provide information a little quicker, but even they had to travel over distance, and then either drop messages or land to pass information across. By far the fastest way to send information or orders was through semaphore (flags) or heliographs (mirrors). For these to work, messages had to be short, in code (in case the enemy also saw them), and, most importantly, visible. In thick fog, the communications of an army were extremely limited. When, as in the first attack on Gaza, insufficient reconnaissance had been carried out, and the plans for each unit had been left relatively vague until proper stock of the enemy positions could be taken, the lack of communications was crippling. It took too much time to gather the information required, and too much time to disseminate it, all hampered by a communications white-out.

Despite the fog, most units managed to find their starting points eventually. The cavalry completed the envelopment of the city and reached the sea to the north by around 10 a.m., and established communications with HQ Desert Column soon after. This had been positioned at In Seriate, along with the HQ of the EF. The co-location of these two headquarters would, rather than improving communications, cause some friction during the battle. Murray, meanwhile, had also come forward, leaving Cairo behind and establishing his HQ at El Arish. Here, he was too far away to actively influence events, but close enough to act as an uncomfortable spectre on the shoulders of his field commanders.

Several small Ottoman patrols or outposts had been encountered and dealt with by the cavalry on their march, although the real prize for the morning fell to the 7th Australian Light Horse:

> When we set out from Magdhaba to cut in between Gaza and Beersheba we rode through a heavy fog and we managed to pass without being observed. A troop of the 7th regiment surrounded a carriage in which a Turkish General was travelling to Gaza. When he was requested to surrender by the sergeant he was highly insulted and stated 'I can only surrender to a gentleman of my own rank'. The sergeant explained in no uncertain words that he would either surrender or be shot. He gave in but only if he was allowed to keep his sword until he could hand it over to someone of his own rank.[38]

The general was the commanding officer of the 53rd (OT) Infantry Division, on its way south from Jaffa to reinforce Gaza. The officer would spend much of the day in complaining about his treatment, or about his escort which had fled at the first sight of the Light Horseman, but he was still a significant intelligence coup.

Elsewhere, an equally surprising, although perhaps less valuable, encounter was made by the QOWH:

> Major Ffrench-Blake with 'A' Squadron moved towards Sharia. On his way he surprised an enemy camp, strictly speaking a de-lousing station, when some 60 prisoners were gathered in without clothes, or a shot fired. It is only in Mr. Kipling's story that men are found courageous enough to fight mother-naked. Breeches and bravery have a strange affinity.[39]

It had been hoped that the actual attack on Gaza could begin by 10 a.m., but while the vast majority of units were in position by then, Dallas was not ready. His reconnaissance of the Ottoman positions had had to wait until after the fog began to clear at 8 a.m. By the time he had returned and summoned his senior commanders it was 10.15 a.m., by which time Chetwode was issuing reminders to Dallas regarding the requirement for a sense of urgency.[40] He issued his final orders to the assembled officers at 11 a.m., but it still took the best part of another hour to arrange his troops properly.[41]

His orders were that the 160th Brigade was to attack from Esh Shaluf directly up the Es Sire Ridge to Ali Muntar. On their right flank, 158th Brigade was to swing north-west from Mansura and then north against Ali Muntar. The 159th Brigade would also start from Mansura, following the 158th Brigade north-west before passing behind them and attacking Clay Hill, to the north of Ali Muntar. A single battalion, the 1/7th Cheshire Regiment from the 159th Brigade, would be held back at Mansura as the divisional reserve. The 161st Brigade (with the 271st Brigade Royal Field Artillery (RFA) attached) were on loan from 54th Division, and were supposed to be held at Sheikh Nebhan on the Wadi Ghazze, but earlier had received orders from 54th Division to cross and take up position at the foot of the Burjabye Ridge. The division's artillery, the 265th and 266th Brigades RFA were positioned at Esh Shaluf and on the plateau around Mansura respectively; the division's third artillery brigade, the 267th, was still being used in the defences of the Suez Canal and would be sorely missed. Those artillery batteries that were available only consisted of four of their usual six guns. Even with the support of six heavy 60-pounders from the Royal Garrison Artillery, the amount of guns that could be brought to bear was woefully inadequate for the frontage that was being attacked.

The infantry began to advance at 11.50 a.m., and at noon the guns began to fire despite having little information on the exact location of the enemy positions. Inevitably, a gap soon opened between the 160th and 158th Brigades as they crossed the valley and went around Green Hill on opposite sides. It was the

158th Brigade, in the centre of the line, that reached the enemy
first, or at least, reached a point where it could directly attack the
enemy. All through the advance it had been under artillery fire:

> During the advance the enemy's artillery opened a pretty hot
> shrapnel and high-explosive fire on the brigade; fortunately
> few casualties occurred during that period. This advance was
> carried out perfectly by the troops, and also the wheel facing
> north. Each battalion as it completed its wheel went quickly
> forward towards its objective till the firing-line was held up
> by heavy rifle fire and machine-gun fire about 500 yards from
> the enemy position. I must point out that the 1,500 yards of
> our advance was in full view of the enemy and an absolutely
> open glacis; the battalion nevertheless worked a magnificent
> advance in splendid order, showing the greatest bravery
> and determination.[42]

Now the troops could themselves engage the enemy positions with rifle and machine-gun fire. The 1/5th Royal Welsh
Fusiliers (RWF),* on the left of the brigade line, had reached the
cactus gardens before Green Hill ahead of the rest of the line
and had to pause as the 1/6th and 1/7th RWF came up in support on its right. Fire from Green Hill soon pinned the whole
line down, and also caused casualties among the two flanking
brigades as they passed. The 158th Brigade's reserve, the 1/1st
Herefordshire Regiment, were brought up to directly assault
Green Hill. However, the weight of machine-gun fire from the
hill pushed them off to the right, leaving the gap between the
158th and 160th Brigades still open and the garrison of the hill
free to keep up their fire on all of the attacking columns.

---

* Welch/Welsh: Both the Royal Welsh Fusiliers and the Welsh Regiment traditionally spelled their titles 'Welch'. However, at the time of the First World War,
the official British Army policy was to use the spelling 'Welsh', and so it is used
here. Both regiments had the spelling officially changed to 'Welch' in 1920, as a
token of thanks from the king for their sterling service during the war.

At this point, about 12.40 p.m., General Dallas made redoubled efforts to locate 161st Brigade, which he had originally sent for just before sending in his main attack. However, 54th Division had not informed him of the change in location, and his staff officers could not find it at Sheikh Nebhan. It would not be until after 1 p.m. the brigade would be found, by accident, at the base of Es Sire Ridge, to where they had moved on the brigade commander's initiative.[43] Now orders were issued for the brigade to advance on Green Hill directly, but it would be 3.30 p.m. before they could march to Mansura, and 4 p.m. before they began their attack. Their deployment also meant the deployment of the 271st Brigade RFA, which proved a much needed boost to the division's firepower.

By then, the 160th Brigade had met with limited success on the left of the line. The 2/10th Middlesex Regiment had taken the area known as The Labyrinth at 1.30 p.m., and now overlooked Gaza from the south. However, when the 1/4th Sussex Regiment had attempted to extend to the right, behind Green Hill towards Ali Muntar, they had been repulsed with heavy casualties. In the centre and the right, the 158th and 159th Brigades had slowly forged ahead against Ali Muntar. The 1/7th Cheshires were now sent forward to reinforce their brigade, and not before time as the forward units were suffering heavily. Where the two brigades met, their respective flanking units – 1/5th Welsh Regiment and 1/7th RWF – had made a lodgement on the lower slopes. Both units had taken heavy losses: the 1/5th Welsh had already lost their commanding officer, most of his senior staff, and three of their company commanders, and by the end of the battle both battalions would have lost around a third of their strength – the heaviest casualty rates in the division.

The remains of two companies had managed to work their way painfully slowly up Ali Muntar to about 200m (220yds) from the Ottoman positions. Captain E.W. Walker, with Lieutenants Latham and Horace Fletcher, and about forty men from the 7th RWF, and Captain A.H. Lee and Lieutenant R.H. Taylor with

about the same number of men from the 1/5th Welsh, had found
an area where they were sheltered from direct machine-gun fire,
but both felt that they lacked the numbers to stage a final rush on
the summit. Both sent for reinforcements, only to be told that
their battalions were fully committed and no one was available
to help add weight to their advance. Deciding to attack anyway,
Walker sent word at 2.30 p.m. for the British barrage on the
positions around the summit to be lifted. He waited an hour
for the shelling to stop, but the message did not get through.
Instead, the two captains had to lead their men not only into
the fire of Ottoman machine guns, but also their own artillery.
Captain Lee reported:

> Worn out and heavily laden (besides their packs the men car-
> ried extra rations, a second water bottle, and extra bandoliers
> of ammunition) the prospect of having to rush the entrenched
> and steep slopes was not a pleasant one, but with bayonets
> fixed and revolvers cocked, off we went with a cheer. The
> Turks evacuated their trenches and ran. The top of the hill
> was reached and we rounded up many Turks. Those who ran
> were fired at and some bowled over. On looking round we
> found ourselves behind Turks who were still firing on other
> oncoming troops, and we got some fine firing at their backs,
> until they withdrew. Our party had reached the top, I suppose
> unobserved, at any rate for a while, for we were troubled by
> British shells and rifle fire from converging troops. These trou-
> bles soon ceased, and Colonel Lawrence of the Cheshires came
> along and took command of the situation ... Water shortage
> was serious, and parties were sent off to collect water bottles
> from the dead, and ammunition from the wounded and dead.[44]

By 4 p.m. the hill top was in British hands. The 1/7th Cheshires
arrived in time to consolidate the British hold on Ali Muntar
and man the defences against an Ottoman counter-attack, which
was just as well, as the attacking brigades, who another officer

reckoned had had seven hours' sleep over the past four days, were exhausted from their attack.

With the capture of Ali Muntar, the two flanking hills were over-run, although not without a fight. At around 4.45 p.m., 159th Brigade took Clay Hill, with the assistance of the New Zealand Mounted Rifles. Although effectively cut off, Green Hill held out until assaulted by the 161st Brigade, who advanced down the long slopes of Es Sire Ridge and up the other side under constant Ottoman bombardment.

The infantry would have gone forward in a style that had been tactically advanced in 1914. The Boer War had impressed on the army the need to move in open order when assaulting entrenched positions. Doctrine was to advance in widely spaced lines, which unfortunately now suffer from the stereotypes of the long ranks of soldiers marching slowly into the mouths of machine guns. In fact, the system, although outdated by the standards of the Western Front, was still more or less valid for the terrain faced outside Gaza. The 1/5th Essex Regiment, from 161st Brigade, are a typical example. They advanced on Green Hill in four lines. The first three were made up from C and D Companies, side by side. Two platoons from each company (each of forty to fifty men) made up the first line, followed probably by the headquarters platoons in the second line, and then the remaining two platoons of each in the third. The fourth line was denser, made up of the remaining two companies and the battalion headquarters. With some 3.7km (2.5 miles) to cover, each platoon started off in a tight column four men wide; this was the most efficient way to move large bodies of men quickly over broken ground. With each column were mules carrying the platoon's heavy (in weight but not calibre) Lewis machine guns. As soon as the columns came under long-range rifle fire, the Lewis guns were unloaded and the mules led to the rear. Each column then spread out into four single files to make smaller targets. Once effective rifle range was reached, the columns swung out into a long line, four platoons wide, with each man three paces from the next. This kept the chances of too many men being hit by a single shell or burst of machine-gun fire to a minimum.

As clear sight was made of the enemy positions, a system of leapfrogging would begin. Alternate sections of each platoon would lay down covering fire, to keep the enemy's head down, while the one next to it dashed forward. Throwing themselves into whatever cover was available, that section would then provide covering fire for its partner as it advanced. Should the enemy fire prove too fierce for an advance, following lines would either move up to add their own weight to the covering fire, or possibly would be able to swing out to either side to move around the flank of the enemy position and attack it from there, although the terrain was generally unsuitable for this at Gaza. If the worst came to the worst, these following lines could also provide covering fire while the front lines pulled back.

In this case, the tactics worked, although at a high cost. Green Hill fell to the 161st Brigade at about 5.30 p.m. After a deal of mopping up and digging in across all three hills, the positions, dominating Gaza, were secured by dusk at around 6 p.m.

While the infantry had been attacking from the south-east, the two mounted divisions had not been sitting idle. From midday onwards patrols had been clashing with Ottoman scouts. There were known to be Ottoman garrisons at Jemmame, about 18km (11 miles) east, at Tel esh Sheria, about 24 km (15 miles) to the south-east, and of course at Beersheba, about 40km (25 miles) south-east. The principal fear was the troops from the latter two places could sweep around in the British rear, cutting them off from their supplies. In addition, it was now known from prisoners that at least parts of the 53rd (OT) Infantry Division were moving south, and that the garrison of Gaza itself was nearly twice the size previously thought, around 3,500 men. In fact, several additional infantry battalions, supported by Austrian artillery, had arrived in the city several weeks earlier.[45]

Kress von Kressenstein's contingency plan for an attack on Gaza was exactly what the British feared. While the 3rd (OT)

Infantry Division was to advance from Jemmame against the British troops to the eastern side of Gaza, pushing them back and reinforcing the garrison, the 16th (OT) Infantry Division at Tel esh Sheria and a mixed force of the 27th (OT) Infantry Division with cavalry support at Beersheba were both to advance west towards Khan Yunis, taking the British in the rear. As news of the British advance reached him at 8 a.m., Kress von Kressenstein had immediately put this plan into action, and by mid-morning most of the relief forces were moving. However, all were a long march from Gaza and it would always be close as to whether they could reach the city by dark.[46]

Under normal circumstances, the cavalry could only hope to delay the Ottoman relief columns. Mounted regiments were small – just over 500 men at full strength – and lightly equipped, and could not hope to stop a determined Ottoman infantry attack in such numbers. However, by full use of their mobility, they could both slow down and annoy superior forces in relatively open ground. The 5th Mounted Brigade's experience was probably typical:

> The Brigade occupied a position on the right of the Imperial Mounted Division, technically holding a line between two places with unpronounceable names. As there was nothing whatever to mark the locality of these places on the ground, their situation was determined by compass bearings and speculation. But in no sense of the term was it a line. About mid-day the enemy began to show signs of activity, and columns of infantry from Nejile or Sharia were reported advancing by the patrols. 'A' Squadron [QOWH] came in contact with them soon after 1 p.m., and, for the next four hours, this squadron was engaged upon some very pretty cavalry fighting. The heads of the columns were not met frontally, but they halted mechanically as a brisk fire from a troop broke out on their flank. Slowly the Turks deployed to the threatened flank, only to find the cavalry vanished into

space while fire opened upon them from another troop, this time in their rear. This method of defence adopted by 'A' Squadron, admirably handled by Major Ffrench-Blake, was fluid to the last degree, but it was most effective. Harried this way and that by their mobile opponents and never given the opportunity to indulge in a frontal fire fight, where their numbers would have given them the advantage, the enemy were unable to make any progress, until finally they gave it up and marched sulkily back to Sharia.[47]

The number and size of approaching Ottoman columns increased dramatically as the afternoon wore on. Just as these troops came within close range of Gaza, the defending cavalry were stripped away, and the already thin shell of the piquet line became egg-shell thin. As early as noon Chetwode, becoming frustrated by the delays being experienced by the infantry, had warned Chauvel and Hodgson that he might call on them to send a brigade each against the north of the city, and had ordered reconnaissance in this direction to be made. At 1 p.m., he took the decision (with Dobell's approval) to make an amended version of this plan a reality. He sent orders to Chauvel to take command of both mounted divisions. He was to move the Imperial Mounted Division north, stretching them to take over the area held by the A&NZ Mounted Division, while the ICC Brigade also moved north to take up a little of the slack. The A&NZ Mounted Division was then to be turned inwards to assault the city.[48]

3

FIRST BATTLE OF GAZA: DISASTER

THE ORDER TO send some of his mounted troops into Gaza from the north and east took an hour to reach General Chauvel. Even then, making the proper adjustments in the line took time. Piquets and patrols needed to be called in and each squadron and regiment concentrated. Each unit then needed to remain in position until other troops arrived to take their place. Chauvel moved his headquarters, too, to be in a better location to supervise the movements of both divisions. It was not until 3.15 p.m. that Chauvel could gather his senior commanders to issue his orders, and so it was 4 p.m. before the attack began.[49]

The 2nd ALH Brigade advanced from the north, from the coast down the Gaza–Jebaliye road; the New Zealand Mounted Rifles Brigade advanced from that road across country into the north-east outskirts of the city; and the 22nd Mounted Brigade struck from the east, towards the ridge north of Clay Hill. The 3rd ALH Brigade, from the Imperial Mounted Division, was also given over to the attack, although it was late joining and would soon be called away.

The cavalry advanced fast towards the northern and eastern outskirts of the city. The horses were taken as far as possible, and this additional speed helped take some of the Ottoman defenders by surprise, including a complete field ambulance unit taken captive by the Wellington Mounted Rifles.[50] In most places the ride took them right up to the cactus hedges (often described as like the 'prickly pear' variety) that here, as in the south, marked the boundaries of the intricate clusters of private gardens and allotments that ran in a broad band around the outskirts. These hedges were thinly held by the Ottomans, who took full advantage of the cacti and the physical protection they provided, as well as the limits they placed on visibility. Trooper Ion Idriess of the Australian Light Horse described the fight for the hedgerows:

> The colonel threw up his hand – we reined up our horses with their noses rearing from the pear – we jumped off – all along the hedge from tiny holes were squirting rifle-puffs, in other places the pear was spitting at us as the Turks standing behind simply fired through the juicy leaves. The horse-holders grabbed the horses while each man slashed with his bayonet to cut a hole through those cactus walls. The colonel was firing with his revolver at the juice spots bursting through the leaves … Then came the fiercest individual excitement – man after man tore through the cactus to be met by the bayonets of the Turks … It was just berserk slaughter … The Turkish battalion simply melted away; it was all over in minutes.[51]

On the left flank of Idriess's unit, the New Zealand Mounted Rifles Brigade had a slightly clearer run, although they also faced the fire of two 77mm Krupps field guns. The Wellington Mounted Rifles stormed these, and Sergeant Clunie recorded that:

> We fixed bayonets and got to them and some of them stood up to it too, but they never had a hope. We were too good for them. We got the guns and some of our chaps turned them round, backed them up again. Port sighted them through the

barrel onto a house where a lot of Turks had gone in and then they stuck a shell in and let go and by joves [*sic*] they created some dust. They tore the house down, and burst in another one and what Turks were not killed came out and surrendered. It was good sport. Then we got some more that were in a trench a few yards further on.[52]

While the A&NZ Mounted Division were pressing further into Gaza, the Imperial Mounted Division was feeling the pressure of the Ottoman relief columns. While the changes in position were taking place, the Ottoman column from Jemmame attacked the weakened outposts on Hill 405, about 2.4km (1.5 miles) east of Beit Durdis, reaching the crest at around 5.15 p.m. This gave them a hole in the outer cordon that could be exploited to attack either south or north-west, hitting the other over-extended cavalry piquets in the flanks and rolling them up piecemeal. Thankfully, the Ottomans now paused, seemingly to bring up their artillery. This gave Hodgson the chance to frantically rearrange his defences. The 6th Mounted Brigade were called up, although they were watering their horses which created some delays. Brigadier General Royston brought his 3rd ALH Brigade back from the attack on Gaza to shore up the line to the north-west of Hill 405, while the Nottinghamshire and Berkshire Batteries, Royal Horse Artillery (RHA) also came up. Together, the two brigades and two batteries enfiladed the hill, and stopped any further advance, although the Berkshire Battery was itself badly mauled by Ottoman artillery.[53] While two of his brigades were concentrated on stopping the enemy at Hill 405, contact with his third brigade, the 5th Mounted, to the south had been lost. The protective cordon around Gaza was now crumbling fast.

At nightfall, about 6 p.m., the situation looked grim to Chetwode and Dobell. The infantry had a toe-hold in the south-east of the city, which seemed secure enough, although they would need to be reinforced and resupplied overnight.

The flank of that position was a worry, though, as at present it hung in the air, with a gap of 3–5km (2–3 miles) between the right flank of 53rd Division and the left flank of 54th Division. Some rearrangement would be needed there. To begin that process, Dobell had already (at around 5.40 p.m.) ordered 54th Division to start pulling back from Sheikh Abbas to a line running roughly along the Burjabye Ridge.[54] Their left flank would then lie about a mile north of Mansura, still leaving a gap between the divisions, but it was hoped the 53rd Division would be able to fill this.

The major question was what to do with the cavalry. The Imperial Mounted Division, with a fighting strength of around 3,000 troopers, was facing known columns of enemy infantry and artillery numbering 10,000 or more men (not including the clear indications that the 53rd (OT) Infantry Division was also heading south) spread over a 24km front. Inside the city was the other cavalry division, also spread out over a large area and now facing the prospect of fighting at night in an urban environment. Both divisions were supported by only light artillery and relatively small numbers of machine guns – although a few armoured car companies provided valuable localised weight of fire – and had to be short on ammunition and water. Some water sources had been found and exploited, so that many (but not all) units had watered their horses, but this information was not made clear further up the chain of command. Instead, Dobell and Chetwode were under the impression that none of the horses had been watered since the day before. Understandably, and prudently, they decided not to risk two entire divisions of cavalry in such precarious circumstances, and at 6.10 p.m. Chetwode ordered Chauvel to gather his men and fall back to the Wadi Ghazze.[55]

Chauvel, and his officers and men, were shocked by what they saw as being ordered to withdraw while on the brink of victory. However, Chauvel set about organising his forces. The Imperial Mounted Division was ordered to remain in place, concentrated at Beit Durdis, until the even more scattered A&NZ Mounted Division could be gathered and marched south. This took considerable time and effort, perhaps giving credence to the idea that they were dangerously scattered and strung out. The 7th ALH Regiment, who would have the furthest to ride anyway, being on the coast north of Gaza, had to retreat some 6.5km (4 miles) just to reach their horses.[56] It was not until 2 a.m. on 27 March that the last Australian units passed Beit Durdis, and the withdrawal of the Imperial Mounted Division could begin. The retreat was unopposed, as the various Ottoman forces halted at dusk and dug in for the night, but just before dawn, at 5.30 a.m., the 3rd ALH Brigade was attacked as it crossed the Gaza–Beersheba road. The timely arrival of the 7th Light Car Patrol helped to push the Ottomans back, and covered the extraction of the brigade.[57] By just after dawn, the last of the cavalry had reached the Wadi Ghazze, after some twenty-eight hours of hard marching and fighting.

While the withdrawal of the cavalry went fairly smoothly, the reorganisation of the infantry was nothing short of a fiasco. At about 5.40 p.m., Dobell had ordered the 54th Division to pull back from its flanking position around Sheikh Abbas to a line along the Burjabye Ridge, about 3.2km (2 miles) closer to the 53rd Division.[58] The left end of their line would now sit just north of Mansura, or about 1.5km south of the positions at Green Hill and Ali Muntar. The fighting around those hills was still going on, and the situation was, to use Dobell's own word, 'obscure' as dusk fell.[59] Only later did it become clear that these key positions had fallen. To help secure the new line, at around 7 p.m. Chetwode ordered Dallas to extend his right flank to meet the 54th Division's left, closing a dangerous gap in the line. It was clearly his intention to keep the two infantry divisions in position overnight, ready to resume the offensive the following day. Unfortunately, in a continuation of the communications problems that had been plaguing the army all day, this plan would go horribly wrong.

To begin with, no one had told Dallas, commanding 53rd Division, of the change in position of the 54th Division; although the message should have been copied to his headquarters it does not seem to have been. He assumed that the left flank of that unit was still around 6.5km (4 miles) away at Sheikh Abbas. To close such a large gap, he would have no choice but to pull south, abandoning all of the day's hard-gained ground. He immediately protested the new orders and requested reinforcements to close the gap, but Chetwode remained adamant. Even during the course of what must have been a robust telephone conversation, neither general realised that the other was acting under a misunderstanding.[60] With great reluctance, Dallas ordered his division to begin pulling back.

On the front lines, this decision was naturally met with resentment and disbelief. The bulk of the units in the division had marched most of the night and fought all day, and taken heavy losses to achieve their objectives. Now they were being asked to give up all of their gains. Only with some difficulty was order restored; units had become mixed together, and casualties among officers and non-commissioned officers created problems. Eventually battalions began to re-form and by 10.30 p.m. Dallas's division was beginning to fall back from the captured Ottoman trenches. He informed Chetwode of his actions, even naming Sheikh Abbas as the point to be reached, but still the confusion went unnoticed.[61]

It was not until 11 p.m. that the 'fog of war' began to lift sufficiently from the EF headquarters to allow a proper appreciation of the situation. It was now realised just how successful the 53rd Division had been in terms of achieving its objectives, albeit at great loss. At the same time, radio intercepts were brought to Dobell's attention, showing messages between the German commander in Gaza, Major Tiller, and Kress von Kressenstein. These had been collected through the day by British intelligence section MI1e (Wireless Intelligence) who had access to listening posts in Cyprus and near Cairo (including an aerial on the top of the Great Pyramid at Giza). They were passed to MI1d (Cryptanalysis), who had long since cracked the Ottoman codes. They had then been passed to Murray at Rafah as they were decoded, usually within fifteen minutes of being sent by Tiller, but had somehow failed to be appreciated by the EF or Desert Column.[62] The messages were increasingly pessimistic, even panic-stricken late in the evening, as Tiller saw his defences crumbling and his troops' morale faltering. Had they been available earlier, it is possible that these messages may have encouraged Dobell to take more offensive action, and much has been made of them in this respect. However, it is difficult to see where he could have got fresh troops from at short enough notice to make any serious moves before dusk, or what else could have been done with the resources at his disposal.[63]

Dobell's reaction to the new information coming in was to order Chetwode to tell Dallas to 'dig in on his present line' while also withdrawing his right flank to meet the 54th Division.[64] Chetwode reasoned that these orders were exactly the same as the ones he had already given Dallas, and did not pass them on. Dallas himself, meanwhile, had discovered at 1 a.m. that elements of the 54th Division were much closer to his old right flank then he had suspected, information that was confirmed by a staff officer from that division. Inexplicably, he made no further attempts to find out what the rest of 54th Division's positions or orders were at that time. His 159th Brigade reached their new positions at 3.30 a.m. on 27 March, followed by 160th Brigade at 4 a.m. and 161st Brigade at 5 a.m. Only then did he ascertain the exact location of the division he was supposed to be joining with.[65] It was at this time that Chetwode was informed of the actual position of the two infantry divisions, and that the scale of the mistake became evident.[66]

Chetwode immediately ordered patrols to push forward into the abandoned positions, an order which Dallas passed on. After little or no rest, units from 160th and 161st Brigades began to retrace their steps. They found that the Ottomans had not realised the British mistake, and that the defences were still empty. A company of the 1/7th Essex managed to reoccupy the positions on Ali Muntar and two companies retook Green Hill without resistance. Other battalions were pushed up on either side to complete the line and, as had originally been intended, make contact with the 54th Division. Their reoccupation was just in time, as strong Ottoman patrols began probing the defences just after dawn. These developed into a counter-attack that saw the Essex men pushed off Ali Muntar and parts of Green Hill before rallying and retaking both. However, a second attack at 9.30 a.m., supported by the forces that had attacked the 3rd ALH Brigade at dawn (and which had already taken possession of Sheikh Abbas), proved too much, and the whole of the position along the ridges south-east of Gaza was lost.[67]

In the midst of these movements, the command structure was again changed. At 8 a.m., Dallas was informed that he was now back under the direct control of EF instead of Chauvel. Shortly after the final fall of Ali Muntar, 54th Division was placed under Dallas's command. He was now ordered to shore up a defensive line consisting of both divisions, ready to hold whatever gains were left while the 52nd Division was brought up from the rear.[68]

The infantry were now in a dangerous position. The two divisions were almost parallel in a long, thin triangle with their support units, artillery, reserves, and camel and mule transport squeezed into a narrow wedge between them; indeed, the artillery were virtually back to back.[69] When Ottoman artillery on Sheikh Abbas began to open fire into this dense mass, the situation quickly became dire. Even if the British had managed to maintain their hold on Ali Muntar, without significant reinforcements to push out to the east and retake Sheikh Abbas it is doubtful if the British position could have held.

At 11 a.m., Dallas informed Dobell that his position was untenable. Still, there was little that could be done during the day, as any moves to withdraw would be clearly visible to the

Ottomans, inviting artillery bombardments and even counter-attacks on the thinning and disordered lines. Only in the
late afternoon did the withdrawal begin, with the camels and
wheeled transport threading back down to the Wadi. At dusk
the artillery followed, and then the infantry at 10 p.m. It took
until shortly before dawn for the last British units to reach and
cross the Wadi Ghazze.[70]

The forces involved were exhausted. They had seen almost
non-stop movement and fighting for two full days, and three
nights. During the second day the *khamsin*, the sweltering
hot wind that blows up from central Africa, had made conditions almost unbearable. Physical conditions aside, the fact that
they had (as they perceived it) taken Gaza and then had their
victory snatched from their grasp by the senior staff was crippling to morale. More than 500 men had been killed, nearly
3,000 wounded and over 500 more were still missing, all to
achieve nothing. While Murray's staff would put out figures claiming some 7,000–8,000 Ottoman casualties had been
inflicted, few believed such claims. In truth, the Ottomans had
suffered only 301 men killed, just over 1,000 wounded, and
around 1,000 more missing or captured.[71]

So what had gone so badly wrong for the British? Some mistakes were avoidable, and some were not. Among those that
were not was the fog in the morning, blamed by many of the
senior staff for delays of up to two hours. There is perhaps an
element of exaggeration in this, and there is certainly the fact
that proper reconnaissance and planning would have negated
many of the delays.

The lack of proper planning and reconnaissance was entirely
avoidable, and was probably mostly a symptom of overcon-
fidence. The expectation that the Ottoman forces would not
stand was perhaps understandable, but it also led to a fundamen-
tally flawed mindset in the commanders. Once battle was joined,
these problems were exacerbated exponentially by serious flaws
in the command and communications systems. At almost every

level, communications broke down at some point. Criticism has been made that Dobell and Chetwode withdrew the cavalry because they were concerned about the need to water them, unaware that water had been found by most units. Surely, this was because this important information had not been passed up through the brigade and divisional staffs and back to the main headquarters. Another example was the use of artillery. Inadequate numbers of guns were available to begin with, and these were then ineffectively used. Infantry units had no, or only very slow, ways to call down artillery on specific targets or parts of the Ottoman defences (which had not been properly mapped anyway, due again to reconnaissance failures). And of course, the biggest breakdown of all was the confusion between the 53rd and 54th Divisions on the evening of 26 March.

A major reason for the breakdowns in communication lays with the staff officers at division and higher levels. First World War staff officers are much-maligned figures in the popular imagination, but they were a crucial cog in the machine. Every piece of information coming into a headquarters, every message, every telegram, every hand-scribbled report, had to be read, comprehended and compared. The progress of units could only be recorded by collating all of these scraps of information and then physically plotting them on a map. Every outgoing message had to be drafted in a standard format and using very specific terminology to avoid any possible confusion, and then despatched to the correct recipient. It was hard work requiring concentration and skill, but all of the higher formations at the 1st Battle of Gaza were short of such officers. Dobell, commanding a force larger than the average army corps on the Western Front, had a much smaller staff than such a force required. At his advanced headquarters he had only three trained staff officers, one or two of whom could be absent at any one time as they directly coordinated with Chetwode or other formations.[72] Chetwode, meanwhile, had only the standard staff to control a single division, while attempted to keep track of three divisions spread over a considerable distance. One of those divisions, the 53rd, was apparently so short of staff that Chetwode could not establish any meaningful communications with it for a whole two hours on the morning of 26 March.[73] Given these staffing levels, it is perhaps unsurprising that vital messages (including the intelligence intercepts) were left unread, or that messages like those ordering the 54th Division to retire were not properly forwarded to the other relevant headquarters.

Interestingly, given the number of avoidable mistakes that were made, much debate has focused on one decision that was perfectly justifiable: the withdrawal of the cavalry from the northern parts of Gaza. It was deeply unpopular with the divisions involved, especially the Australians and New Zealanders who, understandably, felt that they had driven in the defenders and were on the brink of victory. However, their position was far from secure. All units were exhausted after a day and a night's hard riding and fighting, and in need of water and ammunition, both of which would be difficult to bring up to the correct positions in the darkness. The outlying cordon encircling Gaza to the north and east and protecting their rear was stretched dangerously thin, and gaps up to several miles wide were beginning to appear in the piquet line. Should large Ottoman reinforcements arrive in the night – and it was known for certain that the 53rd (OT) Infantry Division was advancing from the north, quite apart from the other large bodies that had been seen – this thin egg-shell of cavalrymen would be unable to do more than offer a token resistance and perhaps delay them a little.

Inside the city, the situation had even more potential for disaster. At least the outlying regiments and brigades were mounted, and could spur to safety. Inside the city the cavalrymen were up to several miles from their horses. They were also spread through unfamiliar streets and buildings, with no cohesive defensive plan or effective means of communication between units. They had not been trained for urban warfare, and even today, when the British Army puts considerable effort into such training, street fighting is only approached with great caution. In the jumble of alleys and houses it would have been very easy for the existing Gaza garrison to launch limited counter-attacks in the dark, isolating and overwhelming the horsemen in penny-packets. With the Ottoman reinforcements from the north hitting them from that side as well, the two brigades in the city would have stood little chance.

In the early 1930s a broad review of the various First World War campaigns was held to create what would now be called a 'lessons learned' report. The officer who studied the 1st Battle of Gaza identified many problems, from the slow and unreliable communications, to the confused command structure, and the insistence of the senior commanders to repeatedly throw reinforcements into already failed assaults on Ali Muntar (although these did eventually succeed). 'The [1st] Battle of Gaza', the author noted, 'should become a classic example of a Battle won by troops, but lost by Staff.'[74]

4

SECOND BATTLE OF GAZA

IT IS HARD to see how anyone could represent the 1st Battle of Gaza as a British victory, but somehow General Murray contrived to do so. In his initial brief telegram to London, he announced that he had driven the railway another 24km (15 miles) towards the Wadi Ghazze before becoming 'heavily engaged' with a force of some 20,000 Ottoman troops. No mention of a deliberate attack was made, and indeed it could easily have been assumed that it was the Ottomans who attacked the British line.[75] This was certainly how Sir William Robertson, the Chief of the Imperial General Staff (CIGS), interpreted it, when he reported the 'victory' to the Imperial War Cabinet on 29 March 1917. Great losses were reported to have been inflicted on the enemy, quite apart from a large number of prisoners taken (which admittedly was true), and the CIGS went so far as to say that no pursuit of the defeated enemy was possible due to water shortages.[76]

The War Cabinet, and in particular Prime Minister David Lloyd George, were not content to let it rest at that. After all, unlike Robertson and many of the other senior military commanders, Lloyd George was an 'Easterner'. He was encouraged in this belief by the new government in Russia, which had

come to power in a revolution in early March, and who prom-
ised to press the Ottomans more vigorously on the Caucasian
and Persian front. Closer to Palestine, a few weeks earlier the
British forces in Mesopotamia under General Sir Frederick
Maude had captured Baghdad. This was a severe blow to the
Ottomans; while their empire was large, their population (and
thus army) was relatively small and already struggling to fight in
Mesopotamia, Arabia, southern Palestine, the Balkans and the
Caucasus. The perpetual hope, from the advent of the Gallipoli
campaign in April 1915 until the last weeks of the war, was that
just one more push would cause the 'sick man of Europe' to collapse entirely. Equally, the fall of Baghdad was a clear victory
to trumpet to a British public who were facing a third long year
of bloody stalemate in France and a growing spectre of starvation as the German submarine blockade tightened its grip. Lloyd
George now scented another opportunity. On 31 March the
CIGS wired Murray for more details, which arrived the next
day and were presented to the Cabinet on the day after that.[77] In
this fuller account Murray at least admitted that he had initi-
ated the battle, although he rearranged his objectives for public
consumption. Taking the Wadi Ghazze was now held up as
the primary objective, followed by bringing the Ottomans to
action, and only thirdly seizing Gaza if possible. The account
of the battle continued to be sanitised, with no reference to how
close they had been to taking Gaza, or of the debacle surrounding the withdrawal of the 53rd (Welsh) Division. On hearing of
this apparently successful but deliberately limited action, the
War Cabinet ordered another attempt on Gaza to be made. This
time, the objective was not just to take the city if possible, but to
rout the Ottomans all the way back to Jerusalem, the capture of
which would have a very inspiring effect in Christendom.

General Murray was now neatly hung by his own petard.
Opposite him, the Ottomans had already begun to improve
their positions, not only reinforcing the defences to the south of
Gaza, but also beginning a line of redoubts and strongpoints out

to the east, strung out for about 19km (12 miles) along the Gaza–
Beersheba road. Turning the flank of these would be practically
impossible, given the lack of developed water sources in that
direction. The Ottomans' skill at creating formidable fieldworks
was well known, and it was clear that not only would any future
battle have to be fought in a direct, head-on manner without the
support of flanking movements, but it would also be against a
well-dug-in and prepared enemy. The sweeping attacks of the
first battle would have to be replaced with dogged, Western
Front-style assaults, for which the army was ill-prepared. Such an
attack required substantial artillery support, but the EF had been
short of guns even for the more limited action seen during the
first battle. Due to these shortages the 74th (Yeomanry) Division
would still not be able to take a proper role in the battle, while at
least one of the three infantry divisions that Murray could use,
the 53rd, was now seriously under-strength. At least his cavalry
had been reinforced; A&NZ Mounted Division regained the 1st
ALH Brigade and the 4th ALH Brigade returned to the Imperial
Mounted Division. In all, Dobell had around 35,000 men with
whom to mount his attack.

The artillery shortage was partially solved. The steady
improvement in the supply situation as the railway and water
pipeline were developed meant that the Royal Garrison
Artillery's complement of 60-pounders could be doubled to
twelve guns, while the addition of the 201st Siege Battery added
two 8in and two 6in howitzers. The artillery detachments of the
infantry divisions were also brought further up to strength; each
now had all three of their designated brigades of artillery, but
each of the brigades' three batteries still only had four of their
six guns.[78] Additional firepower was arranged with the French
Navy, into whose area of responsibility the coast of Palestine
fell. The French supplied the coastal defence ship *Requin*, and
allowed the British monitors *M21* and *M31* to take part in bombarding the Gaza defences, as well as arranging for a suitable
flotilla of escorts.[79]

Other attempts were also made to prepare the army for a Western Front-style battle, although as with the artillery, almost all of the efforts fell short. As well as his persistent (and consistently ignored) assertion that advancing into Palestine would require five fully equipped infantry divisions, on 4 April 1917, Murray had listed his demands for equipment and specialist troops in a telegram to the War Office. He requested more heavy artillery, more signallers, more engineers, and more (and more modern) aeroplanes. Although he stated that he was 'anxious not to hurry' over the preparations for the next assault on Gaza, it was clear that the pressure was on. The Cabinet clearly expected early results, while Murray himself wanted to act before the Ottomans could move up too many reinforcements or prepare too many defences. At the same time, the impending approach of summer must also have been a factor. Murray was working desperately to develop wells and cisterns and stock-pile water in the rear areas and in the Wadi Ghazze itself.[80] The onset of summer would only decrease the natural supply while increasing the demand.

Everything in the lead up to the 2nd Battle of Gaza was done in too much of a rush. Murray had ordered Dobell to come up with a plan, which he did on 3 April. A few changes were made over the following week, but the final orders for the operation were issued on 12 April, with an intended start date of 17 April.[81] In that time, all of the deficiencies of the first battle still had to be solved, and the army refocused from open, mobile warfare towards siege operations and trench warfare. It also meant that even if the equipment and men that Murray had requested had just happened to be on hand in the UK (which was unlikely, with the army in France gearing up for their own major offensive at Arras) and was immediately loaded onto ships, it would not have reached the front in time to play any part in the battle.

Some of the modifications were logical enough, and indeed long overdue. On 9 April 1917 General Instructions were issued to the artillery that included orders to mark their maps up in a grid system, as had been used in France since the early days of the war.[82] This reflected the need for pin-point accuracy in directing not only artillery, but the movement of troops. Old directions such as those given by Chetwode to Dawnay in a letter in February that the position in question was 'near the "M" of Magruntein' were simply not good enough.[83] Other efforts to improve artillery cooperation were less logical, and included instructions that each infantry company should carry two canvas screens, measuring 0.9m by 0.6m (3ft by 2ft), painted in their divisional colours. These should be planted behind the leading troops to indicate their position to friendly artillery.[84] The obvious drawback in this scheme – that what the British artillery could see, so could the Ottomans – must have been pointed out by someone (or perhaps many people) closer to the firing line, as two days later a second order was issued requiring the screens to be cut in half and used as flags instead, and stating that they 'will in no case be planted in the ground'.[85]

Great efforts were also made to improve cooperation with artillery and commanders through the use of aircraft. During the first battle, No. 14 Squadron, Royal Flying Corps (RFC) and No. 1 Squadron, Australian Flying Corps (AFC) had only been able to provide twenty-one serviceable aircraft: twelve aged BE2s and nine slightly more modern Martinsyde Elephants. Five of these aircraft were designated for general reconnaissance work under the direction of HQ EF, six for artillery cooperation, and six for general patrol work, with the rest in reserve. They had been spread too thinly, with too many gaps between patrols, and although some valuable reconnaissance work had been done, the artillery and patrol work was far from a success. Their opponents across the lines, *Flieger Abteilung* (FA) 300, had far fewer aircraft but of much newer and better designs. Fresh two-seater Rumpler C.1s (not Halberstadts, as often quoted) had just arrived to reinforce those already at the front, while the Germans also had two or three designated fighters – Fokker E.IIs or Pfalz E.IIs. These were outdated 1915-vintage monoplanes, while the Rumplers were technically reconnaissance aircraft, but all were fast and had forward-firing guns. They easily out-classed the British machines, shooting one down and damaging two more.[86]

After the first battle, more British aircraft were brought forward, and in the intervening weeks they were busy photo-graphing the front to aid in the production of accurate maps, and in an exchange of bombing raids with the Germans on each others airfields. Appeals were made to London for even a small number of the most modern types of fighters to be sent out to help secure air superiority.[87] Such requests came at a bad time, as the RFC in France was preparing for the Battle of Arras. Here too they had been falling behind in the technological race, and all of the newest machines were needed to simply keep pace with the Germans. Through the first quarter of the year, the RFC's losses doubled each month, culminating in what would become known as 'Bloody April', when over 250 aircraft (and over 400 aircrew) would be lost.[88] In Palestine, the best that could be done was to bring up more flights, until they were able to supply seventeen BE2s and eight Martinsydes by 17 April, and twenty BE2s, nine Martinsydes and two Bristol Scouts by 20 April.[89]

The only new weapons that Murray would be able to bring into play were two that were already present in the country, and were ones that in many ways epitomise Western Front battles: tanks, and poison gas. The latter was a particularly cold-blooded decision, and Murray dithered over the issue for a considerable period. Although he had requested 12,000 poison gas shells (and an equal number of 'tear gas' shells) in January 1917, this was at least partly so as to have a stock on hand for retaliation in case the Ottomans used gas.[90] Now, to use poison gas against troops known not to have any protective equipment was a hard deci-sion to make.

The tanks were also already on hand, having been sent out over the winter. It had been decided not to use them for the first battle, as this was expected to be a mobile battle leading to a general pursuit of the enemy, in which the tanks would not have the ability to keep up. None of the eight machines were in their prime. The plan had been to send twelve new tanks, but this was later reduced to eight, all obsolete Mk. Is. Their crews were drawn from E Company, Heavy Branch Machine Gun Corps. They were called forward from their depot (which were briefly known during the First World War as 'tankodromes' before 'tank park' regrettably became the standard term) near Kantara, on the Suez Canal, to Khan Yunis and then Deir el Belah.[91] Little effort appears to have been made to integrate the tanks fully into the plan, or arrange coordinated actions with them. Actions in France had already shown how vulnerable tanks could be to enemy artillery fire, and the necessity of acting in close harmony with supporting infantry and artillery in order to be effective. Other costly lessons had included the need to use tanks in large concentrated groups, with the ideal sub-unit within that being four tanks, as well as the dangers of over-estimating the ability of tanks and assigning them too many objectives. All of these lessons would be completely ignored during the coming battle. Indeed, the 'Special Instructions – Tanks' issued by Eastern Force HQ declared that:

> Tanks must be regarded as entirely accessory to the ordinary methods of attack, i.e., to the advance of infantry in close co-operation with the artillery.
>
> Any modifications or alterations required in the plan of attack when tanks are employed must be such as will not jeopardise the success of the attack in the event of the failure of the tanks.[92]

On the one hand this is perhaps understandable; tanks were new and unfamiliar weapons, of known mechanical frailty and untried in desert combat conditions. It would be terrible for the attack of a brigade or even a division to fall to pieces at a critical juncture simply because a tank had broken down. On the other hand, by not making any allowances for the tanks in the plan at all, they were being almost certainly doomed to failure.

If the rushed preparations and lack of reinforcements did not cause any misgivings among the men of the EEF, an order issued a week before the start of the second battle probably would have. In line with the policy operating in France, each unit would leave a cadre of men behind. They would act as a pool of reinforcements or, ominously, as an experienced core around which to rebuild any units that had taken severe losses. Every infantry battalion was leave either their commanding officer, his second-in-command, or the 'fittest' of the four company commanders behind to lead this cadre. With him would be at least four other 'company officers' (i.e. fighting officers as opposed to supply, signals, etc. officers) including at least one company commander and one second-in-command, as well as two company sergeant majors, the most senior non-commissioned men in each company. Each company would then leave an additional sergeant, corporal and lance corporal, and three privates from each platoon. On top of these, 10 per cent of the specialist troops (i.e. signallers, scouts, machine-gunners) would also be left behind. Apart from surely casting a pessimistic impression on the men, this was also a hefty pro-portion of soldiers to take from what were already mostly under-strength units. Even more importantly, it eliminated some significant sections of the chain of command on the eve of a battle. Just when soldiers would need to see familiar faces, and have a clear idea of whom to report to, listen to and follow, the whole structure of their company and battalion would be changed.[93]

With all of these considerations, it is hard to see the coming action as anything but predestined to fail. Everything was too rushed. There was not enough change where change was needed, and too much where consistency and familiarity would have been most advantageous.

Kress von Kressenstein's forces now manned a formidable line of defences, held by some 49,000 troops, of which about 18,000 were front-line riflemen, supported by machine guns, artillery, and about 1,500 cavalrymen.[94] The 3rd (OT) Infantry Division had come forward from Jemmame to permanent positions at Gaza. The defences south and east of the city, especially around Ali Muntar, had been considerably built up, with new redoubts and trenches built from Es Sire Ridge to the sea, including along Samson Ridge. The confused areas around Ali Muntar, already made complicated and formidable by the cactus hedges, had been improved and fortified, and the codenames for the new trench systems – The Maze, The Warren and The Labyrinth, speak for themselves.

East of Gaza a tight series of trench systems covered the area over which the British cavalry had passed a few weeks before. Known as Beer Trenches, these stretched for several miles to Khan Sihan, where a short gap existed before the line reached Atawine Redount. These positions were garrisoned by the newly arrived 53rd (OT) Infantry Division. They did not form a continuous line but as they were sited along a stretch of high ground they effectively dominated the area before them, as well as the apparently empty gaps in between. At the eastern end, the 16th (OT) Infantry Division held the Hairpin and Hureira Redoubts, and then a small detachment at the far end held Beersheba. Behind the line, the 3rd (OT) Cavalry Division was in reserve at Jemmame, although it was brought up to Tel esh Sheria on the evening of 17 April.[95]

The 2nd Battle of Gaza opened late on 16 April, with the various British divisions moving forward from south of the Wadi Ghazze towards their concentration points to the north. On the far left, 53rd (Welsh) Division (under Brigadier General Mott, after Dallas' resignation) moved forward up the coastal sand dunes between the Gaza–Rafa road and the sea. They advanced until their right met with the 'Eastern Attack' force, formed from 52nd (Lowland) and 54th (East Anglian) Divisions, together under the command of Major General W.E.B. Smith (OC 52nd Division). This had advanced to a line running from Sheikh Abbas on the right, through Mansura and onto Kurd Hill on the Es Sire Ridge. This move had meet with some resistance. The 157th Brigade had to clear Ottoman piquets off El Burjabye Ridge. This had been done by patrols from the brigade every night since 9 April, and so initially the Ottomans read nothing special into the attack.[96] However, once the full brigade became visible in the dawn on Mansura Ridge, artillery fire began to fall among them. To their right, 163rd Brigade of 54th Division faced a stiffer task in clearing the Sheik Abbas Ridge. Although supported by two tanks (one of which was knocked out) some 300 men were lost clearing this area.[97]

On the eastern flank of 'Eastern Attack' was the Desert Column. The Imperial Camel Corps Brigade moved up from Abasan el Kebir to bridge the gap between the infantry and the Imperial Mounted Division, whose first objective was the height at Tel el Jemmi (Tel Gamma). This tel* not only sat on or near the banks of two wadis, but was also an excellent command post. It gave clear views for many miles around, while conversely, in a relatively flat landscape, being a first-class navigation point for messengers or stretcher parties to find quickly. Chetwode lost no time in establishing this as the headquarters of the Desert Column. Further east, the A&NZ Mounted Division gathered at the prolific springs at Shellal. These had been abandoned by the Ottomans in March, leaving behind a machine-gun post dug into the ruins of a Byzantine church overlooking the springs. Underneath the post was found the remarkable sixth-century mosaic that was later taken back to Australia and is now on display in the Hall of Valour in the Australian War Memorial.

By dawn on 17 April most of the initial objectives had been seized. The infantry held a line from Sheikh Abbas to the sea,

---

* A 'tel' is a tall mound created by villages being built on top of each other over the course of thousands of years. Usually fairly small in circumference, they can be very high and steep.

and the Desert Column had taken possession of the two vital water sources on the eastern flank. From Tel el Jemmi, the Imperial Mounted Division had pushed north into touch with the eastern end of the Ottoman defensive line: the Atawine and Hairpin Redoubts. The A&NZ Mounted Division had come into touch with the most easterly enemy position, the Hureira Redoubt, and then swung further south to protect the open desert flank from the Ottoman garrison at Beersheba. Two patrols of the QOWH, from 5th Mounted Brigade, had even crossed between the Hairpin and Hureira Redoubts to cut the telephone and telegraph lines. Two lieutenants, R.M.F. Harvey and Jack Parsons,* each led a five-man patrol out at midnight on a 6-mile ride through enemy lines. Parsons had encountered an Ottoman patrol and made a fighting retreat, while Harvey managed to destroy a lengthy section of line before running into a patrol and making it back to British lines at the gallop.[98] Apart from any annoyance value, this raid also forced the Ottomans to rely on wireless communications, which could be easily intercepted and read by Military Intelligence in Cairo.[99]

The Ottomans also attacked the British lines of communications. Soon after dawn on 19 April, a Rumpler C.1 (serial 2631) flown by Oberleutnants Gerhard Felmy and Richard Falke landed by the railway and pipeline near Bir Selmana. They laid charges on both, and on the telegraph and telephone posts. On detonation, the communications lines came down, but the pipeline was only scratched while the charges on the railway failed to explode. The German pilots retrieved the latter, and, placing them on the pipeline, tried again. This time, a hole was blown in the pipe. The pilots then escaped back to Ottoman lines, taking a piece of the pipeline as a prize.[100]

The rest of 17 April was spent digging in, and at dusk the cavalry withdrew (leaving piquets behind) to their respective bases, where the springs and wadis were being developed to supply

---

* Better known at the time as a Warwickshire County cricketer.

adequate water for the horses. At dawn on 18 April they were again in position close to the enemy, while the infantry continued to dig in along their advanced line. At the same time, stores, ammunition and artillery were brought up. The British and Ottoman artillery kept up sporadic fire throughout the day. By bringing his forces across the Wadi Ghazze and spending the best part of two days setting them up largely within sight of the Ottoman defences, Dobell had of course lost any chance of surprise in his attack. However, it is debatable how much surprise could really be achieved, given the British inability to keep German reconnaissance aircraft from their airspace.

It is also doubtful how much of an advantage mere surprise would have been against the Ottoman defences. As it was, if nothing else Dobell had ensured that his men would not face the long march that had preceded the first battle, and would therefore hopefully go into action on time and relatively fresh. This they did at dawn on 19 April. At 5.30 a.m. the British artillery opened a barrage, supported by the naval guns off-shore. It was a fairly ineffectual affair; with fewer than 150 guns to cover a frontage of 13,700m (15,000yds) and only limited ammunition, the shelling was too light to make any difference.[101] For the first ninety minutes the 4.5in howitzers kept up a steady fire of gas shells – around 2,000 in all, spread across twelve of what were deemed to be the tougher defensive posts or largest artillery positions. As with the main bombardment, the concentration was too low; the gas evaporated or dissipated long before the necessary density could be built up to have any effect, and it seems likely that the Ottomans did not even know that gas had been used.[102]

At 7.15 a.m. the 53rd (Welsh) Division advanced, followed by the Eastern Attack at 7.30 a.m. In both cases, most units had to advance for an average of 1,800m (2,000yds) across ground that was 'perfectly open grass-land, quite smooth and as flat as a lawn';[103] this as the best part of a thirty-minute march at the standard infantry rate of 3mph. Sergeant Thomas Minshall of the 10th King's Shropshire Light Infantry was stirred by the sight of the long lines advancing:

> The air and earth fairly shook, shells of all calibres up to 11 inches, tore slits into the elaborate Turkish defences, the battleships pouring a deadly fire into the forts on the hills around the city, and our comrades commenced to advance about 8.30 a.m. [*sic*]. I saw the men walking across the plain before Gaza, every man a hero, they moved forward with splendid steadiness through a shower of shrapnel and high explosives and owing to the open ground many brave fellows dropped never to rise again as I watched them advance.[104]

Perhaps of crucial importance to his account, Minshall's battalion was part of 74th (Yeomanry) Division, which was kept as a reserve and did not take any part in the advance themselves. Those who did found a less romantic reality: the plain was swept by artillery and machine-gun fire, and the Ottoman defences were virtually untouched by the bombardment. On Eastern Attack's flank, the Imperial Camel Corps Brigade had been attached to 54th Division, while the two mounted divisions were given orders merely to 'demonstrate' in front of the Ottoman lines. This entailed creating enough of a threat that the Ottomans would be compelled to keep their line fully manned, and thus not able to send troops west as reinforcements. The cavalry were also to guard the open flank against any counterattacks from Beersheba.[105]

The 53rd (Welsh) Division had the most successful day of any of the attacking formations. Despite stiff resistance, and with the aid of two tanks (although one broke a track very early on and was of little use) the division took the small Sheikh Ajiln hill on the coast, and the much larger Samson Ridge at around 1 p.m. This ridge ran parallel along the south-western side of Gaza, but separate from the main defences. Once on the ridge, the division did not have the strength to cross the valley and assault the El Arish Redoubt opposite, although the single remaining tank made an attempt. The female* Mk.1, named 'Tiger', ran amok for several hours, at times with Ottoman infantry literally banging on the side trying to get in. Every crew member was wounded, and at one point Lieutenant Dunkerley of the Royal West Kents, on board as a guide, had to take the controls and drive the tank, despite having a wound himself. Eventually, having fired 27,000 rounds of ammunition, the tank withdrew. The division, however, made the sensible decision to dig in with the gains already made and, by early afternoon, their artillery had been diverted to supporting the 52nd Division to their right.[106]

The 52nd (Lowland) Division needed that help very badly. The 155th Brigade managed to gain a foothold on Outpost Hill by about 10 a.m. Their supporting tank tipped over, but a reserve was brought up in its place. An Ottoman counter-attack pushed the Scots back at about 11 a.m., but they managed to rally and take the hill. Unfortunately, Outpost Hill was just that, an outpost in front of the main line. As with the Welsh by the coast, crossing the gap into the main defences proved impossible. By dusk around seventy men under the command of Lieutenant Robert Anderson were all that remained, mostly from the 4th Battalion King's Own Scottish Borderers (KOSB), with a few others from the 5th Battalion KOSB and the 5th Royal Scots Fusiliers. Anderson made the decision to withdraw, ensuring that the wounded were successfully evacuated but paying with his own life. The 4th Battalion suffered six officers and 155 men killed, and only nine officers and fifteen men wounded. The highly unusual ratio (usually more men would be wounded than killed) speaks of the weight of Ottoman fire, making it impossible to recover wounded men or drag them into cover. The 5th KOSB lost even more heavily: twenty-one officers and

---

* Female tanks were armed with four machine guns; male tanks had two machine guns and two 6-pounder guns.

322 men killed or wounded. That night, the battalion mustered at less than company strength. The two other battalions in the brigade – 4th and 5th RSF – suffered a combined casualty total of around 500 men.[107]

Further along the line, the 54th (East Anglian) Division paid much the same cost for even less gain. Two companies of 1/10th London Regiment, from 162nd Brigade, broke through just to the east of Ali Muntar at 8.30 a.m., and advanced north until they actually crossed the Gaza–Beersheba road. However, two battalions of Ottoman infantry counter-attacked and pushed them back. Further east two companies of the 1/5th Norfolk Regiment followed a tank into a redoubt a mile north-west of Khan Sihan. The tank was quickly knocked out by artillery fire, and the supporting battalions –1/4th Norfolks and 1/8th Hampshire Regiment – were pinned down too far back to give any support. Eventually the last battalion in the brigade, 1/5th Suffolk Regiment, was sent forward. Their commanding officer, Lieutenant Colonel F.H.A. Wollaston, found there was nothing that could be done:

Our Brigade's objectives was [*sic*] trenches and a couple of redoubts about 2,000 yards to our front. The 4th and 5th Norfolks commenced the attack with some of the Machine Gun Company following a Tank, this Tank got into one redoubt and did very good work but it was knocked out a few minutes later and the crew came out of it burning. Some men also got into the redoubt and took a few prisoners but could not hold it. The 8th Hants soon went up in support and after that little is known of what happened; the Brigade was spread about in small parties and as far as could be ascertained most of them were either killed or wounded. The Turks seem to have reserved their machine-gun fire for certain places and the troops were caught by this fire from every direction and on coming to these selected spots they were simply mown down. In the afternoon men were seen retiring and we ... were sent forward. Machine-gun fire

from the left enfiladed us practically the whole way and was
as hot as anyone could wish for, but by some marvel hardly
anyone was hit. We arrived at the line where the remains of
the Hampshires were and finding that it would simply be a
case of the Battalion being wiped out like the remainder, we
decided to dig ourselves in where we were (at this place the
bullets just cleared our heads).[108]

By the time the 1/5th Norfolks could be extracted, the three
battalions had suffered 1,500 casualties, including two of
their commanding officers and all twelve company commanders.[109] The Imperial Camel Corps, supported by the 4th ALH
Brigade, managed to push through east of Khan Sihan and seize
a section of the Ottoman line, but only briefly. As elsewhere,
the Ottomans merely withdrew further into their defensive
positions while their artillery plastered the breach, and then
mounted an overwhelming counter-attack. By mid-morning
the British artillery were running short on shells, and were
unable to provide the kind of barrier-barrage that was needed to
protect captured positions, or break up Ottoman attacks.[110]

To the east much of the cavalry became bogged down assaulting Sausage Ridge, which ran south from Hairpin Redoubt
and protruded between the two divisions. The southern end
was taken by the New Zealand Mounted Rifles, but the attack
was held up at the redoubt itself. This was never meant to be
a serious assault; the cavalry divisions were weaker in numbers
and more spread out than the infantry. They lacked the firepower in either artillery or riflemen to put enough pressure on
well-entrenched positions and were only supposed to keep the
Ottomans on that flank from helping their comrades further
west. However, Brigadier General Hodgson, commanding the
Imperial Mounted Division, attacked in earnest, and in so far as
it kept the defenders of Hairpin and Atawine Redoubts in place,
his attacks worked. Indeed, more than worked, as a considerable
Ottoman force gathered and counter-attacked at 2 p.m., forcing

the cavalry to retreat.[111] At about the same time, the 3rd (OT) Cavalry Division under Colonel Essad Bey launched its own counter-attack, looping around the A&NZ Mounted Division's open right flank.

What followed was a confused fight by small units spread over a large area, with both sides considering themselves outnumbered and in a desperate situation. At around 1,500 strong, it was the Ottoman cavalry who were greatly outnumbered in total, but as the British cavalry was so far spread out, locally the Ottomans could enjoy superiority. Rafael de Nogales, a Venezuelan mercenary and adventurer on the staff of the Ottoman division, presented their side of the affair in dramatic tones:

> A mounted aide de camp emerged from a cloud of dust, dashed down in our direction, reined in, saluted and handed Colonel Essad Bey the order to advance. It was tantamount to a sentence of execution, and we all knew it. I glanced swiftly over the faces of those officers; and the look on their bronzed countenances of unmoved control, of utter fearlessness, remains for me one of the most cherished memories of my four years beneath the Crescent.[112]

In fact, although the 1st and 2nd ALH Brigades fell back, covered by the 22nd Mounted Brigade and their own machine-guns sections, which Nogales characterised as 'heroic' and who 'protected his [i.e. the enemy's] retreat with remarkable boldness and sangfroid',[113] no great gains were made and the counter-attack petered out.[114]

While the battle had raged, General Murray had been keeping an eye on affairs from Khan Yunis. Even from this detached position, it was clear by 4 p.m. that no further gains could be made that day, while at the same time word was reaching him from Cairo that Ottoman wireless chatter was indicating a large-scale counter-attack that night or the following morning.[115] In fact, by the time that this latter information reached

Murray, Kress von Kressenstein had already abandoned the idea, but this did not become known until later. In the meantime, Murray ordered Dobell to cease all operations and dig in. All ground taken that day was to be held 'without fail', and, with fresh stocks of ammunition brought up overnight, the attack would resume in the morning.[116] In practical terms this was impossible, and at dusk the few pieces of the Ottoman lines still in the British hands, except Samson Ridge and Sheikh Ajiln in 53rd (Welsh) Division's area, were abandoned. During the night Dobell reported to Murray that, in consultation with Chetwode and his divisional commanders, he was of the belief that any further attacks would be futile. Murray had no choice but to postpone the renewal of the offensive for twenty-four hours, then another, and then altogether.[117]

In truth, the Eastern Force was in no fit state to fight any further, even if 74th (Yeomanry) Division was committed to the firing line. Some 6,444 men had been killed, wounded or were missing. Of the latter – 1,576 men – the Ottomans would only report 272 as prisoners, bringing the total of British killed to around 1,800. The 54th (East Anglian) Division had borne the brunt (2,870), followed by 52nd (Lowland) Division (1,874). By maintaining a relatively sensible stance on Samson Ridge, 53rd (Welsh) Division's casualties were limited to nearly 600 men. The Imperial Mounted Division lost 547, the A&NZ Mounted Division just over 100, and the Imperial Camel Corps Brigade suffered 345 casualties. Ottoman casualties came to just over 2,000, of whom 400 were killed.[118]

The principal reasons for the failure have already been highlighted. Insufficient artillery was a major factor, and symptomatic of the generally rushed and under-resourced nature of the battle. Inexperience in such warfare was also a contributing factor, from the commanding generals underestimating the task ahead, to smaller details such as failure to use the tanks or calculate the use of gas shells properly. In the short term, though, it would be Dobell who paid for the failure.

On 21 April, Sir Charles Dobell was relieved of command of the Eastern Force, and ordered home to the UK; this despite his warnings before the battle that his forces were too weak and the enemy's positions too strong.[119] He was replaced by Lieutenant General Sir Philip Chetwode, who was himself replaced as commander of the Desert Column by Major General Sir Harry Chauvel, who thus became the first Australian to command a corps-sized formation in the British Army. It was left to Chetwode and Chauvel to consolidate the line, rebuild their forces, and make the best they could out of the small gains achieved. Murray, meanwhile, returned to his headquarters in the Savoy Hotel, Cairo.

5

OTTOMAN PALESTINE

THROUGH THE SECOND half of the nineteenth century, a growing
Zionist movement had agitated for a formal return of the Jews
to Palestine, or better yet Palestine to the Jews. By no means
all of the international Jewish community supported such a
move; indeed, their own internal differences and divisions are
as confusing and as contradictory as those of the governments
they lobbied. To take Britain as the most relevant example,
leaders such as Theodor Herzl and Dr Chaim Weizmann had
spent decades lobbying influential politicians or Jewish figures
for the Zionist cause, even while Jewish pillars of the establishment such as the Rothschilds were broadly against it. Opinion
was divided before 1914, but the political machinations became
a positive quagmire after war was declared. The question now
had repercussions on the war with the Ottoman Empire, on
the alliances with Russia and France (and less so, later, Italy
and America), and on the growing relationships with the Arab
nationalists, all of which groups were themselves divided.
The Prime Minister, the War Office, the Foreign Office, the
Treasury and innumerable newspaper editors, financiers, and
lobbying groups all had their own views, and many would

show a disturbing willingness to communicate with the outside interested parties on their own initiative with no coordination inside their own organisations. Policy was decided from a heady mix of idealism, conservatism, and perhaps most of all pragmatism. The only question on which all of these groups in Britain agreed was, that whoever did rule Palestine after the war, it must not be the French.

But the French would get Syria. They had stated their interest in the country very early in the war, which was why the Syrian and Palestine coasts came under the operational control of the French Navy. This was confirmed in the Sykes-Picot Agreement, which had been negotiated between Britain and France over the winter of 1915–16, and formalised in May 1916. Around the same period, a series of agreements were made with Sharif Husein bin Ali, the Emir of Mecca, as part of the campaign to spark a revolt in Arabia. This guaranteed British support for an independent Arab state, although in suitably vague geographical terms to allow Britain leeway later to redefine the parameters of their backing. In November 1917 the Balfour Declaration was added to the mix. This stated, in its entirety, that:

> His Majesty's Government view with favour the establishment in Palestine of a national home for the Jewish people, and will use their best endeavours to facilitate the achievement of this object, it being clearly understood that nothing shall be done which may prejudice the civil and religious rights of existing non-Jewish communities in Palestine, or the rights and political status enjoyed by Jews in any other country.

For the Zionists it fell short of promising a new Jewish nation, and for the Arabs it went too far in assuring Jewish immigration into their lands. It also left unstated but implied that the British intended the rulers of the post-war Palestine to be themselves.

The country was too important as a buffer zone to defend the
Suez Canal and as a route to the oil fields of the Middle East,
apart from any less practical sentimental, religious or cultural
attractions, to leave to anyone else's control.*

But what manner of a country was it that so many people
were vying to rule? For one thing, it was not a country, only a
vaguely defined area within the Ottoman province of Greater
Syria. Palestine in 1917 was a largely empty country, certainly in
comparison to the same area today. Estimates as to the population
vary, partly due to the lack of any systematic censuses, and partly
because Palestine was part of the larger Syrian governmental
area. The best estimates say that perhaps 640,000–650,000 Arabs
lived in Palestine, with around 90,000 Jews.[120] About 75,000 of
the Jews were fairly recent immigrants, mostly from Eastern
Europe and Russia, where violently anti-Jewish attitudes
prevailed.[121] Some of these immigrants had joined existing communities, but others had established their own. Zionist groups
across Europe and America funded new settlements and kib-
butzim; in 1909 one of them, the Jewish National Fund, had
purchased a parcel of land from the Ottomans at Tel Aviv. By
the outbreak of war, some 200 houses stood on the site, with a
population of around 2,000 immigrants.[122]

Then, as indeed now, the question of immigration and settlement was a contentious and emotive issue. Many Arabs were
worried about the levels of Jewish immigration, although that
did not stop some of them from selling land to newcomers.
However, this was just one of several questions over the future
of the country that were being debated in the coffee shops

---

* This is very much the rough guide to the international politics surrounding
Palestine during the First World War, and many complete volumes can (and
have) been written on the subject without fully teasing out all of the machinations and manoeuvring, and their contemporary and modern implications
and results. For more information, the author recommends Norman Rose's *A
Senseless Squalid War*, and Barbara Tuchman's classic *Bible and Sword*.

and drawing rooms of Palestine. Since the rise to power in the Constantinople of the 'Young Turks' a few years before the war, with their pro-Turkish policies, dissatisfaction had increased in the region. The Arabs were feeling increasingly neglected as a political voice, although a majority retained a basic loyalty to the Ottoman Empire. One option was to attempt to negotiate for greater devolved powers while staying within the Ottoman Empire, but there were also strong nationalist elements looking at potentially joining an independent Syria, or even an independent Egypt.[123]

Political activism and debate was quickly driven underground by the arrival of Djemal Pasha as the new governor of Syria and commander of the 4th (OT) Army. He entered Jerusalem on 18 December 1914 and established his headquarters in the Augusta Victoria Hospital, which had been built on Mount Scopus on the orders of Kaiser Wilhelm II as a hospice for German pilgrims just before the war. From here, in his own words, he maintained a 'strong rule', but a fair one. In his memoirs he records that:

> The policy I desired to see pursued in Syria was a policy of clemency and tolerance. I left no stone unturned to create unity of views and sentiments in all the Arab countries.[124]

Elsewhere, he is recorded as having stated his policies to be: 'for Palestine, deportation; for Syria, terrorisation; for the Hedjaz, the army.'[125] His actions seem to bear the latter statement out rather than the former, and would earn him the nickname of 'The Slaughterman'.[126] The war would definitely bring some benefits to Palestine and Jerusalem, including the widespread expansion and improvement of infrastructure such as roads, railways, water supplies, electricity, telephones and the telegraph. It would bring modernisation and Westernisation in those areas, and others too, such as the broader adoption of Western

timekeeping over the traditional Arab and Ottoman methods.* Of less directly military interest, it also led to a greater
demand for news and books, with the number and circulation of
newspapers increasing.[127]

However, these improvements came at a heavy cost. Djemal
Pasha immediately began to crack down on revolutionaries
and dissidents, real or imagined, who he believed to be plotting with the Entente Powers or simply for their own ends. On
30 March 1915, two soldiers were hanged at the Jaffa Gate in
Jerusalem, ostensibly for spying for the British, although simple
desertion was a more likely cause.[128] In August 1915 a wave of
arrests spread across Syria, with those apprehended being put
before military tribunals. Eleven Arab leaders, including politicians and the Mufti of Gaza, were sentenced to death, although
some of the sentences were commuted in deference to the age
or status of the accused. Around 60 others were condemned
to death in absentia, including newspaper and journal editors
in Egypt.[129] Those who were not commuted where publically
hanged in Beirut. More hangings followed in May 1916, in Beirut
and Damascus.[130]

Not all punishments were so harsh, but they were bad enough.
The Ottomans had stopped all Jewish immigration into Palestine
on the outbreak of the war. At the same time they began exiling
Jewish leaders or activists. David Ben Gurion, a Russian immi-
grant who had studied law in Constantinople, had begun to raise
a Jewish unit for the Ottoman Army, but was exiled to Egypt
when it became known that he was a Zionist. He later joined

---

* Until the First World War, the Ottomans maintained a system much like that
of the Romans. Days were split into two periods, starting at dawn and dusk. Day
and night were divided into twelve equal parts regardless of their actual length,
so an hour became longer in summer and shorter in winter. The Western system
was already in use by some government and military institutions, and became
more widespread during the war. For one thing, the spread of electricity meant
that dusk no longer meant the end of the practical working day, and for another
much more precise timings were needed for military operations.

the British Army and served in Palestine in 1918, going on to become crucial to the founding of the state of Israel, as well as the first Prime Minister. The general Jewish population also suffered. Some 18,000 Jews were expelled or fled during the war, of whom 12,000 were sent by ship from Jaffa to Alexandria.[131] At Passover, 1917, all Jews were expelled from Jerusalem and Jaffa, while Djemal ordered the expulsion of Christians and destruction of Christian sites in Jerusalem as the British Army approached in November and December 1917. The Jewish population of Jerusalem alone dropped by 20,000 throughout the war, although curiously the numbers of another persecuted race, the Armenians, doubled during the same period as refugees from further north sought new lives.[132]

Although it is perhaps the best documented, Jerusalem was not the only town to suffer. In the late summer of 1917, Rafael de Nogales rode from Beersheba to Jerusalem, and found:

> During this trip, which took me also to Ramleh, Jaffa and several other points, I could judge of the ruin caused by deportations, epidemics and looting. Jaffa, for instance, was a dead city, practically evacuated save for a few German families and the civil authorities, who had remained under pretext of guarding the town and who were sacking it right and left in complete accord with their master, Djemal Pasha.[133]

Before 1909 Christians and Jews had been exempt from conscription into the Ottoman armed forces, paying higher taxes instead. Even after that, the draft had been imposed lightly on non-Muslims, but in 1914 that changed and young men of all religions and creeds were called up to serve. In the spring of 1915 the policy was again reversed. Christians and Jews were not to be trusted in front-line units and were put instead into unarmed labour battalions, expected to perform menial tasks. Alexander Aaronsohn, a Palestinian Jew of Rumanian descent, had been a reluctant conscript but had felt some small pride in

the performance of his co-religionists and the Christians, compared to the poor showing made by their Arab comrades. Being
moved to a labour battalion ended that:

> The final blow came one morning when all the Jewish and
> Christian soldiers of our regiment were called out and told
> that henceforth they were to serve in the *taboor amlieh*, or
> working corps ... We were disarmed; our uniforms were
> taken away, and we became hard-driven 'gangsters.' I shall
> never forget the humiliation of that day when we, who,
> after all, were the best-disciplined troops of the lot, were first
> herded to our work of pushing wheelbarrows and handling
> spades, by grinning Arabs, rifle on shoulder.

Aaronsohn bribed his way to a discharge soon after, but many
others were not so lucky. While labour battalions worked with
the army, Jewish and Christian civilians were conscripted into
'garbage battalions' to work in the towns and cities. Many of the
conscripts were older men, too old to serve in the army, but who
under the local customs and culture should have been accorded
respect and a certain level of privilege. Even as a Muslim Arab,
Private Ihsan Turjman of the Jerusalem garrison recorded how:

> This morning while walking to my work at the Commissariat
> I came across several Jewish citizens, almost all above 40 years
> of age, holding brooms and cleaning streets. I was horrified
> by this scene.[134]

Khalil Sakakini shared Turjman's horror, to see men forcibly
given such menial tasks:

> Today a large number of Christians were recruited as garbage
> collectors to Bethlehem and Bait Jala. Each was given a broom,
> a shovel, and a bucket and they were distributed in the alleys of
> the town. Conscripts would shout at each home they passed,

'send us your garbage.' The women of Bethlehem looked out
from their windows and wept. No doubt this is the ultimate
humiliation. We have gone back to the days of bondage.[135]

Clearly, outrage at this act was not confined merely to those
affected, and spread through the wider community. Some, like
the Arab Turjman, even seem to have found some kind of soli-
darity in the Ottoman Empire's treatment of its subject people.
There was beyond doubt inherent discrimination against them
all, and most importantly for this region against the Arabs. Even
in the army (of which they made up around one-third) they were
looked down upon as second class, even after many Arab units
performed with distinction at Gallipoli and elsewhere. Rafael de
Nogales was a Venezuelan mercenary in Ottoman service, and
came without the inherent world-view of most Ottoman officers, yet even he felt that:

Neither rhyme nor reason avails with the low-caste Arab
recruit. He is traitor, liar, and deserter by nature. The only way
to subjugate and rule him is to pump him full of lead or lay on
the lash. The contrary is true of the Bedouin of the desert and
the Moor of the rocky plain, who are the embodiment of courage, chivalry, and knighthood.

In fact, Nogales was fairly enlightened by Ottoman terms, in not
only drawing a distinction between the different types of Arabs
but also praising some of them.

But while Arabs made up around a third of the rank and file
of the army, they only provided about 15 per cent of the officers, and these were often looked upon with distrust. The small
numbers were generally due to the relatively poor education
available in the Arab provinces of the Ottoman Empire, compared to the European and Turkish lands. Efforts had been made
to change this from the 1870s onwards, with military schools
being slowly established across the empire, in part to solve the

perennial and chronic shortage of trained officers for the army. The resulting Arab officers were frequently distrusted and seen as potentially disloyal, both by the Ottomans and by the British, who both believed that secret societies of Arab officers were plotting revolution. During the war, this impression was assisted by the defection of a small but prominent number of Arab officers who, after being captured by the British, opted to join the Arab Revolt rather than go to prisoner of war camps. (Interestingly, attempts to recruit Arab soldiers from the prison camps proved largely unsuccessful.) However, the bulk of the Arab officer corps remained steadfastly loyal; of the seventy-five Arabs who graduated from the Military Academy in 1914, just one would desert during the war. On the other hand, thirty-two of them not only opted to remain in what became the army of the Republic of Turkey after the break up of the empire at the end of the war, but also then fought for the Republic during the Turkish War of Independence.[136]

While this proves that broad stereotypes and racial divisions cannot be drawn across the Ottoman Empire, there can be no doubt that there was a very definite undertone of discontent among the various minorities, even if it usually fell short of open revolt or disobedience. Ihsan Turjman was probably not alone in questioning, in September 1915:

> What does this barbaric state want from us? To liberate Egypt on our backs? Our leaders promised us and other fellow Arabs that we would be partners in this government and that they seek to advance the interests and conditions of the Arab nation. But what have we actually seen from these promises? Had they treated us as equals, I would not hesitate to give my blood and my life – but as things stand, I hold a drop of my blood to be more precious than the entire Turkish state.[137]

However, that did not stop him serving loyally until his death in late 1917.

Less passive was the Aaronsohn family. After leaving the army, Alexander had escaped to Egypt in August 1915, and tried to get British Intelligence interested in an organisation growing under the encouragement of his brother. Aaron Aarohnson was a noted botanist, and conducted agricultural research. His work, sanctioned by the Ottomans, allowed him to travel freely around the country. He used this freedom to map the country, to build up connections in scattered Jewish communities, and to gather information on garrisons and defences. Alexander initially failed to overcome British suspicions that he was an Ottoman agent trying to spread disinformation, but a visit by another member of the group, Avshalom Feinberg, later in the year convinced them. When Feinberg returned to Palestine – being landed at night on the coast – in November, arrangements for a scheme for visual signals on the coast had been agreed. Unfortunately, this broke down almost immediately, and it was not until February 1917 that communications were re-established.

By then, the group had been formalised as the Netzah Yisrael Lo Yishaker ('Eternal one of Israel will not lie', Samuel 15:29) or 'Nili' organisation. Their network involved twenty-three regular agents with many more sources and contacts, spread from Damascus to Beersheba. There were a series of regional cells, where one member acted as the hub to collect and collate information to pass on to Aaronsohn's headquarters in Atlit, on the coast south of Haifa. From here, messages and reports were passed out to the Royal Navy, although this system was slow and sporadic. In the seven months that the Nili group was at its most active – March to September 1917 – only nine rendezvous with ships could be made. Naturally, this negated much of the immediate use of the reports, and by that time the five- or six-week-old information had often already been received or surmised from wireless interceptions, aerial observation or other human intelligence sources. Where the Nili group was invaluable was in confirming this other information. So reliable were their reports that they were considered the litmus test for all other sources.

In late August or early September 1917, two Arab agents were captured by the Ottomans as they landed on the Palestine shore. Under interrogation they revealed not only their own tasks and contacts, but also knowledge of the Nili.* From this, Aziz Bek, head of counter-intelligence for the 4th (OT) Army, managed to begin to unravel the network. Aaron Aaronsohn was out of the country at the time, and escaped, but his sister Sarah was among those arrested. She withstood four days of torture before managing to end her own life. Others were tortured and executed, and the most reliable direct source of intelligence for the British in Palestine ended.[138]

The simmering discontent below the surface in Syria was heightened by other circumstances of the war. The sudden arrival of thousands of troops stretched the capacity of the land to support them. Due to the logistical inefficiency of the empire, the army was forced to fall back on local resources. Djemal Pasha recorded in his memoirs that he ordered the 4th (OT) Army to pay promptly and in cash for all food and supplies rather than simply requisitioning them, as the Ottomans did elsewhere.[139] But, if this command was issued, it was soundly ignored. All that could be said for the army policy of living off the land was that it was non-discriminatory. Christian Jerusalemite Wasif Jawhariyyeh recalled that:

> Food prices rose dramatically due to the army's tyranny and despotism. They confiscated the foodstuffs stored in the foreign establishments they had seized, as well as grains, oils, and even textiles from markets and from Jerusalem's well-known merchants, on an incredibly large scale. Since the goods were

---

* A more common story has the Ottomans intercepting a pigeon carrying a coded message from Nili. The most recent academic study – Yigal Sheffy's excellent *British military intelligence in the Palestine Campaign 1914–1918* – offers the more convincing story of agents being apprehended while landing. A captured pigeon, even with a deciphered message, is extremely unlikely to lead back to any particular individual or location.

seized without payment, this confiscation was called 'assistance to the military'.[140]

The family of the Muslim Turjman also suffered, with their lands just outside Jerusalem being plundered, despite their having at least one son in the army:

> Soldiers are stealing wood from our land in Karm al A'raj. Not satisfied with dead wood, they started tearing branches from our olive trees. Who do we complain to? The officers claim they cannot control their subordinates. Of course not. Officers are busy in taverns getting drunk; then they go to the public places [brothels] to satisfy their base needs.[141]

'Requisitioning' could take place on large or small scales. Alexander Aaronsohn witnessed an incident where:

> A Turkish soldier, sauntering along the street, helped himself to fruit from the basket of an old vender, and went on without offering to pay a farthing. When the old man ventured to protest, the soldier turned like a flash and began beating him mercilessly, knocking him down and battering him until he was bruised, bleeding, and covered with the mud of the street. There was a hubbub; a crowd formed, through which a Turkish officer forced his way, demanding explanations. The soldier sketched the situation in a few words, whereupon the officer, turning to the old man, said impressively, 'If a soldier of the Sultan should choose to heap filth on your head, it is for you to kiss his hand in gratitude.'[142]

Given the low pay of soldiers it is perhaps inevitable that abuses took place. An Ottoman private received 85 piastres a month.[143] In comparison, the British government forwarded to soldiers who had been taken prisoner 1,000 piastres a month from their own pay, and even then this often proved insufficient as shortages became more acute and prices rose. And it did not take long for those shortages to start. Even without all of the extra people to feed, there was also the cessation to all imports from outside the empire and many of those from within. As early as April 1915, Turjman was recording in his diary that 'money is scarce and the stores are empty'.[144] As the year progressed, the situation worsened:

10 July 1915
The government is trying (with futility) to bring food supplies, and disease is everywhere ... Jerusalem has not seen worst days. Bread and flour supplies have almost totally dried up. Every day I pass the bakeries on my way to work, and I see a large number of women going home empty-handed. For several days the municipality distributed some kind of black bread to the poor, the likes of which I have never seen. People used to fight over the limited supplies, sometimes waiting in line until midnight. Now, even that bread is no longer available.[145]

20 October 1915
People are dying of hunger. All essential foodstuffs are missing, including material produced in other Ottoman provinces. Citizens can no longer bear this situation.[146]

17 December 1915
I haven't seen darker days in my life. Flour and bread have basically disappeared since last Saturday. Many people have not eaten bread for days now. As I was going to the Commissariat this morning, I saw a throng of men, women, and boys fighting each other to buy flour near Damascus Gate. When I passed this place again at midday, their numbers had multiplied.[147]

Some small relief was available through the religious or social organisations in Jerusalem. The American Colony, for example, maintained a soup kitchen and gave work and training to the unemployed, as well as channelling money for relief efforts from international sources. Even after the entry of the United States into the war, Djemal Pasha allowed them to continue their good work unhindered.

The year 1915 would be particularly bad, as other factors also came into play. At the worst possible time, Egypt and Palestine also fell under invasion by swarms of migratory locusts. Coming out of Africa, these insects literally stripped the country bare, devouring all in their path. Aaronsohn recalled:

> Not only was every green leaf devoured, but the very bark was peeled from the trees, which stood out white and life-less, like skeletons. The fields were stripped to the ground, and the old men of our villages, who had given their lives to cultivating these gardens and vineyards, came out of the synagogues where they had been praying and wailing, and looked on the ruin with dimmed eyes. Nothing was spared. The insects, in their fierce hunger, tried to engulf everything in their way.[148]

The locusts came in March, destroying the year's crops. The swarm's size was beyond measure, probably billions of insects blotting out the sky as they passed. Turjman watched their progress with horror:

> The locust invasion started seven days ago and covered the sky. Today it took the locust clouds two hours to pass over the city. God protect us from the three plagues: war, locusts and disease, for they are spreading through the country.[149]

The swarm had already passed through Egypt, where rapid action had been taken. The concern was not just the swarm itself, but its legacy. The locusts laid eggs in shallow holes in the ground, and while mounted patrols monitored and fol-lowed the swarms, the *fellahin* of Egypt were mobilised to sift and turn the topsoil behind them, killing off the eggs before they could hatch. At the same time, *fellahin* were also employed to kill adults, being paid by the weight collected, and after an intensive effort lasting from February into June the threat was finally contained.[150]

Similar efforts were made in Palestine, under the direction of Aaron Aaronsohn. His brother's undoubtedly biased account does not show the effort in a good light, and lays the blame for its failure squarely with the Arab farmers:

> The menace was so great that even the military authorities were obliged to take notice of it. They realized that if it were allowed to fulfil itself, there would be famine in the land, and the army would suffer with the rest. Djemal Pasha summoned my brother (the President of the Agricultural Experiment Station at Atlit) and entrusted him with the organization of a campaign against the insects. It was a hard enough task. The Arabs are lazy, and fatalistic besides; they cannot understand why men should attempt to fight the *Djesh Allah* ('God's Army'), as they call the locusts ...
>
> In spite of these drawbacks, however, he attempted to work up a scientific campaign. Djemal Pasha put some thousands of Arab soldiers at his disposition, and these were set to work digging trenches into which the hatching locusts were driven and destroyed ... It was a hopeless fight. Nothing short of the cooperation of every farmer in the country could have won the day; and while the people of the progressive Jewish villages struggled on to the end – men, women, and children working in the fields until they were exhausted – the Arab farmers sat by with folded hands. The threats of the military authorities only stirred them to half-hearted efforts. Finally, after two months of toil, the campaign was given up and the locusts broke in waves over the countryside, destroying everything ...[151]

In his diary, Turjman (although from the point of view of one not directly involved) gives further details on the government's campaign. All citizens aged 15–60 were required to collect 20kg of locust eggs, he recorded, while fines had to be paid for every kilogram uncollected.[152] These fines, he wrote approvingly, were gradated to fit the income of the individual.[153] He also records a conversation with two of his relatives, both army officers, who disapproved of the scheme, and felt it wrong for the government to compel people to take part in such a campaign even when it was for the common good.[154]

While the Ottoman campaign to deal with the locusts seems to have been less efficient than that of the British in Egypt, by the autumn the swarms had either been dealt with or moved on. They left devastation and starvation in their wake, and 1915 would be remembered in the region as the Year of the Locusts.

If the Arabs did see the locusts as a plague sent by God, it was just one of several. Diseases, many no doubt aggravated by poor diets, also spread across the land, with local outbreaks of cholera and typhus.[155] Other, perhaps inevitable, diseases also followed in the wake of the soldiers who arrived. Venereal diseases, known euphemistically as 'social diseases', became prevalent in the city. A significant factor in the spread was the increase in the number of prostitutes, particularly as prices rose and desperate women whose husbands had been conscripted were forced to find alternative means of support.[156] Such behaviour disturbed many religious and social leaders, although others seemed less concerned as they joined in the high-life of the city. While the general population and the common soldiers went short, Djemal Pasha entertained his officers and high society in style. To the suffering lower classes, his parties and celebrations became topics of great discussion and resentment, and most likely not a little exaggeration. As Turjman recorded in his diary, such events cast doubts on not

only the characters of those involved, but also the righteous-
ness and justice of their cause:

25 April 1915
Yesterday HQ sent several military vehicles to Latron to
bring alcoholic drinks. More than 100 officers were invited,
and the military band played throughout the meal. It's hard
to take seriously Djemal Pasha's (and his retinue's) claim to
devotion to Islam and of wanting to liberate Muslims from
the British yoke. Every day we read a circular warning soldiers and officers against frequenting cafes and beer halls,
upon threat of imprisonment and expulsion from service.
All this while the commanders are swimming in debauchery
and drunkenness.[157]

27 April 1915
Djemal Pasha issued an order today, in celebration of the
anniversary of Sultan Mehmet Rashad V's ascension to the
throne, to distribute mutton and sweets to members of the
armed forces ... This was followed by another circular issued
by Rusen Bey [Albanian commander of the Jerusalem garri-
son] cancelling the very same order since not enough rice and
meat can be obtained from the depots. It seems that rice and
meat can always be found for the officers.
    To celebrate the anniversary a number of notables and their
ladies were invited to Notre Dame. An orchestra performed
while liquor flowed. A number of Jerusalem prostitutes were
also invited to entertain the officers. I was told that at least
50 well-known whores were among the invitees. Each officer
enjoyed the company of one or two ladies in the garden com-
pound. While this was happening, our brothers were fighting
in the Dardanelles.[158]

The arrival of the British in December 1917 was greeted by
most of the population with relief if not always joy. With

communications once again open with Egypt and the rest of the world, trade slowly resumed and supplies flowed in. The British had gone to extreme lengths to establish efficient and adequate logistical support for their troops, and so the unpaid requisitioning of food and material ceased. While the political situation and future governing of the country remained very much in the air and a cause for concern for several years to come, daily life began to improve in most areas, although perhaps not quite all. The new, essentially secular society brought with it uncertainty, and an unfamiliar level of freedom for women. Writing in 1920, Khalil Totah and Omar Salih Barghouti also recorded that the British brought less welcome legacies:

> During the war we witnessed the spread of social diseases among city folks, and we thought that this was a national product [of the war]. But when the German and Austrian soldiers arrived we found that they were worse [than us]. We attributed their behaviour to their contacts with the Turks. And when the British Army arrived, we found that they were even more degenerate, for there is no vice and immodesty that is beyond them. We concluded that war is the source of this moral corruption, especially since the city population, and especially those who live in the vicinity of army camps were much more degenerate than those who lived in villages and towns away from military centres.[159]

How welcome some of the longer-term changes and decisions made by the British were is still heavily debated, especially as their repercussions remain to this day. However, that is another, longer story.*

---

* The author would recommend Roberto Mazza's *Jerusalem: From the Ottomans to the British* for a discussion of the shorter-term legacy.

6

EGYPT 1917

WHILE THE OTTOMAN territories in Palestine and Syria suffered under the influences of the war, entering into a spiral of hunger, disease and oppression, the experiences of neighbouring Egypt were much more varied. The war presented a mixture of opportunity for some, and hardship for others. If nothing else, 1917 at least saw the end of the direct threat of enemy action against Egypt, with the final defeat of the Senussi in the Western Desert.

Britain had occupied Egypt since the 1880s, although at least nominally the country had remained a semi-independent part of the Ottoman Empire. The British Agency had complete control over the country's finances, and thus by extension the rest of the government. Over time, the civil service, army, coastguard and other areas of public office had become increasingly dominated by Britons, and adapted to British principals and procedures. On 2 November 1914, the day that Russia declared war on the Ottoman Empire in response to an Ottoman attack in the Crimea, Martial Law was declared in Egypt. Six weeks later, on 18 December, the country was officially declared to be a British Protectorate, and all ties to the old empire were cut. The anti-British *Khedive*, Abbas Hilmi, who was at that time in

Constantinople anyway, was deposed and his uncle, Hussein Kamel, appointed in his place. To complete the separation from the Ottomans, his title was changed from *Khedive* to *Sultan*. The existing post of British Consul was also changed to reflect the new relationship, becoming British High Commissioner. Sir Milne Cheetham held this post temporarily from the outbreak of the war, but was replaced by Sir Henry McMahon in early 1915. On 1 January 1917 he was himself replaced by Sir Reginald Wingate, formerly the Governor of the Sudan. Under Martial Law, however, power in the country was centralised into the hands of the army.

From September 1914 this meant General Sir John Maxwell. An old Egypt hand, he knew and was known by Egypt and the Egyptians. He proceeded with a light hand amid British fears that the declaration of war against the Muslim Ottoman Empire would see widespread Islamic rebellions in Egypt, Sudan, and even India. Together with McMahon, Sultan Hussein and the Egyptian Prime Minister, Hussein Rushdi Pasha, he worked hard to dissipate tensions, and minimise the effects of the war on Egypt. The country was promised that as little impact would be made on daily life as possible, although inevitably this promise could not be kept. Immediately, regulations were issued ordering each farm to dedicate a certain percentage of their land to the growing of food crops, as opposed to the more lucrative cotton.[160] Regional boards were also established to buy up food at fixed prices, which proved unpopular. Various of the Capitulations, the laws decreeing that Egyptian police and legal services could not interfere with Europeans, instead handing them over to the various embassies and consulates to be tried or punished, were suspended. This had a positive effect over all, although resentment simmered that they had not been revoked entirely. Censorship was imposed in the press, effectively shutting down nationalist newspapers and publishers. By extension, the censorship added to the nationalists' grievances, while also closing many of the important channels for communication and discourse between political factions and with the government, heightening discontent and creating a pressure cooker of pent-up frustrations.[161]

The arrival of the army in large numbers also provided mixed blessings. Individual Egyptians, especially in the major cities, faced increased mistreatment and abuse at the hands of the British, Australian and New Zealand troops. Some of this was clearly intentional and deliberate, but far more was simply ingrained habit as a result of the casually racist mindsets of the age. Few white men would have questioned the basic belief that the locals – 'Gypos', 'Wogs', and even 'Niggers' – were simply beneath them, and could be treated accordingly. Naturally, such treatment would hardly be popular with the Egyptians. On the other hand, the influx of tens, later hundreds, of thousands of soldiers led to lucrative new markets for local traders to exploit, dealing with either individual soldiers or the army as a whole. This did not just cover goods, but also services. The railways and ports expanded rapidly, requiring staff and labour; the number of local employees working in the harbour at Port Said alone rose to 15,000 by 1917, a situation reflected at Suez, Alexandria, and the new harbour being constructed at Kantara.[162] Equally, local industry grew partly to provide material and goods for the expanding infrastructure and for the army, but also to process raw materials such as tobacco, cotton and sugar, which before the war would have been sent to European factories. For the first time, Egypt developed a significant industrial base, and industrial workforce.[163]

These new markets and new industries led to a growth in the economy. Even though expenditure also rose, government revenue increased even more. The financial year of 1915–16 saw a government surplus of over £1.1 million, rising to nearly £2.7 million the following year. However, these figures hid a rising crisis at the lowest levels. The economic boom, and the successes of the army in reconquering the Sinai Desert, led to problems from 1917 onwards. Some were simple issues such as the overstretching of the railway network; as the army built their railway across the desert and expanded the system in central Egypt, the supply of rolling stock and engines could not keep up. Services had to be cut, affecting both commercial and personal travel. Others sprang from more complicated roots, and interacted to heighten the problems. Probably the most serious of these for the majority of the population was the growing pressure on the *fellahin*, the Egyptian agricultural peasants.

By 1917 the army was requiring not only more food, but was also desperate for more transport animals. That year the cereal harvest was poor, but the army still insisted on taking their full quota, leaving the *fellahin* short of cereal for their own consumption or trading. As shortages increased so did the prices on the open market, but the army continued to only pay a fixed, relatively low, price. This robbed the *fellahin* of higher profits at the same time as it increased the cost of living, a distressing cycle to become trapped in. To add further hardships, a Purchasing Commission for Animals was established in November 1917. All landowners and peasants were required to bring their beasts of burden before inspectors, who could compulsorily buy any that were deemed fit for army use.[164]

At the same time as the *fellahin* were seeing their relative profits decline and their animals taken away, with the resulting fears for how they would manage in the coming year, some of the larger landowners were flourishing. Many found ways to circumvent the rules on acreages, and had quietly increased their cotton crops at a time when prices were four or more times higher than they had been at the start of the war. For the average peasant, seeing the rich get richer by flouting the rules that were making them suffer, while at the same time adding to the problem of food shortages and high prices, resentment was inevitable.[165] While meat and sugar remained plentiful throughout the war, by the end of 1917 the shortages of wheat, maize and fuel were causing widespread suffering and discontent.[166]

Many of the resentments and problems came together in one large, high-profile, issue: the Egyptian Labour Corps (ELC), and its sub-unit, the Camel Transport Corps (CTC). The ELC had been established soon after the outbreak of war, to provide a body of labourers to work on improvements in the defences and infrastructure of the Canal Zone, and also to act as herdsmen and handlers for the army's ration and baggage animals. For the first two years of the war, employment in the ELC had been a relatively attractive proposition. Wages were good, and contracts set at a three-month period. Discipline could be harsh, including physical beatings, but overall it offered the chance to accumulate an appreciable sum of money in a fairly short time-span.[167] Rations were provided, and a canteen system established to allow labourers to supplement or vary their issued food. The profits from the canteens went into a fund to provide aid to men who had been injured while serving with the ELC, and the widows and families of those who had been killed. By May 1917 some 186,000 men had served with the ELC, and nearly another 60,000 with the CTC. Most had served within Egypt, although some had been sent overseas on six-month contracts; as of June 1917, some 10,000 were in France, 8,000 were in Mesopotamia, 1,000 at Mudros in the Aegean, and around 600 in Salonika. This experience of being sent far from home for longer periods was about to become much more widespread.[168]

By the middle of 1917, the war had moved a long way from Egypt's main centres of population along the Nile Valley. Fewer men were inclined to volunteer, given the general perception that the war was now far away and, true to Britain's promise, nothing more would be asked of them. Those that did volunteer spent longer in travelling to and from the army, especially given the common delays caused by shortages of trains. It became obvious to the British commanders that something would have to be done to ensure sufficient labourers and animal handlers would be available for the offensive being planned for late autumn. Indeed, without sufficient Egyptians helping in the rear areas, the big push may not even be possible. Therefore, steps were taken to ensure a sufficient supply. Contracts were arbitrarily extended to six months, including for those already serving, while pressure was placed on the Egyptian Government to conscript labourers rather than relying on volunteers. It seems that the British intention had been for the Egyptians to utilise the existing draft system used for the Egyptian Army, which called up only a fraction of those eligible each year. However, instead the government drew up set quotas, and passed the issue down to the regional governments. These in turn issued quotas to towns and villages, leaving it to mayors and headmen to provide enough people. Unsurprisingly, being forcibly removed from their homes to serve in someone else's distant war (especially when working their land was becoming ever more important and difficult) proved deeply unpopular with the *fellahin*, and the blame was levelled squarely at the British.

The treatment of the ELC became a major issue across Egypt, even entering into popular culture. One widespread song that remained popular even after the war, although admitting that the wages were good and the back-pay ('profit') welcome, summed up the feelings of those who were forced to go far away, and into harm's way, for the sake of someone else's war:

Welcome back to safety
We went and returned safely
Blow your horn, oh, steamboat, and anchor
Let me off in this country [Egypt]
Who cares about America or Europe
There is no better than this country
The ship that is returning
Is much better than the one that is departing

Welcome back to safety
We went and returned safely
Who cares about the British Authority, it was all for profit

We saved as much as we could
We saw the war and the violence
We saw the explosions with our very eyes
There is only one God and one life, and here we are
We left and now we returned[169]

Such issues were a golden opportunity for Egypt's nationalists. At the same time that they were finding such fertile ground in both issues and audience, the very existence of the ELC, as well as industrialisation and other employment opportunities, was bringing about changes to make the *fellahin* more receptive to their ideas. For the first time since the 1850s Egypt saw large-scale movement of population. Many of the current generations had never strayed far from their own villages, but now they saw their country and met other people from all across it. As with the soldiers of Britain, Australia and New Zealand, and all of the Ottoman provinces too, a heightened awareness of the outside world was created, and with it a new sense of national identity was born. Quoted in *The Storyteller of Jeruslaem*, the Egyptian historian Salah Issa has asserted that:

They became attuned to life in the big city, in which they … would realize their dream of a more hopeful life than the life of village drudgery they came from … War gave them the opportunity to meet men from other regions which they had only heard about, and to travel in open markets and city boulevards which they had not dreamt of seeing before.

As this nationalism grew, the British failed entirely to connect or communicate with it. Censorship and controls on political activity closed many channels, while an increasingly physical distance also developed, not just between the government and the people, but also between the British military authorities and the Egyptian politicians and bureaucrats with whom they were supposed to work. This distancing had started when

General Murray replaced Maxwell, and became worse when General Allenby replaced Murray in the summer of 1917. One of Allenby's first actions was to move the headquarters of the army from Cairo out to the far side of the Sinai, to be closer to operations. This proved popular with the troops, but made direct communications with the Egyptian government much more difficult. It also reinforced the tendency for those ultimately responsible for administering the Martial Law to see Egypt purely in terms of being a base of operations for the army, there to support the campaign, rather than a country needing careful and sympathetic running as an end in itself.

At least the British reactions to the rise of nationalism remained relatively light-handed. Just two nationalists were executed during the war. In April 1915, Mohammed Khalil attempted to assassinate Sultan Hussein Kemal, but his bullet missed and Khalil was arrested and executed the following month. In July 1915 a further attempt on the sultan saw a bomb being thrown at him in Alexandria, although it did not explode. Two men were arrested and sentenced to death by the British military authorities, but their sentence was commuted to hard labour for life on the sultan's insistence. The other man to be executed was civil servant Saleh Abdel Latif, who stabbed and seriously wounded government minister Ibrahim Fathi Pasha in September 1915. In both cases, execution would almost certainly have been the sentence passed by the civil courts in peace time. Apart from these few extreme cases, by the end of 1917 just fifty-eight men had been deported or exiled from Egypt for their nationalist or anti-war activities, while somewhere over 500 more had been imprisoned or had their movements in other ways limited (including being banned from certain militarily important areas).[170]

In higher political terms, the only major potential crisis of 1917 was when the sultan died. Hussein Kamel, who had been ill earlier in the year, died on 9 October 1917, and the prospect was briefly raised that his son, Prince Kamel-El-Dine Husein, a known nationalist, could succeed him. However, some ground work had already been laid by all sides, and the prince refused the offer on the basis of his own unwillingness to help the British in any way. Instead, the throne passed to the late sultan's brother, Ahmed Fuad. Although also a nationalist, Fuad was far subtler in his approach to the issue, and was willing to work within the system to finally secure Egyptian independence.

While the internal politics of the country churned on, and preparations were made to continue the campaign on Egypt's eastern border, a military and political solution were also devised for the lingering Senussi threat in the west.

The Senussi were an Islamic sect whose influence stretched across North Africa. Under the leadership of the Grand Senussi, Sayyid Ahmed al-Sharif, members of the sect had been resisting the Italian invaders in Libya since 1911. From 1914, they came under increasing pressure from the Ottomans and Germans to also attack the British in Egypt. Sayyid Ahmed al-Sharif was initially very reluctant, having nothing particularly against the British and being hesitant to open a new front in his war. However, the pressure increased, and with it the flow of supporting troops, arms and gold, until November 1915 when the actions of a German submarine forced the issue. After sinking a British patrol boat, HMS *Tara*, and delivering the crew into the hands of the Senussi, the submarine then attacked the Egyptian Coastguard station at Sollum, precipitating general fighting. Initially, the British and Egyptian forces fell back along the coast, consolidating their forces at Marsa Matruh. Preoccupied with the fighting at Gallipoli, few troops could be spared for this new campaign. Those that could be fought a series of inconclusive skirmishes and actions with the Senussi, at least some of which could be said to have been British defeats.

Only in January 1916 did the British begin to gain the upper hand, and by the end of March they had retaken Sollum and rescued the crew of HMS *Tara*. With the coast secured, attention turned to the inland areas, where Senussi forces had occupied several of the large oases that dotted the otherwise barren Western Desert. These were slowly isolated and pushed back, often simply by using long-range patrols of armoured cars, light patrol cars* and Imperial Camel Corps (ICC) to intercept Senussi supply columns and cut their lines of communications. Skirmishes occurred, but the biggest danger was usually the desert itself. Geoffrey Inchbald, an officer with the ICC, would record:

> There was no water, no growth and no sign of life, nothing but gravel, rock and during the day-time a burning shimmering heat which distorted everything into fantastic shapes and images. Things were not made any easier by the fact that we were supposedly in enemy territory and had received orders to be always on the strictest guard and never to show ourselves on any skyline and I must admit that, as our trusty camels bore us further and further into this dreadful wilderness, we began to feel very small and lonely.[171]

The land could vary from flat, open plain to tangles of dunes hundreds of feet high and miles long. Such dunes could be almost impossible to climb (even without the orders not to appear on the skyline) and great detours were needed to navigate through them. With the objectives and bases of the patrols usually being small oases or outposts, it was all too easy to miss them and become lost in the vast wilderness.

However, the campaign worked and by early 1917 the only Senussi force still active was at the Siwa Oasis. This oasis was in fact a large depression, about 16km (10 miles) square and including the settlements of Siwa and Girba and the long valley in between. Under Sayyid Ahmed al-Sharif and his senior remaining commander, Muhammed Saleh Harb, its garrison consisted

---

* Light patrol cars were flat-bed light trucks with a machine gun fitted in the rear.

of about 1,200 men. On 21 January General Murray ordered preparation to be made to launch a coordinated attack on Siwa with cameliers and cars. It was estimated that it would take a month to gather the resources and make the plans needed to take such a force across 320km (200 miles) of desolate desert. But within days intelligence was received that Sayyid Ahmed al-Sharif was preparing to leave and return to Libya. If a move were to be made, it had to be done immediately, and so the cameliers were dropped and the task force was ordered to go with motor transport alone.[172]

The force left Marsa Matruh on 1 February 1917. It consisted of the eleven Rolls-Royce armoured cars of the Light Armoured Car Brigade, Nos 4, 5 and 6 Light Car Patrols (each with six Ford cars), and over eighty support vehicles including ambulances, supplies and headquarters staff, under the command of General Henry Hodgson.[173] At noon the next day, after covering over 290km (180 miles), the convoy arrived at the 'Concentration Point', about 21km (13 miles) north of the Shegga Pass, which led into the valley between Siwa and Girba. Here the force was to split. The bulk of the fighting vehicles – eight armoured cars and two of the Light Car Patrols – plus headquarters, signals and medical vehicles, led by Major L.V. Owston, were to descend the Shegga Pass. For this they were guided by Captain Leopold Royale, now of the Royal Flying Corps but formerly an officer with the Egyptian Coastguard. They were to strike the main Senussi camp, believed to be near Girba, while a smaller force swung around the edge of the depression and took up position to the west. This smaller force – three armoured cars, No. 6 Light Car Patrol and an ambulance, under Captain C.G. Mangles – was to take up position overlooking the Manassib Pass, which lay on the direct route between Girba and Jaghbub. This later place was on the Egyptian-Libyan border, and was a holy site for the Senussi. It was presumed that the Grand Senussi would fall back this way, and would then be cut off by the blocking force, allowing the main body to catch up and deal with them.

The attack began at dawn on 3 February. As the main force descended onto the floor of the depression, six of the armoured cars spread out in pairs to scout the way forward. This initially lay over a salt-plain, where several of the cars broke through a thin crust into boggy ground below and had to dig themselves out. As they reached the far side of the plain they entered a tangled country of tall dunes and rocky outcrops, with narrow, windy tracks between them. Driver Sam Rolls recalled that:

> Driving down the camel track between those overhanging heights, ignorant of what lay behind the next bend, and in constant expectation of being met with a hail of lead, was nerve-racking work.[174]

Although taken by surprise by the appearance of the British force so close, the Senussi reacted fast, taking to the high ground with machine guns and two mountain guns. These targeted the narrow tracks, pinning the advancing armoured cars down. With poor visibility confounded by the restricted view from the cars, the scouts could only inch forward, struggling to spot the sources of the incoming fire. They frequently stopped to allow the lighter Fords to catch up in order to dismount their machine guns and haul them to the tops of outcrops to provide covering fire. It was hot, confused and noisy work:

> My gunner took a snatch at his gun-belt to make sure that his next cartridge was well home in the breech, and then swung his turret in the direction from which the sound had come. But at that moment a deafening rattle of rifle-fire came from the other side, and a hail of bullets crashed against the armour and the wooden rifle-boxes at the rear. My gunner struggled to bring the turret round again, but it was jammed through the car being at that moment in an inclined position, for she was running sideways on a slope. The gunner swore and muttered, but in a few moments we

came on level ground, and there I halted the car. The turret
swung round with a jerk and the gunner fell in a heap on top
of me. Then I cursed too, and the suppressed excitement in
that little steel cylinder was terrific. In another moment the
gunner was on his feet and blazing away at the rocks with
a reckless expenditure of ammunition ... The unholy din
inside the steel cylinder during the action, chiefly caused by
the firing of our own gun, was such that weeks passed before
I became free of the sense of a continual metallic clanging in
my ears.[175]

The fighting lasted all day with little progress made. Only at
the following dawn, after a final flurry of fire, did the Senussi
withdraw. Their actions had given the Grand Senussi, who had
been at Siwa with around one-third of his men, time to withdraw. After taking a day to carefully sweep the area and rest, the
British entered Siwa Oasis at dawn on 5 February.

After so long in the desert, the experience of entering the area
of the oases was profound. 'We had come out of the wilderness
into a veritable Garden of Eden,' wrote Sam Rolls:

Along a deep valley cut in the yellow rocks a mass of dark
palm trees stretched for mile upon mile to the eastward.
This paradise of colour and shadow was the Siwa Oasis
... The road soon entered between avenues of trees, heavily laden with limes, figs, olives, pomegranates, oranges,
lemons, and other fruits; and the rows of date palms
extended for miles about us. We drove across quaint little
wooden bridges which spanned the irrigation channels of
cool clear water, and passed several lakes bordered by green
fields and more orchards.[176]

The town itself was an equally strange spectacle. Generations of
families had built and lived on exactly the same spots, leading to
multi-layered houses where the lower levels were derelict:

The castle-like town was built of mud, and on its decayed walls tier above tier of little wood-and-mud houses were stuck like swallow's nests. Some of the crumbling mounds looked like huge ant-heaps, swarming with brown human beings instead of ants.[177]

At the town the soldiers were met by the local leaders and enthusiastic residents, and welcomed and feasted. The next day, 6 February, the column returned to the Concentration Point, and on 8 February arrived back in Marsa Matruh.[178]

The second column had less success. The ground leading to the Manassib Pass proved too rough for two of the armoured cars, which had to be left behind. The final car and the Ford trucks managed to edge nearer and arrived over the pass at 7 p.m. on 3 February. The following dawn they successfully ambushed a Senussi caravan, but the survivors warned their comrades and all of the forces fleeing from Girba were directed towards a second pass to the south, out of the reach of the British forces.

The action cost the Senussi an estimated forty men killed and 200 wounded, and the British three officers wounded. More than that, it finally destroyed any credibility that the Grand Senussi still had. Increasingly his supporters ebbed away to join his nephew, Sayyid Muhammed Idris. The son of the previous Grand Senussi, Idris had only been a child when his father died. His uncle, with popular support, had taken the title, but after Idris came of age a growing ground-swell of support wanted the title passed back to the original heir. Idris had been against the war with the British from the start, writing to General Maxwell soon after the campaign started offering to open negotiations. Such talks had started in July 1916, although due to an Anglo-Italian agreement any negotiations had to be joint ones. The issues with the British were fairly simple, but the questions over the fate of Libya were far more complex. Talks broke down in September, but restarted the following January. The British victory so soon afterwards merely confirmed the hopelessness of the Senussi position, and terms were quickly agreed. The Senussi would end hostilities with the British, return all prisoners, and confine their Egyptian presence to the holy site at Jaghbub. Still, Libya remained a sticking point, but with the Anglo-Italian alliance against them, Idris bowed to the inevitable and a tri-partite agreement was signed on 14 April 1917, bringing peace.[179]

For the Grand Senussi, this was merely a formality. With his followers and power leaking away, he fled to the Libyan desert where he remained until August 1918, when he escaped to Constantinople in a submarine. For the British, it meant that their western border in Egypt was finally secured, and they could concentrate their attention on the east. Here, they could more gainfully employ their armoured cars and cameliers not only in the Sinai and southern Palestine, but also in Arabia.

7

ARAB REVOLT

A REBELLION HAD broken out in Arabia in June 1916, led by Sharif Husein bin Ali, the Emir of Mecca. In the opening months of the fighting the Arabs had captured Mecca as well as the critical ports of Jeddah, Rabegh and Yanbu on the Red Sea coast, allowing communications with the outside word, and in particular the British in the Sudan. The Sharif's forces were large but poorly equipped, with few modern rifles and no artillery or machine guns. With the capture of the ports, weapons and advisors began to flow in, including by the end of the year a detachment from No. 14 Squadron of the Royal Flying Corps, artillery batteries from the Egyptian Army, thousands of rifles, dozens of machine guns, artillery pieces, and millions of rounds of ammunition for them all; millions of pounds of rice and flour; grenades, explosives and detonators; wagons, boots, saddles, mess tins, buttons and water-bottles; and prodigious piles of British gold. For the British the new front in Arabia was another opportunity to drain away Ottoman resources for relatively little cost. While equipment was fairly cheap for the British – especially as many of the weapons were old ones deemed too worn out for use by the army, or of Japanese types – they knew that any men or material that the Ottoman Empire committed to the campaign would be sorely missed elsewhere. British, and thus Christian, troops were a different matter, particularly so close the Muslim holy sites at Mecca and Medina, but as the campaign moved north that problem slowly faded.

The Sharifian army waxed and waned in both numbers and successes over time. It was a complicated mix of tribes and families, many of whom had age-old grievances with each other, and who came and went from the alliance at will. Their traditional style of war-fighting was raiding. Committing themselves to the steady, constant effort that modern warfare demanded, with pitched battles, discipline and standing armies, was largely alien to them. They were also highly territorial, and often unwilling to fight outside their traditional tribal lands. Numbers steadily declined through the autumn, and by the end of the year the situation was grim. In October 1916 a British delegation was sent to make an assessment of the situation. This consisted of Ronald Storrs, a civil servant with the Egyptian Government, and Captain Thomas Lawrence of the Arab Bureau, a part of the British headquarters' intelligence organisation. Lawrence, having travelled through the Middle East during his pre-war studies and work as an archaeologist, while also covertly mapping certain areas for the British Army, spoke Arabic and knew a certain amount about Arabic culture and politics.*

---

* Despite being the most written about Briton of the twentieth century (apart from possibly Sir Winston Churchill), Lawrence is an enigmatic figure. His character is rife with contradictions: a man who craved obscurity and yet wrote widely about his exploits; a man who felt himself to be physically weak – and indeed was often struck with illness during the war – and yet who performed feats of great strength and endurance; he was haunted by self-doubt, but was equally determined to play a critical role in shaping the future of the Arab peoples. Unfortunately for historians, he was also a proven liar and embellisher in his letters, reports and memoirs, while at the same time often being the only witness to record the events he described. There is no space here to fully discuss Lawrence's character or his impact on the Arab Revolt, but the author would recommend: James Barr's *Setting the Desert on Fire*, Michael Asher's *Lawrence: The Uncrowned King of Arabia*, and Michael Korda's *Hero: The Life and Legend of Lawrence of Arabia*.

Lawrence and Storrs toured the Arab forces, speaking to the Sharif himself and his sons Ali, Feisal and Abdullah, each in the field with their own armies. They returned to Cairo to advise that the revolt was doomed unless British aid and advice was stepped up. The Arabs could not defeat the Ottoman forces in the field as they were, and serious changes were needed. Lawrence was sent back to Yanbu to talk to Feisal, the Sharif's middle son. Fresh from defeat in the field, he was preparing defences with the aid of *Bimbashi* Herbert Garland of the Egyptian Army. By chance, the Ottoman efforts in Arabia were also starting to flag, mainly due to supply shortages, and Feisal's forces were given a respite long enough for Lawrence to persuade him to make one more effort. In early January 1917, Feisal's forces struck up the coast to the port of Wejh, 320km (200 miles) north. At the same time a small Royal Navy flotilla took 500–600 Arabs north by sea, with the intention of making a coordinated attack on the port on 23 January. In the event, Feisal's men were delayed by a day, but the naval commander decided to attack anyway. The Arabs and 200 armed sailors were landed under the command of Major Charles Vickery and Captain Norman Bray and successfully took the port.

Taking this port 160km (100 miles) north of Medina was a tremendous strategic victory for the Arab cause. It placed a large force effectively behind the Ottoman garrison at Medina, between them and the rest of the Ottoman Army. A stretch of 320km (200 miles) of their sole supply line, the Hedjaz railway, now lay open to Arab attack. With this life line under threat, the Ottomans were forced onto the defensive, and the Arabs could take the initiative. Raids began on the Hedjaz railway; *Bimbashi* Garland had laid the first mine at a point 240km (150 miles) south-east of Wejh on the night of 20/21 February, while Lawrence was back in Cairo.[180]

The question now loomed as to what should be done next. With the revolt taking hold and beginning to spread outside the immediate area of Medina and Mecca, the leaders found themselves at a series of crossroads regarding the future conduct of the campaign, and even its ultimate goals. By moving to the north, the Arabs were now within easy range of the tribes of the Hedjaz and northern Arabia, and of those of Syria. Raising and then uniting these tribes would be hard work; an intricate web of blood feuds, rivalries and quarrels flowed between them, while a recent proclamation by the Sharif had managed to alienate many. In October 1916 he had been declared King of the Arab Nation at Mecca. The announcement threw the British government into a panic, as it did the French. The title implied sovereignty over vast areas well outside the confines of the Arab Peninsula, including Syria. It also threw many of the fearsomely independent Arab tribes into uproar, and some refused to recognise the title. Abdul Aziz Ibn Saud, for example, was a strong rival of the Sharif and controlled the Nejd region of central Arabia. He refused to recognise the Sharif's new title, and although the British managed to maintain strong links with the sheikh, any hopes of uniting the Sharifian and Saudi forces were destroyed. After much debate, the British official response was to recognise the Sharif as King of the Hedjaz, a title that clearly stated where they saw the limits of the revolt as being.[181]

While Ibn Saud refused to actively join the revolt under the Sharif's leadership, other of the great sheikhs even worked against it. Ibn Rashid, the Emir of Hail, ruled an area to the north of the Nejd, and had been a close ally of the Ottomans since the 1890s. His forces worked to keep the Ottomans in Medina supplied, although these efforts ended in April 1917 when a large convoy was ambushed near Hanakiye by the pro-Sharifian Emir of Zeid. Four mountain guns, over 3,000 fully laden camels, over 3,000 sheep, and hundreds of prisoners were taken, after which Ibn Rashid withdrew his forces to join the Ottoman garrison at Madain Salih, on the railway 320km (200 miles) north of Medina. Here he gradually lost both prestige and support, and turned from a source of supplies into a drain on already scant Ottoman resources.[182]

However, there was enough support being offered to the Sharifians by tribes to the north to encourage plans for expansion in that direction, and this drew greater international attention to the revolt. The French had been monitoring progress, and had sent small numbers of troops and advisors to assist the Arabs, but the British had worked hard to keep them at a distance. Now that Damascus lay within the possible scope of the revolt, an area that the French had already, under the Sykes–Picot agreement, ear-marked for their own occupation, that interest was renewed. Lawrence had returned to Cairo after the capture of Wejh, and was there accosted by Edouard Brémond, the Chief of the French Military Mission to the Hedjaz. Brémond wanted to land an Anglo-French force at Aqaba, on the tip of the eastern fork of the Red Sea, and then advancing inland to take Ma'an, where a garrison of 6,000 Ottomans stood astride the railway. Lawrence opposed the idea on two counts. Firstly, Aqaba stood between high cliffs that were heavily defended against attack from the sea, and secondly, by placing an Anglo-French armed force at Ma'an the revolt would be blocked from moving further north, and he suspected that this containment of the Arabs was the true purpose of the French. Rebuffed, Brémond nevertheless travelled to Arabia to visit Feisal, who also refused to countenance the idea, although small numbers of French Algerian troops continued to serve with the Arabs. What Feisal did instead, at the end of February, was to ask Cairo formally for Lawrence to be returned to him as liaison officer.[183]

This Lawrence was happy to do. He had already identified Feisal as the most promising Arab commander, from the British point of view, being open to outside aid and advice, with an aggressive streak (although equally prone to bouts of doubt, which Lawrence felt he could handle), and a conviction that the revolt should move as far north as it could to include the fullest possible amount of the Arab world. The British High Command was also happy for a man with proven influence over Feisal to return to the field. Intelligence had reported that the Ottomans were considering pulling their garrison out of Medina. Between the garrison and the Hedjaz Expeditionary Force, guarding the railway and keeping communications open, somewhere over 15,000 Ottoman troops were tied up by their decision to maintain a presence in the holy city. For General Murray, gathering his forces to attack Gaza, the sudden appearance of this many Ottoman troops either on his open right flank, or even behind Gaza itself, was a dangerous prospect. For the British it was far preferable to keep these troops pinned down in a strategic dead-end, where the Ottomans could not make any serious gains; indeed, if the situation was handled correctly, even more Ottoman troops could be sucked in. Therefore it was imperative that everything should be done to make withdrawal as difficult as possible, while at the same time easing the direct pressure on the Medina garrison. Sending back to Arabia a man with proven influence over at least one of the Arab leaders was an excellent idea.

Lawrence talked Feisal into keeping his focus on moving north, in part by disclosing the existence and basics of the Sykes-Picot agreement. The only way to prevent the French from taking Damascus and Syria in any post-war arrangements would be for the Arabs to physically move north and seize those areas for themselves. Having convinced Feisal, Lawrence set out to visit Abdullah at his camp in Wadi Ais, in order to attempt to talk him around as well. The journey would involve crossing the railway, which could be attacked on the way.

It took five days to reach Abdullah's camp, and it was a night-marish journey for Lawrence, who fell ill on the way. Boils and dysentery plagued him to the extent that, after reaching his destination on 15 March 1917, he spent ten days prostrate in his tent. Abdullah was deeply suspicious of all European attempts to meddle in Arabian affairs, and any attempts to persuade him to bring his force north failed, while any urging to attack the railway was wasted. His men had already destroyed a railway bridge 113km (70 miles) north of Medina a few weeks earlier.[184] With that part of his mission a failure, a still weakened and sickly Lawrence turned his party for home on 26 March. He was joined by Sharif Shakir and some men from his Utaybah tribe and a single field gun. Two days later they arrived near the station of Abu an Naam, a typical post consisting of a water tower, the station buildings, and a small garrisoned fort, made of barracks and storerooms built around a central courtyard, with a parapet along their roofs. The garrisons of these posts were usually quite small, although they were generally active. Stations were 21km (13 miles) apart, and parties from each fort patrolled to the halfway points to the next station to the north and south each day. At Abu an Naam, though, extra tents stood around a nearby mosque, enough for an estimated 300 Ottoman soldiers. This was too strong a force for the Arabs to attack directly, so instead mines were laid on the rails to the south and the telegraph wires were cut. At dawn, the field gun opened fire on the station, damaging the buildings and the water tower and causing casualties among the troops. Soon after, a train in the station tried to escape, but hit the mine. However, the Arab machine-gunners left to cover the site had disappeared in the night, and the crew were able to edge the locomotive back onto the tracks and make good their escape. While not a complete success, Lawrence reckoned they had caused about seventy casualties and closed the line for three days.[185]

Lawrence set another mine – which initially failed to explode – and blew up a bridge and around 200 rails on the rest of the journey home to Wejh. His mission had not been a success; Abdullah had refused to come north and instead remained focused on Medina, and his attacks on the railway had been fairly small affairs. However, the question of preventing the withdrawal of the Medina garrison soon became moot. Although orders had been sent to the garrison to evacuate, the military commander, Fakhreddin ('Fakhri') Pasha, and the new Emir of Mecca (Constantinople had, understandably, publicly renounced Hussein), Sharif Ali Haider, protested the order

vociferously, believing that the symbolic and religious importance of Medina outweighed any military effort needed to
maintain the garrison. Even before Lawrence had set out to see
Abdullah, the order to withdraw had been rescinded.[186] On the
other hand, the Arab forces in the field around Medina remained
incapable of taking the city by force.

While the flap over Medina had ultimately been a non-event,
it had allowed Lawrence time to assess the ability of the Arabs
for field operations, and it was during this time that he formed
his doctrine for using the tribesmen for guerrilla raids. The
Arabs could not face heavy weapons fire or even massed infantry,
especially not in prepared defensive positions. But they could
do valuable work in hit-and-run raiding, stinging and hurting
the Ottomans in small actions along a considerable frontage
before disappearing back into the desert, and thus tying down
large numbers of regular troops and substantial resources in
defending the railway. Already *Bimbashi* Garland and Lieutenant
Colonel Stewart Newcombe were busy leading bands attacking
the railway, as were the Arab forces further south. Other British
officers were soon to arrive to help with the raids, while still
more worked coordinating logistics and organising the forces
at Wejh, where British troops, including armoured cars, were
beginning to arrive, and where the flight from No. 14 Squadron
RFC had moved from Yanbu. Although the year had started on
a slightly shaky note, the tools needed to turn the Arabs into a
formidable fighting force were now at hand.

But the question as to where that force should be directed
remained. For several months discussions dragged on, but
increasingly Feisal, under Lawrence's influence, was preparing to break with the pattern on which the British, French, and
even his father and brothers, were intent. In mid May Lawrence
embarked on the first stage of a journey that, he hoped, would
lead to delivering Aqaba into Arab hands. With him were
Sharif Nasir, brother of the Emir of Medina and a man who
had already been scouting and raiding to the north, and more

importantly Auda Abu Tayyi, whose Howaytat tribe controlled large swathes of the land through which they were
about to travel, and who had a fearsome reputation as a warrior, cut-throat and bandit.[187] Neither Lawrence nor Feisal
let Colonel Cyril Wilson, Britain's political officer with the
Arabs, know of their plans. While he may well have sympa-
thised, Wilson would have had to have told Cairo, who would
not. Britain had already identified Aqaba as an important spot
for themselves to occupy after the war, to help secure the
approaches to the Suez Canal.[188]

It would, by any stretch of the imagination, be a hard march
to reach Aqaba. None of the Bedouin currently serving the
revolt would move so far north out of their tribal lands, and
so Lawrence, Nasir and Auda had, apart from servants, just
seventeen men with them, mercenaries from the Agayl tribe.
They would ride north-east, across the railway and deep
enough inland to mislead any Ottoman spies as to their intentions, before sweeping back down on Aqaba. This circular route
would also allow the group to raise supporters and troops on
the way, for which purpose they carried a considerable amount
of gold. This would be the only heavy baggage they would
take, though. The route would be long and harsh, including a
five-day trek across the waterless wasteland known as al-Houl
('The Terror'), and so no machine guns, artillery or baggage
train could be taken.

The Terror lived up to its name. 'We, ourselves, felt tiny in it, and
our urgent progress across its immensity was a stillness or immobil-
ity of futile effort,'[189] Lawrence wrote later about marching:

Over monotonous, glittering sand; and over those worse
stretches, 'Giaan', of polished mud, nearly as white and
smooth as laid paper, and often whole miles square. They
blazed back the sun into our faces with glassy vigour, so we
rode with its light raining direct arrows upon our heads, and
its reflection glancing up through our inadequate eyelids.[190]

Eventually the party reached the far side, although Lawrence at one point had to turn back to rescue an Arab who had fallen from his camel, and for which act Auda roundly berated him for being so foolish.[191] Fresh water was found in the Wadi Sirhan, and for several days the party moved north down the wadi, regaining their strength and looking for Howaytat camps. Along the way various members of the party rode off to search the surrounding area and visit and talk to different groups to raise support. After finally settling at Nabk, Lawrence himself left the camp on 5 June to scout north to Damascus. His intention was to gain intelligence on both the Arab and the Ottoman situations in eastern Syria, although he took the opportunity to strike at the railway on the way. On a loop of over 885km (550 miles), he destroyed a railway bridge and met with tribal leaders, returning to Nabk on 18 June 1917.[192] A second, shorter, trip ended with a failed attack on a railway station at Atwi, but, with 700 Arabs now under arms, everything was set to begin the operations against Aqaba.

To start with, a force of Howaytat under Sheikh Gasim Abu Daumayk attacked the Ottoman force at Fuweilah, which guarded the road south-west from Ma'an through the Jabal al Batra hills and into the Wadi Itm, which in turn led to Aqaba.

The attack initially went badly, but then an Ottoman counter-attack struck the Arab camp and a dozen women and children were killed. Enraged, the Arabs renewed their attack, taking the fort and killing all inside. With the road now open, Lawrence, Nasir and Auda struck at the railway to the east, destroying ten bridges in the hope of distracting the Ottomans from the actions to the west. This part of the plan failed, and a battalion of 460 Ottoman troops, from the 178th (OT) Regiment, was dispatched from Ma'an to recapture Fuweilah and reopen the road to Aqaba, which they did before camping outside the fort. By chance, this camp was only 3.2km (2 miles) from Aba al Lissan, where the two Arab forces were to rendezvous after their raids. At dawn on 2 July, the reunited Arab forces attacked.

The Ottoman battalion was taken by surprise, but soon rallied and took up defensive positions. The Arabs, scattered in a loose cordon around the Ottomans, kept up a hot fire all day, but this was exactly the kind of pitched battle that Lawrence had previously decided that the Arabs should avoid. Thankfully for the Arabs, the Ottoman artillery rapidly ran out of ammunition, but the small arms fire was still enough to keep the attackers pinned down, unable to move as they lay under the hot summer sun all day. Lawrence and many others had to at least temporarily withdraw from the firing line suffering from the heat. But the Ottoman troops were just as pinned down, unable to move, and one side or the other would need to make a radical move to break the deadlock. This came late in the day, after Auda asked Lawrence of his opinion of his tribesmen, and Lawrence replied that 'they shoot a lot and hit little'. Enraged by the insult to his men's abilities, Auda gathered fifty of them and charged down the slope towards the enemy. Behind him, Nasir and Lawrence quickly gathered a further 400 men and followed in a pell-mell rush into the Ottoman positions. In the process, Lawrence accidentally shot his camel in the back of the head, and by the time he recovered his senses from the tumble it was all over. Some 160 Ottomans had been killed, and 300 captured.

Over the next four days, the Arab forces advanced down the Wadi Itm, clearing out a series of Ottoman outposts along the way. The first, the telegraph station at Quwayrah, surrendered without a fight, while the second, at Khadra, had to be stormed. The others between there and the main Aqaba defences, at the mouth of the Wadi above the port, were abandoned. The whole time the Arab forces were swelled by more and more tribesmen, attracted by success and the scent of plunder. According to Lawrence, his force doubled by the time they reached Aqaba on 5 July, and doubled again by the time they could persuade the garrison to surrender the following day. On 6 July 1917 the Arabs occupied Aqaba, just 275km (170 miles) south of the British Army outside Gaza, and 1,125km (700 miles) north of Medina.[193]

That night, Stewart Newcombe and Captain Henry Hogarth
led a series of raids along the railway either side of Al Ula, about
320km (200 miles) north of Medina. They led a mixed force of
Arabs, Egyptian and Indian soldiers, French Algerian troops,
and, perhaps most surprisingly of all, the newly arrived Ja'far
al-Askari. This Arab officer had been in the Ottoman Army and
had led the Senussi for the bulk of their campaign against the
British, before being captured. As a prisoner, he had seen reports
of Djemal Pasha's execution of Arab nationalists in Syria, and had
volunteered to join the Arab Revolt. That night, they destroyed
some 4.8km (3 miles) of rails, and made further attacks on the
nights of 8 and 10 July. Al Ula itself was not attacked, although
a small flight from No. 14 Squadron RFC bombed the station on
11, 12 and 16 July.[194]

Meanwhile, Lawrence had struck off north to carry the good
news to Cairo. Whatever concerns there may have been about
post-war politics were rapidly overcome once the fait accompli
was presented. Lawrence arrived on 10 July, and met with
Gilbert Clayton, head of the Arab Bureau. Just two days later,
he was in front of General Sir Edmund Allenby, who had arrived
two weeks earlier to replace General Murray. Taking time out
of what must have been an extremely busy schedule, Allenby
listened to all that Lawrence had to say, and promised to give
his report full consideration. After another two weeks in Cairo,
Lawrence returned to Arabia with a new plan, worked out by
himself and Allenby. Feisal's forces would now become a dis-
tinctive group, the Northern Army, effectively an army corps
separate from the other Arab forces. The base at Wejh would
be closed and Aqaba would become the new base of operations
(supplies had begun to arrive by sea as early as 13 July), and the
whole force would become northern-facing. Fresh troops and
resources were quick to arrive, include Ja'far to train and lead a
small cadre of regular Arab troops. This force contained small
numbers of other former Ottoman prisoners of war, including
Nuri Bey, another Ottoman officer who had led the Senussi.
Lawrence was to write to Clayton that Ja'far was:

On the whole fairly sensible, I think, & shows more com-
prehension of the Arab point of view than any of the other
Syrian officers. Captain MacIndoe criticizes his force rather
bitterly, but their real object is not so much to engage the
Turkish forces on equal terms, as to stiffen the Bedouin resistance, by providing the comforting spectacle of a trained
reserve, and to impress the Turks with the fact that behind
the Bedouin screen lies an unknown quantity, which must be
disposed of before they can conquer Aqaba.[195]

In fact, the regulars would become more than that. Although
no more than 5,000 men strong at any time, organised into two
'divisions', and with some distinctly irregular habits (many of
the tribesmen from the Hedjaz mountains or the Yemen refused
to wear the uniform, or any other, trousers)[196] the regulars
would fight pitched battles in 1918, and add exactly the kind of
stiffening and support that Lawrence felt the tribesmen needed.

Nor was Captain J.D. MacIndoe, a Scots Guardsman attached
to the staff, the only one to be distressed at the sight of the Arab
regulars. On arriving at Feisal's camp with his armoured car
unit, Driver Sam Rolls was shocked to recognise both Ja'far and
Nuri Bey, who he had fought against in the Western Desert the
previous year:

> I gripped the arm of a man standing next to me; he was star-
> tled and tired to shake me off. 'Look!' I exclaimed.
>
> 'Look at what?' he said brusquely.
>
> 'That's Ja'far Pasha!' I cried, amazed. 'I know him well.
> We captured him near Sollum and sent him to Cairo. He was
> leading the Senussi against us!'
>
> Then my eye fell on another of them. 'Good God! And
> there's Nuri Bey!' I cried. 'The cunning dodger! Now, what's
> the game here?'

More than once I had chased Nuri on his piebald horse in
the Libyan Desert, and but for his clever choice of ground I
should certainly have caught him. How these two had managed to reach their present position was a mystery to me. I
felt an impulse to rush to Lawrence and confess my great
discovery to him.[197]

All was later cleared up, and Rolls would later happily remi-
nisce (through translators, including Lawrence himself) with his
former enemies.

Rolls had felt no such disquiet when he first met Lawrence
at Aqaba. His unit had arrived three weeks previously, and had
been delayed while they made a track suitable for their cars to
climb from the port to Wadi Itm. It had been a frustrating and
hard time, with little idea as to where they were or what they
supposed to be fighting for or achieving. Late one day there
arrived 'a group of dishevelled Arabs, mounted on richly har-
nessed camels':

'Yalla! Imshi! Clear off!' I shouted to the first of the Arabs,
who was making his camel kneel.

He paid no heed, so I swung my hands at him, palms forward, as one shoos chickens. He had left his camel now, and
seeing me doing this he hastened towards me, which struck
me as strange. Looking now, for the first time, full into his
eyes, I had a shock. They were steel grey eyes, and his face was
red, not coffee-coloured like the faces of other Arabs. Instead
of the piercing scowl there was laughter in those eyes ... He
placed his hand for a moment on my shoulder. 'My name is
Lawrence,' said he, 'I have come to join you.'

I had never heard of Lawrence. Who had? Nobody knew
what he had done or was doing ... but this unexpected meeting meant more to me than the most sensational and true
reports could have meant ... In this moment my carking anxi-
ety and the feeling of purposelessness and of boredom left me

completely, and I never knew it again throughout the war. My first sight of Lawrence brought me ease and happiness, a most satisfying feeling that my little labours had a purpose, and a fine one.[198]

Ja'far himself only mentions Lawrence fleetingly in his memoirs, even though it was Lawrence who initially facilitated Ja'far's joining the Sharifian forces. However, he would later describe the Arab reaction to this influential man:

We all appreciated his courage and devotion to duty at all costs to his life and comfort. He gave us a good and concrete example of self sacrifice for the common cause and the benefit of others. He appeared very reserved, sometimes even cynical and sarcastic, but only against those who were not sincere and true in their dealings with him.

A simple man, he did like simplicity in almost everything. This is why he was so attractive to and attracted by the Bedouins of the desert.[199]

Under the supervision (direct command was impractical) of Allenby, Feisal's men would raid deep into Syria against the railways and other supply lines of the Ottomans. Once the offensive that Allenby was planning for the autumn began, they would protect his right flank while continuing to raid behind the lines. The other Arab forces would continue as before, and continue to come under the supervision of the High Commissioner in the Sudan.[200] There was some concern over how the Emir of Mecca would take this abrupt appropriation of one of his sons and his army, but on his return Lawrence met with Hussein and received his full blessing. After all, he now had British sanction and support to spread his influence and control deep into Syria.[201]

8

TRENCH WARFARE

AFTER THE END of the 2nd Battle of Gaza, both sides hurriedly worked to dig in and improve their defences. Immediately south and south-east of Gaza the temporary British line that had been used as a jump-off point was turned into a proper trench system, with multiple lines, barbed wire and communications trenches leading back towards the Wadi Ghazze. The jumbled terrain disallowed regular lines, and each side held outposts, hills and spurs that jutted into, or even sat detached within, no-man's-land. By the time they reached Sheikh Abbas, the lines were up to 3.2km (2 miles) apart, and then widened considerably as the Ottomans stuck to the Gaza–Beersheba road and the Egyptian Expeditionary Force's (EEF) lines cut down to the south, to keep close to the water sources along the Wadi. The British trenches petered out a few miles beyond the important springs at Shellal, by which time they were 14km (9 miles) from the nearest Ottoman positions at the Hureira Redoubt, although two strong parallel lines of outposts and redoubts carried on to the south-east, protecting the open flank. All along the front the artillery on both sides kept up sporadic bouts of spite against enemy trenches or rear areas, while the German pilots of FA-300s made full use of their continuing air superiority to bomb and strafe British positions, camps, dumps and patrols. Both artillery and aircraft caused a small, steady trickle of casualties, although beyond doubt the latter were more feared. Seeming to roam and attack at will, the feeling of nakedness and defencelessness that a diving aeroplane engendered in those on the receiving end caused much greater damage to morale than physical harm.

To the east of Shellal, the strings of outposts and the wide open space between the lines were held by the cavalry. The springs at Shellal, sitting on the edge of the Wadi Ghazze, were taken as a base camp, although as yet they were under-developed. Even by midsummer, Sergeant S.F. Hatton of the Middlesex Yeomanry would record it as being:

> Just a dirty spot upon a dust-laden wind-swept filthy plain. It was grit, grit everywhere – grit and chlorine in the tea, grit and chlorine in the stew; but grit without chlorine on the bread and jam. Water was very scarce as it was the dry season, and a wash twice a week was a luxury; but by saving a little tea one could shave every day.[202]

In fact, the springs at Shellal (which means 'cataract' or 'water-fall') were in the process of an immense development, along with massive cisterns to hold the 200,000 gallons (over 900,000 litres) a day that would eventually be pumped out.[203] So prolific would they become that today the 'dust-laden wind-swept filthy plain' is a lush green holiday camp and golf course, and the water is more palatable now that the army has stopped chlorinating it against disease. A few miles south-east down the Wadi, which at this point was around 18m (60ft) deep and 75m (80yds) wide, the Tel el Fara sat on the southern bank like a redoubt. Raised above the surrounding banks and giving excellent views in all directions, this tel was appropriated by A&NZ Mounted Division as their base. The cavalry divisions were rotated regularly, usually monthly, to allow men and horses time at rest camps on the coast. And rest was certainly deserved, as when they were deployed they saturated the area with patrols and played deadly games of cat-and-mouse with their Ottoman counterparts in the scattered hills and wadis. Units from section-size up to multiple divisions took part in raids, ambushes and reconnaissances across the area.

It was a continuous effort requiring confidence and an aggressive spirit, and was generally enjoyed by all of the Australian, New Zealand and British cavalrymen who took part. But it was also a job that needed skill, judgement and luck. Henry Bostock was a member of the Scout Troop of the 3rd ALH Brigade, and as such was more active than most in this intricate little war:

> Next morning reveille was at 1 a.m. The Scouts formed the advance screen on the march to el Karm and continued in a south-easterly direction until we met the Turkish cavalry at dawn. We chased them back several miles, exchanging shots on horse back, and took up a position near Beersheba. We held this all day, got some good shooting and had some narrow escapes. I was considered the best marksman in the troop and [was] often called upon. We often wondered why the whole Turkish cavalry regiment was not ordered to cut us off. They were armed with lance, sword and rifles. Perhaps our horses were too fast.

After returning to camp at 11 p.m., the Scouts were up again at two next morning to act as supports for an ambush set by the 8th Light Horse Regiment, but the Turks were too cunning to be trapped.[204] A few nights later Bostock was wounded, and one of his colleagues killed, when his night-time patrol literally ran into an Ottoman patrol in the dark.

In May a series of raids were launched against the Ottoman railway that ran south-east from Beersheba towards El Auja on the Egyptian border, and then past it to Kossaima. The area south of the border had been abandoned by the Ottomans earlier in the year, although a small garrison remained at El Auja and was supplied by rail. In fact, the rails and sleepers (equally valuable in a country with a limited industrial base and facing a severe shortage of wood) south of El Auja had already begun to be torn up, for reuse in the expanding rail network supporting the Gaza–Beersheba defensive line.[205]

However, General Murray did not know this. Reconnaissance reports from the Royal Flying Corps stated that the lines were still in place, misinterpreting the impressions of the freshly removed rails as tracks that had been covered with a thin layer of sand. Murray only saw a potential back door around his flank and into the Sinai Desert, where an Ottoman attack, or even large-scale raid, could cause havoc with his lines of communications. Indeed, intelligence was reporting that reinforcements were arriving in southern Palestine, and it seemed a distinct possibility that some of these might be directed into such an attack. General Chetwode, commanding Eastern Force, was more dubious, feeling that any Ottoman advance along that line would leave their own lines of communication so vulnerable that they risked being cut off and defeated.[206] Murray was insistent, however, perhaps due to the pressure he was himself receiving from London to be more aggressive and pro-active on this front, and he pressed Chetwode into forming a plan. This came to consist of a two-pronged attack on the railway, with the 1st ALH Brigade escorting the combined Royal Engineer contingents of the A&NZ and Imperial Mounted Divisions to Bir Asluj, about 19km (12 miles) south of Beersheba, and the Imperial Camel Corps (ICC) Brigade attacking El Auja. Meanwhile, the rest of the Imperial Mounted Division would create a diversion south of Beersheba, while an artillery bombardment would be carried out on Gaza.[207] This plan eventually evolved to include three days of diversionary attacks along the whole front, and the deployment of the entire A&NZ Mounted Division.

Interestingly, a few days after the serious planning began, cast-iron evidence arrived that the rails had been removed. No. 16 Company of the ICC Brigade (reinforced with members of No. 2 Company) had launched their own raid across the Sinai to the railway at El Auja on 6 May 1917. The six-day patrol destroyed a railway bridge and several wells, and captured some Ottoman rail workers. Both the prisoners and direct observation confirmed that the rails had gone.[208] Regardless of this, diversionary operations began on 19 May, and on 22 May the main raiding forces left their respective bases, the ICC Brigade from Rafah and the A&NZ Mounted Division from Tel el Fara. Following the pattern set in the long-range raids in the northern Sinai six months earlier, the attacking forces rode all night to come up on their target areas at dawn, having rounded up and secured the local civilian populations first. In the event both main parties were delayed by several hours, but no direct opposition was met although the Imperial Mounted Division experienced some light skirmishing just south of Beersheba. The demolition work took only a few hours, and by dusk all of the forces were withdrawing as planned, although the cameliers were subsequently delayed when an RFC aircraft made a forced landing nearby. The brigade camped out overnight while the aircraft was repaired, and returned to Rafah the following day. Behind them, some 21–24km (13–15 miles) of railway embankment and nine bridges or culverts, as well as a considerable amount of Ottoman stores, had been destroyed.[209]

The military value of destroying a railway that was already being dismantled is open to debate, but the raid proved that the British, and the cavalry in particular, where still capable of long-range operations in the desert, and that such operations were possible on the open flank south of Beersheba. If nothing else it proved that Murray and his army were still capable of undertaking large-scale aggressive action. Unfortunately, it also acted as a warning to the Ottomans. Rafael de Nogales was on the staff of the 3rd (OT) Cavalry Division at Beersheba:

Now some Bedouins arrived to tell us that the enemy cavalry had taken El Khafir by surprise ... This news, which fell like a bomb at our headquarters, finally disposed of the comfortable theory that the enemy would not dare advance by the south sector.[210]

Between May and September 1917, the Ottoman forces in this isolated garrison would be reinforced, their front-line strength more than doubling from 1.6 riflemen per yard of frontage, to 4.2 riflemen.[211]

In the west, the infantry were also active in the confined spaces between the lines outside of Gaza. By day machine guns and snipers waited for opportunities to fire, while artillery regularly engaged in sporadic bombardments. At night British patrols probed and mapped the Ottoman lines in the darkness, while attempting to stop Ottoman patrols from doing the same. The Ottomans could also attempt to tap onto the many telephone lines that had been left scattered across the area by the British in the early battles, some of which were still connected to their main communications system.[212] Not infrequently, British patrols encountered Ottoman soldiers, including officers, attempting to cross the lines and surrender.[213]

Trench raids were also mounted to test the defences, bring in prisoners for questioning, and keep up the offensive spirit. Such raids evolved out of the probing patrols which often involved lobbing grenades or firing a few rounds at the enemy trenches, but soon escalated into something else entirely. On 5 June 1917 the Ottomans mounted the first serious raid, against a small British outpost, about 160m (180yds) in front of Umbrella Hill. This lay on the edge between the coastal sand dunes and a wooded area on the side of Es Sire Ridge. The ground was heavily broken and covered in scrub, and so in daylight an eight-man piquet was kept out in front to warn of any enemy attack. At just after 6.15 a.m., after the usual morning 'stand to' had been stood down, the sentries had been replaced and the daily routine begun, Ottoman snipers killed the two men of the 1/5th Royal Scots Fusiliers (RSF) from the piquet who were on watch, and a party of around twenty Ottoman soldiers rushed the rest. Their approach route was carefully chosen so that the first the troops in the front line knew of the attack was when they saw them pour into the outpost, struggling with the remaining Scottish soldiers. A rescue force was swiftly organised by Second Lieutenant J.M. Craig, of the 1/4th RSF but attached to the 1/5th, but by the time they had reached the outpost three of the piquet were dead, two dying and three missing. A second Ottoman force opened fire from close by to cover the retreat of the main raiding group, while longer-range machine-gun and artillery fire began to fall around them. Several of the rescue party were themselves wounded, and Craig repeatedly braved the barrage despite being hit himself to bring wounded soldiers in before British artillery managed to suppress the enemy fire. For his selfless bravery, he was later awarded the Victoria Cross.

It had been an impressively well-organised raid. The lines of approach and retreat had been carefully selected, the time of day when the British were likely to be the most relaxed chosen, and the covering fire for the retreat well laid down. However, the British retaliatory attack less than a week later would take trench raiding in Palestine to an entirely new level.

In truth, it was not strictly a retaliatory attack, as this operation had been in planning for several days before the Ottoman raid, but revenge certainly became a motivation. The scheme was the idea of Lieutenant Colonel Alexander Kearsey DSO, of the 1/5th King's Own Scottish Borderers (KOSB), part of the 155th Brigade. He had noticed how isolated one of the Ottoman forward positions, known as the Sea Post, was. As the name suggested, this was at the extreme end of the Ottoman line, right on the Mediterranean coast (although a smaller position – Beach Post – sat a short way behind and to the west of it, almost on the waterline). With the enthusiastic approval and support of his brigade and divisional commanders, Kearsey built a replica of the Sea Post behind British lines, based on aerial photographs. Even before the Ottoman raid opposite Umbrella Hill, he had teams of men training across this full-size mock-up. His plan was thoroughly tested, modified where necessary, and approved. It went ahead after dusk on 11 June, and was a model trench raid.

For some days previously, British artillery had been using high explosives and shrapnel to cut holes in the Ottoman wire by day, while sporadic machine-gun bursts discouraged them from repairing them at night. At 5 p.m. on 11 June, a brief barrage of seventy-seven shells was fired at the gaps. After dark, a British patrol set out to check the holes, and sweep no-man's-land for Ottoman patrols. At 8.20 p.m., they reported all clear, and the two main assault parties set out under the overall command of Lieutenant Turner. These two forces, under Lieutenants McGeorge and Mackinnon, each consisted of fifteen riflemen (some armed also with axes, in case of unexpected obstacles) and two bombing parties totalling another fourteen men. These crept out and took up position about 200m (220yds) from the Sea Post. At 8.54 p.m. another brief barrage, just two minutes in duration, struck the wire, allowing the two raiding parties to dash forward another 100m (110yds). There followed a two-minute gap, and then another two-minute barrage fell upon the post itself. At the same time, diversionary actions opened further east along the brigade's lines. Careful monitoring had revealed that the Ottoman night-time distress signal was three red flares, and a spot in the 1/5th RSF trenches had been chosen from where such a signal could be launched which, when seen from the main Ottoman observation posts on Ali Muntar, would appear to have come from their Umbrella Hill positions. Sure enough, believing that their post there was under attack, Ottoman artillery immediately began shelling the area ahead of Umbrella Hill. This barrage would cost the Royal Scots three men killed and one wounded, but it also kept Ottoman attention on the wrong area of their line. At the same time, slightly further east, the 1/5th Highland Light Infantry began to pull ropes which were attached to dummies that they had seeded across no-man's-land. The figures lurched up and down in the light of further flares, drawing more fire and attention.

With the situation suitably muddied, if not utterly chaotic, the barrage lifted from the Sea Post and resumed 200m (220yds) beyond to the north and the east, blocking any possible Ottoman attempts to counter-attack from those sides. This work was supported by the 155th Machine Gun Company, who would fire some 10,600 rounds across no-man's-land to suppress enemy movement. The raiding parties of the 1/5th KOSB rushed in to the Sea Post. The bombardment had pushed most of the defenders underground, and the dozen that remained where killed or wounded in a brutal flurry of bayonets and axe-blows.* Even as the Scots poured in, Lieutenant H. Burt led a supporting bombing party on, around the Sea Post and astride the four communications trenches that ran back towards the main Ottoman lines. In these, they pulled down the parapets to create trench-blocks, over which they could lob their bombs, and which they vigorously defended against the few Ottoman soldiers willing to risk running through the blockading barrages. In one trench, an attempt by some of the Sea Post garrison to retreat led to the bombing party being attacked from both sides, but they drove both sets of attackers off. Meanwhile a reserve assault party moved up ready to back up either of the main assault parties, as did a support party ready to give covering fire. Supporting parties of signallers, more bombers, and extra axemen also moved forward, while a reserve party readied itself in the British lines in case of disaster.

With the Sea Post isolated and occupied, the main task of destruction began. As the raiders had gone in, the support party (under Captain J.B. Penman, also in overall command of the raid) followed across no-man's-land. They included a booty

---

* The troops had advanced with full magazines, but no round in their rifles' chambers, so that no accidental shots could alert the Ottomans.

party who began searching for enemy papers, weapons and equipment, while two demolition parties also arrived and began to destroy the Post systematically. Many Ottoman soldiers were found to have taken shelter in deep dug-outs. Those that could be were enticed out and taken prisoner; those who could not where buried as the dug-outs were blown. The trenches and barbed wire entanglements were also destroyed where possible, and mines were laid in the wire above the main post* and on the trench-blocks in the communications trenches. Happy that the work was complete, Penman blew the recall signal on his whistle, and, covered by the supports and reserves, the bombers, raiders and demolition men withdrew to their own trenches. Meanwhile, a beach party (with their own beach party reserve), had attacked the Beach Post, and now withdrew as well.

The raid had taken just fifteen minutes from the lifting of the second barrage to the recovery of the last raider into their own trenches, where a tot of rum awaited every man. Just one of the raiders had been wounded, accidentally injuring his own foot with an axe, while 60–100 Ottomans were estimated as killed. Regrettably, an over-enthusiastic bomber had blown up the headquarters dug-out before it could be searched, but at least they had brought back a dozen prisoners for questioning, while a Lewis gun that had fallen into Ottoman hands during the 1st Battle of Gaza, and which was being used by them in the Post, was also brought back. Including the enlarged Regiment Aid Post established near the scene, but not the men of the supporting nine artillery batteries, the machine-gunners, or the several battalions involved in decoy operations, the raid had involved over 370 officers and men (all of whom had been issued a white arm band for ready identification at night; after all, the Ottomans also wore khaki uniforms). (See Appendix C.) Captain Penman and Lieutenant Mackinnon were awarded the

---

* They had been intended for use in the trenches, but in the event they proved too congested for the Royal Engineers to work.

Military Cross, and Privates A. Paul and J. Dickson the Military Medal. Several others were mentioned in despatches.[214]

Such raids became a regular occurrence, although few were so successful for such light casualties. In between this activity, the men in the front lines and rear areas settled down to trench warfare. Their experiences could vary greatly depending on where they were. Depending on the location and orientation of their trenches, dug-outs, or even their camps, which tended to be tucked away in wadis and ravines where possible to protect them from air observation and attack, they could be stifling heat-traps or breezy areas of shade. All of them were dust-blown, and sand storms could make life a misery. The worst were the *khamsin*, the furnace-like blasts of hot air that swept up across the Sinai, and could last for several days. Even on the best of days the heat could be oppressive, making any form of work uncomfortable or even dangerous. Thomas Minshall, 10th King's Shropshire Light Infantry, recalled:

> We were working at full pressure trenching and wiring in the burning sun, the hot winds parched the men's lips until some were overcome with the heat and had to be carried to our position. To see big strong men crying like little children for water, 'precious water,' was terrible.[215]

And that was only in late April, before the start of the summer.

Throughout, soldiers were plagued by flies and other wildlife. Fleas and lice were rife and an unavoidable fact of life, despite the efforts of 'delousing' units which steamed clothing to kill off the unwelcome guests while the soldiers themselves were scrubbed down. Scorpions were common, as were giant centipedes (up to a foot long), and even tarantula spiders. Care had to be taken in putting on boots and clothes in case such creatures had decided to shelter in them, and likewise when laying out blankets for sleep. Just as much care would be needed on awakening, in case any had decided to take advantage of the sleeping soldier's body-warmth at night. These three poisonous creatures in particular were favourites for capture, and pitting them into fights against one another to much excitement and betting. Other common local insects, such as dung-beetles, were largely left unmolested.

To support the men in their efforts, water continued to be pumped in from Egypt via the pipeline across the Sinai, although this system was rapidly proving inadequate. Local sources were developed – existing wells expanded and new wells dug – but it was slow work, and water was generally scarce. The official ration was a gallon (4.5 litres) per man per day. Of this, the majority, five pints, went to the cookhouse for the preparation of meals and the steady supply of tea that the army required. This left two pints for drinking – generally issued one before dawn and one after dusk, with drinking water in daylight hours discouraged – and just one pint for personal hygiene. This was the seldom-met ideal, and even when it was delivered it left very little room for waste. Lieutenant James Mackie of the 2/4th Somerset Light Infantry had served in India before his battalion was posted to Palestine, and so was no stranger to hot climates, but even so he found that:

> The great difficulty up here is to get water. It all has to be brought up on camels & all ranks are allowed one gallon per day for all purposes. This has to do everything – washing drinking – cooking etc. We don't waste very much I can assure. We use about a pint every morning to wash, shave & clean our teeth in & then this water is used by our batmen to wash socks etc in before it is thrown away. We can't afford water to wash our plates in but sand makes a very good substitute & you can get them just as clean by rubbing them with sand as by washing them in water. As a matter of fact they don't want much cleaning for we clean them fairly well with bread before we finish our meals for even a drop of gravy is too valuable to waste.[216]

Inevitably, when supplies ran short hygiene tended to lose out first. Sickness spread through the army, with diphtheria and scarlet fever far from unknown, and stomach and heat- or sun-related illness common. By far the most common complaint was septic sores. Trooper Victor Godrich of the QOWH recalled:

> Every man in the fighting forces was covered in septic sores on their hands, faces and legs – all in bandages. My own hands did not properly heal until the cold weather in December ... If one's hand was accidentally knocked against a saddle, a large piece of skin came off. The result was an open sore that would not heal. The swarms of flies settling on the sore did not improve matters, so we had to use bandages for self-preservation.[217]

So prevalent were these that Godrich recalls a sick-parade by his entire regiment to have their sores examined: 'The first line were "bad" cases, wrecks etc. The second line "fairly bad" and the rear rank "not so bad."'[218] So many were afflicted that the vast majority had no choice but remain on duty, with only the very worst cases being sent back for treatment in hospitals. Meanwhile, rest camps were established along the coast so that units could be rotated, spending at least some time in the cooler, healthier climate on the shore, and taking advantage of the sea for frequent bathing. A few lucky men even managed to obtain short trips back to Egypt, although leave to home – be it the UK, Australia or New Zealand – remained a distant fantasy.

Back in Cairo, General Murray and his staffs were just as active, fighting their own paper war with London. Pressure was still being put on the EEF to take offensive action, despite Murray's constant, and correct, insistence that nothing could be done with the resources he had available. The two battles outside Gaza had proved that he did not have the strength in either artillery or infantry to break through the Ottoman lines, and indeed the situation was now made worse by battle casualties. Slowly, the situation began to be rectified. Artillery began to arrive from the UK and Salonika, enough to at least allow the 74th (Yeomanry) Division to enter the line as a combat formation. Other units also arrived from Salonika. The 60th Division began to transfer across in mid June, while the 7th and 8th Mounted Brigades began to arrive later in the month, allowing a complete restructuring of the cavalry from two divisions into three. The A&NZ Mounted Division, under Major General Edward Chaytor, now consisted of the 1st and 2nd ALH Brigades and the New Zealand Mounted Rifles Brigade; the Australian Mounted Division was formed under Major General Henry Hodgson, with the 3rd and 4th ALH Brigades and the 5th Mounted Brigade; and the Yeomanry Division was formed under Major General George Barrow, with the 6th, 8th and 22nd Mounted Brigades, while the 7th Mounted Brigade remained independent and reported directly to HQ Eastern Force. Meanwhile various garrison units from Egypt, Aden and India began to be gathered to create a new infantry division, the 75th, under Major General Philip Palin. This initially consisted of three brigades, but each of three battalions as opposed to the usual four, and it was without artillery. To make this formation possible, the garrison of the Suez Canal was stripped back to almost nothing.[219]

At the same time, two more exotic units also arrived in Palestine. Italy and, particularly, France both had interests in the region and sent contingents to represent them in the field, giving them a direct involvement in the campaign and thus a larger say in any post-war settlements. The French were determined the acquire Syria, and their detachment arrived in late May and consisted of the 5/115th Territorial Regiment and the 7/1st and 9/2nd Algerian Tiralleurs, with supporting artillery, cavalry, engineers and medical units, under Colonel de Piépape. The Italians meanwhile had expressed an interest in acquiring parts of the Smyrna coastline of Anatolia, but the British War Cabinet made it clear that any such claim had to be backed by a commitment of troops to the theatre. It was hinted that the Italians may like to make up the one or more infantry division that Murray was still appealing for, especially as the Cabinet felt that Italy was not pulling its weight in the war effort as whole. Instead of an infantry division, though, a contingent of 500 men was sent, under Colonel Francesco d'Agostino. (Later, in September, the possibility was raised of the EEF acquiring a brigade of Chinese troops, although nothing came of this.)[220]

The newly arrived or formed divisions – 60th and 75th – immediately began to undertake training to acclimatise themselves to desert operations. The 75th Division, gathered from scattered units, also needed to drill and train itself into acting as a coherent formation, as did its constituent brigades. It was hard work for all. W.N. Hendry of the 2/14th London Regiment (London Scottish) was immediately sent with his unit to a desert camp:

> Here we stayed for some weeks, training all the time, with exercises, drills and skirmishes in the mornings. We laid down in the sweltering heat all afternoon, or sometimes walked the three miles to a canteen … It was a very rare occasion when meals were really plentiful.[221]

This latter issue was also rapidly becoming a problem. While Murray was at last beginning to receive the troops that he needed to break the Gaza–Beersheba line, he also had to supply them. The army was still being fed by the single-track railway across the desert, which was running at thirteen trains a day. Six of these were needed for the maintenance of the railway itself or for hospital trains, leaving just seven trains for bring up supplies for the fighting forces. Once the two new divisions entered the line, the demand for supplies would increase dramatically, and while it was confidently predicted that these trains could provide enough food, fodder and stores to supply five infantry and three cavalry divisions, there would soon be six infantry divisions with the Eastern Force. Some small slack was available on the line, enough perhaps for three more trains a day, which should have proven sufficient to supply an extra two divisions, but running such a tight service left very little room for stock-piling or safety margin in case of disruption. The water situation was even worse. By May the pipeline was pumping 600,000 gallons (2.7 million litres) of water out of Egypt every day, yet just 36,500 gallons (166,000 litres) was reaching the end of the pipeline in Palestine. The rest was being used to keep the rear areas, including the railway itself, the Egyptian Labour Corps and support troops supplied. Thankfully, good sources of water were being developed at Shellal and Khan Yunis to make up the deficit, but it was still a tight margin. Murray requested permission to double the railway immediately, and to expand the water system, but permission for neither project was forthcoming from London.[222]

Despite such inconsistent support from the War Office, who were still pressuring action on the Palestine front, Murray and his staff proceeded with their plans to renew the offensive after the summer had passed. By late May, the thinking was to split Eastern Force into two separate army corps in order to act across a wider front, and there was a loose plan to unleash one of the corps against the line at or just west of Beersheba, turning the inland flank of the Ottomans before rolling up their line, and then advancing north.[223] This option had briefly been discussed during the advance on Gaza at the start of the year, but was now being revisited, perhaps not least because of the success that the mounted divisions had enjoyed on that flank when raiding the Ottoman railway earlier in the month. Indeed, the two primary officers behind developing the plan were Sir Philip Chetwode and his chief-of-staff, Sir Guy Dawnay, who had overseen the raid. However, although troops were now forthcoming in sufficient numbers, the situation regarding artillery, aeroplanes, and logistics were still seriously wanting. Murray was still grappling with these issues when he received a telegram on 11 June informing him that he was being relieved of command.

He would remain on only for as long as it took for his replacement, General Sir Edmund Allenby, to arrive.

On 28 June 1917 Sir Archibald Murray handed over command, and returned to the UK. He would not see active service again, spending the rest of the war as General Officer Commanding-in-Chief for Aldershot Command, and retiring in 1922. His service in Egypt and Palestine had certainly been mixed. Building on foundations laid by his own predecessor, Sir John Maxwell, he had fought a competent if unimaginative campaign to secure the Sinai Desert, taking a slow and careful approach that was more than warranted by the extreme conditions in which his army found itself. During this campaign, and into the early summer of 1917, he has also laid his own solid foundations for the supply and operation of the army in southern Palestine, a fact that Allenby would freely acknowledge. However, his performance before Gaza had been greatly lacking, and it is hard to envisage any new offensive under Murray being more than a similarly limited and pedestrian affair. Perhaps most importantly, he had also lost the confidence of the government.

9

ALLENBY

IT WAS CLEAR after the 1st Battle of Gaza that Sir Archibald Murray had lost the Prime Minister's confidence. David Lloyd George felt strongly that the campaign in Palestine needed to pushed forward vigorously, for the effect success would have on morale quite apart from any strategic purposes. He felt that the 'liberation' of the holy sites of Christianity, and in particular Jerusalem, from the Ottomans would serve as a tonic across all of the allied nations. At his direction, the Chief of the Imperial General Staff (CIGS), General Sir William Robertson, would remind Murray on 2 April 1917 that:

> Everyone now feels the strain of war, and the strain is increasing; therefore the moral effect of success is of great importance ... Success in Palestine will have inspiriting effects in Christendom.[224]

On 5 and 6 April 1917, two special meetings were held by the Prime Minister with the Secretary for War, the Foreign Secretary, and several other prominent MPs and members of the Privy Council, as well as the CIGS. In these, it became clear that Lloyd

George thought that Murray lacked an aggressive spirit and
wanted him replaced, but other ministers argued against this,
pointing out that he had been very successful in Egypt and that
the War Office and Cabinet must bear some of the blame for any
failures as they had not provided all of the support Murray had
requested. The CIGS was less supportive, but voiced concern at
replacing a commander on the brink of a battle. Lord French, the
former commander of the British Expeditionary Force (BEF) in
France, for whom Murray had been Chief of Staff, was consulted,
but although his opinion backed up that of the Prime Minister, it
was clear that there was not enough support to move to replace
Murray. The best that Lloyd George could achieve was suggesting
that the CIGS begin looking for possible replacements, suggesting Lieutenant General Sir William Birdwood (commander of the
I ANZAC Corps in France) or someone like Major General Sir
William Bridges (the Australian commander of the 1st Australian
Division, who had been killed by a sniper at Gallipoli). Both of
these officers were (or had been) aggressive, and had a command
style that included regular visits to the front line and popularity
with their men, in contrast to Murray's aloof style.[225]

After Murray's second failure to take Gaza, Lloyd George
found himself in a much stronger position. In the same meeting of the War Cabinet that Murray's failure was announced,
the Prime Minister again raised the subject, and suggested
Lieutenant General Jan Smuts. A South African who had fought
very successfully against the British in the Boer War of 1899–
1902, Smuts had recently arrived in London after commanding
the campaign in German East Africa. With his experience in
open warfare he was thought to be the ideal candidate, although,
when asked, Smuts felt differently. Protracted discussions followed.[226] After taking two weeks to think it through, Smuts
replied that he was concerned that the campaign would not
receive enough resources to ensure success, especially if the
trouble in Russia, where the government had recently been
toppled by revolution, continued. Lloyd George countered

that, should the situation in Russia worsen, even to the point of them withdrawing from the war effort, it would only make the importance of Palestine greater. He had no hopes of anything being achieved in France in 1917, and proposed making Palestine the leading subsidiary campaign.[227] Even with this reassurance, Smuts finally rejected the idea. This was reported to the War Cabinet on 5 June, and with it came the instruction to inform General Sir Edmund Allenby that the job was his.[228]

For Allenby, this came as none-too-welcome news. Allenby was an experienced cavalry officer; commissioned in 1882, he had served as a junior officer in campaigns in Bechuanaland (1884–5) and Zululand (1888) before passing the Staff College exams in 1896–7, a rare accomplishment for a cavalry officer at that time. After graduating, Allenby served briefly as a staff officer in Ireland before being sent to South Africa for the 2nd Boer War (1899–1902). During the war he established a solid reputation for his grasp of open, mobile warfare against the small Boer guerrilla bands that plagued the more ponderous British Army. During these three years he fought many successful small actions, and rose from the rank of major to brevet colonel, commanding a mixed column of cavalry, infantry and artillery. He returned to England after the war, and in 1905 was promoted to brigadier general, commanding the 4th Cavalry Brigade. Four years later he was again promoted, to major general, and was soon after appointed the Inspector General of Cavalry, responsible for overseeing cavalry training and standards across the army. During this period he began to build a no-nonsense reputation, with a forthright, even harsh, manner and a fearsome temper when displeased, earning him the nickname of 'The Bull'.

On the outbreak of the First World War, Allenby had been appointed to command the Cavalry Division of the BEF in France. The Cavalry Division was not a peacetime formation; it consisted of four brigades of cavalry (plus supporting Royal Horse Artillery) who had seldom worked in unison, and a staff who were thrown straight into their work with no time for training or familiarisation, deploying to the continent within weeks of the division's formation. Despite these handicaps, Allenby's command performed well in the opening campaign in Belgium and northern France, even if problems in communications meant that Allenby himself lost contact with large parts of his division for extended periods. By the end of the year Allenby was commanding the Cavalry Corps, of two divisions, and in May 1915 he took over V Corps, then engaged in the 2nd Battle of Ypres. In October he rose again, to command the newly formed Third Army.

Allenby was still in command of the Third Army in early 1917, when it was decided to launch a series of attacks on the Germans on both the Eastern and Western Fronts. This grand scheme would have hopefully seen the Germans drastically overstretched, and subsequently overwhelmed, but it began to fall apart in February when the Russians announced that they would be incapable of taking part. In March, the Germans themselves added to the problems by staging an orderly withdrawal from a large stretch of the front opposite both the British and French armies, to the heavily fortified Hindenburg Line. This threw Anglo-French planning into turmoil, but the French were determined to push ahead anyway. Civil and military discontent within France was reaching dangerous levels, and a victory was sorely needed. The French Chief of the General Staff, Robert Nivelle, convinced the British to proceed, and on 9 April the 2nd Battle of Arras was launched in heavy snow in the British sectors, aimed at drawing off German reserves before the main French attack a week later. Allenby's forces were positioned in the centre of the British line, just east of Arras itself.

The initial attack by the Third Army was a remarkable success, penetrating 6.5km (4 miles) into the German lines, although problems in moving the reserves forward prevented any chance at a clear breakthrough. Further north, the Canadian Corps in First Army managed to take and hold the dominating feature of Vimy Ridge, although to the south the Fifth Army met with less success. Over the next month a series of further attacks were made, but none were as successful as the earliest phase, and casualties began to mount rapidly. On 16 May the offensive was halted. The French, meanwhile, had launched the Nivelle Offensive on 16 April. This also met with some initial successes, but by 25 April major operations were halted as French casualties in nine days exceeded those suffered by the British in five weeks. By the end of May a widespread mutiny had broken out in the French lines, with tens of thousands of soldiers refusing to take orders. This was part of the background against which Lloyd George was so desperate for victory, and it also brought to a head several problems between Allenby and the British commander in France, Sir Douglas Haig. The two, who had known each other since Staff College, did not work well together. The appointment to Palestine was an ideal opportunity for Haig to replace Allenby.

However, Allenby initially viewed his recall to London and the offer of the position of General Officer Command (GOC) EEF as a demotion. He was, after all, being taken away from the main fight against the principal enemy, and shunted off to a sideshow on the other side of Europe. Only after a long discussion with Lloyd George in person did he begin to come around, and by the time he left England to take up his new command he was fully enthused about the idea. To convince him, Lloyd George had used (apart from his natural and considerable charm) the same arguments with which he had attempted to woo Smuts.

There was no hope of any decisive blow being made in France for the foreseeable future; the French Army was in disarray, and the British would be able to do little more than hold the line on their own. The Russians were fading fast from the war effort, and could possibly even collapse altogether. In April the United States of America had at last joined the fight against Germany, but it was unlikely that they would be able to put troops onto the Western Front in any significant numbers until the following year, or possibly even 1919, while much of their heavy equipment, artillery and aeroplanes would have to be provided by the British and French. Meanwhile, they would have to move all of their troops and supplies across the Atlantic, at a time when the German submarine threat was reaching almost disastrous levels, with British shipping taking unsustainable losses.

In Mesopotamia, the British forces had taken Baghdad in March 1917, a serious blow to Ottoman morale, but there the campaign had halted as the forces involved regrouped. Even should that front begin moving again, there was little of real value to be gained by further advances. The campaign in Salonika, in Macedonia, had seen British successes so far that year, but the government was inclined to reduce the forces in that theatre, to decrease the amount of shipping needed to supply the troops and enable that tonnage to make up losses elsewhere. Therefore, Palestine would be the primary theatre for 1917 at least, and possibly into 1918. Lloyd George promised him opportunity and resources to achieve his ends, and perhaps most tempting of all, the chance of truly independent command. Allenby would be running the show, able to experiment and innovate without senior commanders changing his plans or opposing his ideas. The temptation was too much to resist.

It was at this meeting that, according to Lloyd George's own diary, he instructed Allenby to deliver Jerusalem to the British (and other allied) peoples as a Christmas present. Lloyd George's fixation on Jerusalem had been evident in his instructions to Murray, and it was certainly an accurate sentiment. The British public were facing shortened rations, increased air raids, and continuing lack of success in France. While the state of the French Army was kept a closely guarded secret, even without that news the outlook was grim. Any victory by the end of the year would be a welcome fillip to morale and sprits at home, although the symbolism of retaking the Holy Lands would doubtless add to the effects.

Allenby arrived in Egypt on 27 June, 1917. He immediately began to stamp his own approach and personality on the army. He certainly made an impressive sight. Lieutenant Charles Armstrong of the Warwickshire Yeomanry would describe him the following year:

'The Bull' was at that time in his 57th year, but with his cap on, looked many years younger. A magnificent figure of a heavy man, he had the complexion of a girl, fine featured, with expression stern almost to grimness, eyes that seemed to look through you and sum you up at a glance, very smartly turned out, even in this terrific heat and dust.[229]

His crusade to reinvigorate the army started right away at his own headquarters in Cairo. Lieutenant Colonel Gerald Badcock recalled his whirlwind arrival:

He arrived in Cairo on Wednesday, June 27, and in less than forty-eight hours he had made the acquaintance of every officer in every branch at GHQ. He came round our Directorate, for instance, accompanied by General Campbell (our DQMG). He went to each person's office, shook hands with you, and had a few minutes' chat about your work and so on. I cannot adequately describe the far-reaching effect this simple act had on all such small fry like myself; you felt instinctively that there was nothing you would not try your best to do, and from the date of his arrival as our Commander-in-Chief a totally different atmosphere permeated our whole existence. He went everywhere, saw everything, and possessed moreover that faculty – as wonderful as it is rare – of always remembering everyone he had ever met.[230]

This first-hand knowledge of his staff led directly to a shake-up of the headquarters. Some officers were sent home, others reassigned to units closer to the front. One of those sent home (in September) was Major General Arthur Lynden-Bell, Murray's Chief of Staff, with whom Allenby shared a number of significant differences of view-point. He was returned to England for reasons of ill health, and Major General Louis Bols, who had been Allenby's Chief of Staff in France, was brought out to replace him.

One front-line officer, from the Imperial Camel Corps, recorded with approval:

> Allenby's arrival in Egypt was a breath of fresh air, which was soon to take on the dimensions of a gale … I paid a visit to Shepheard's [Hotel, in Cairo] a few months before Allenby's arrival and again a short time afterwards, and the difference was truly amazing. I have never seen or thought it possible to see such an array of brass gathered together as I found in the bars and dining rooms on the first occasion, nor so few as on my second visit. The removal of all this dead wood made a tremendous impression on the army's morale …[231]

Allenby did not confine his energy to the headquarters. Within weeks he was touring the front lines, visiting units and talking to (and more importantly listening to) officers at all levels. The same camelier, Geoffrey Inchbald, had his unit inspected by the new commander soon afterwards:

> After the inspection Allenby insisted on speaking personally to each of the officers and we all dismounted and went up to him in turn. He leant down, shook us by the hand, said a few words of encouragement and departed, as he had come, in a cloud of dust followed by his staff.[232]

Although not directly addressed on such a personal level, these visits were also appreciated by the rank and file. Corporal Victor Godrich of the QOWH records that his outpost in one of the front-most areas of the army received a visit on 7 July:

> The very fact of the GOC having a look at the front line was unheard of up till then … Sir Archibald Murray was a fig-urehead to us, no more in the front line than Kitchener, but Allenby was a real live GOC moving about among us … He earned our gratitude by ordering all the beer in Egypt up to the

men in the front line when he discovered we could not get it. Only small matters when viewed from an armchair in England, but big things to us in those dry, dusty days in Palestine.[233]

The availability of beer, and better rations, figures in many memoirs, and was symptomatic of Allenby's willingness to listen to all and any complaints, act on the most important, and to get to know his troops as bodies of men rather than markers on the map. Gunner Anthony Bluett:

Shortly after his arrival there was a notable increase in the quantity and quality of our rations, and beer in barrels – yea, barrels – came up the line for the troops.

I am not going to suggest that the two events were in point of fact connected, but I know that the sudden and welcome change was universally attributed to General Allenby, and that thenceforward the EEF was 'on him,' as the phrase goes, to a man.

I wonder if many of our big commanders realised as fully as did General Allenby the enormous influence the 'personal touch' had on the troops they commanded? Just to see your chief wandering about more or less informally, finding things out for himself, watching you – not on parade, but at your ordinary daily jobs; to know that he was not above getting out of his car to ask a question personally, or, during operations, to sit on a gun-limber digging his bully-beef out of a tin with a jack-knife, like any other man. These things went a mighty long way.[234]

After many months of simply being ordered around by a distant and unseen authority, Allenby gave the impression that the high command did at last care about the troops, and about what the men who actually had to do the job had to say about how it should be done.

Allenby is often said to have brought a new, aggressive spirit to the army, and to have restored their confidence, but these statements need some qualification. That the army in its lower levels already had an aggressive, forward posture is quite evident in the myriad of localised but intensive raids and skirmishes in which they had been engaged along the entire front. It was any larger-scale aggression as an army that was being stymied, as Allenby immediately recognised, by being starved of adequate resources by London. Likewise, this small-scale warfare speaks volumes about the troops' confidence in themselves as soldiers. Where Allenby really made a difference was in their confidence in their higher command. After the fiascos at the two battles for Gaza, this was indeed sorely needed. The senior commanders, especially Murray, were seen as out of touch with the realities on the ground; the very fact that at no point had Murray been to see these directly for himself but rather lived all the way back in Cairo was a major factor in this.

However, the 'Allenby Effect' can be over-stated, and was not universal. Some men simply soldiered on as usual, regardless of the changes at the top:

> There is a passage in The Seven Pillars of Wisdom which gave me some amusement when I read it. Lawrence talks about the 'calm drive and human wisdom of Allenby, who was the man the men worked for, the image we worshipped.' This is a ridiculous exaggeration. The men certainly worked for Allenby – they had no option to do otherwise. But we did not worship him because we did not know him or even General Bols, his Chief of Staff. The average ranker could barely visualise the meaning of an Army Corps; the grand personages who commanded them were usually quite unknown to us. General Bulfin and General Studd used to pay us visits when we were in the trenches, but Allenby was quite unknown to us and what we had heard of him did not endear him to us.[235]

This seems to be very much a minority opinion, although valid for all that. It is also worth noting that the author, Bernard

Livermore of the 2/20th London Regiment, had only just arrived from Salonika and thus had not taken part in the first assaults on Gaza. Perhaps these experiences lent perspective to others.

As well as raising morale and reducing the headquarters staff, Allenby sent his impressions, ideas and plans to the CIGS in London on 12 July 1917. His assessment was that any attack on Gaza would be prohibitively costly, while the western end of the Gaza–Beersheba line was equally heavily fortified. The eastern end of the line, before it reached the garrison town of Beersheba, seemed the weakest point. To break this line, Allenby laid out demands for another two infantry divisions (based on the assumption that 75th Division would not be combat-ready until the very end of the year) and 7,000 replacements to bring his existing six divisions (including the 75th) up to full strength; for significant amounts of artillery to bring his existing divisional artillery up to full complement, and create new heavy artillery units that would be commanded above divisional level, and so could be easily moved to where they were most needed; three squadrons of 'the latest' aircraft for the Royal Flying Corps; numerous Royal Engineer detachments, wireless and signals units, and ten new medical units – hospitals, Casualty Clearing Stations and Sanitary Sections. He also required permission and materials to double the railway and the pipeline across the Sinai. His intention was to be ready to mount an offensive in September.[236] A rather ambitious target, this early date was partly so as to make the most of the brief period between the end of the worst of the summer heat and the start of the rainy season in late October or early November, and also partly due to intelligence coming out of Palestine. A large Ottoman force, bolstered by German and Austrian units, was being gathered in Syria in preparation for a counter-offensive against the British in Mesopotamia. An attack in southern Palestine could cause some or even all of these forces to be siphoned off into defensive operations there, spoiling the Ottoman plans.

Over the next month compromises, changes and improvements were made. Typical of Allenby's thorough approach, the various schools of instruction* were visited and assessed, and changes made to modify or update courses, while many instructors (seen as out of touch) were rotated out to active units to improve their own knowledge. However, few reforms were so easy, as most of the changes that Allenby wanted to make relied on outside factors. Only one new infantry division could be spared – the 10th (Irish), from Salonika – although efforts would be made to bring the 75th up to full strength. The work on the railway and pipeline could begin straight away with what resources were at hand, while the additional materials required would be ordered immediately but would take time to be delivered. As Murray had found after the 1st Battle of Gaza, guns, shells, aeroplanes and other material could not simply be magicked into existence, and compromises had to be made based upon the production capacity of the factories at home, and what was needed by or could be spared from the other fighting fronts. The number of artillery pieces was eroded, although not severely, and the amounts of different types of shells also modified by London. Robertson, who as CIGS was the conduit between Allenby and Lloyd George, found himself increasingly in a bind as he continued to pass messages and requests between the two, while attempting to stem Allenby's demands and ambitions on the side. As a 'Westerner', Robertson believed that the Palestine front was a distraction, and in his unofficial correspondence with Allenby continued to attempt to limit the scope of the latter's plans and requests, even while officially passing to him, on 10 August 1917, the War Cabinet's instructions to mount an offensive aimed at reaching the Jaffa–Jerusalem line, if not further, at the earliest opportunity.[237]

---

* There were many of these, for officers, NCOs, machine-gunners, 'bombers', signallers and other specialists, as well as more general ones such as the Trench Warfare School at El Arish.

One of the most important responses to Allenby's requests, although even this was a compromise, was the revitalisation of the Royal Flying Corps in Palestine. The Middle East Brigade of the RFC, under Brigadier General Geoffrey Salmond, had responsibility for all British military aviation in Palestine, Mesopotamia, East Africa, and the Hedjaz, and for the training organisation in Egypt. Salmond had been appealing for months for more aircraft, and of more modern types, as the Germans in Palestine in particular continued to dominate the air. *Flieger Abteilung* (FA) 300, with their fewer but better aircraft, continued to take a toll on the British and Australian airmen opposite them, one of whom recorded that:

> We were, so it was said, the Suicide Club. You know: roosters to-day, and feather dusters to-morrow. Anyway, the average casualty hours over the line were something like five or six ... After which it was the hospital or sad slow music.[238]

This was an exaggeration, but even so Ottoman command of the air allowed them to freely observe troop movements, new artillery positions, new supply dumps, and all of the other obvious signs of an impending attack. In order to achieve any kind of surprise in his proposed attack, Allenby needed control of the air.

Some small modernisations were made over the summer of 1917. At the end of May, two D.H.2 pusher-type single-seat fighters arrived in theatre. Totally outdated by Western Front standards, they at least made a start towards giving No. 14 Squadron an offensive capability. The following month two more types, both single-seat fighters with tractor engines, arrived in larger numbers. The Vickers F.B.19 'Bullet' had been tested on the Western Front and found to be underpowered and with poor visibility, but was deemed suitable for use in the 'sideshows'. The Bristol M1c, on the other hand, was a fast and capable fighter, but it was also a monoplane. Since a series of pre-war accidents, the RFC had been wary of monoplanes and were reluctant to adopt any into general front-line use, although again it was good enough to be sent to the desert. Although these three types allowed the British to begin defending their airspace (although lack of numbers, and an early warning system based on binoculars and telephones, made that defence far from solid), none of them had the ability to escort British aircraft on long-range observation, reconnaissance or bombing operations over the Ottoman lines.[239]

Such long-range raids and flights occurred regularly as the British gathered intelligence on Ottoman movements and defences, photographing and mapping the areas over which it was hoped the army would soon be advancing. Bombing raids were also carried out. On 23 June 1917, seven aircraft bombed the German airfield at Er Ramle (Ramleh/Ramla) to keep FA300 grounded while three Short seaplanes from HMS *Empress* bombed a supply dump at Tul Karum. Three days later, eight aircraft (four BE2cs flying without observers to make them lighter and thus longer ranged, and four Martynsides) bombed an Ottoman headquarters on the Mount of Olives, just outside Jerusalem. Five of the aircraft were lost on the way home; one due to engine failure north of Beersheba, one with an engine failure after landing to pick up the pilot of the first aircraft, one from a broken undercarriage after landing to pick up both of the stranded pilots, and two more due to running out of fuel after circling the other three to see if they could assist. Miraculously, the first three pilots were rescued by a patrol of the Australian Light Horse, and the other two were picked up by two of the remaining aircraft.[240]

On 11 July, after Allenby added his voice to Salmond's, permission was received to create a new squadron for service in Palestine, No. 111 Squadron. The pilots for the new squadron were to be found from the existing squadrons or the training organisation in Egypt, while at least some of the new aircraft and the engines would be sent out from the UK. (One major factor in the delay in getting new aircraft out to Palestine had been a serious backlog in the aircraft and engine production systems in the UK. Existing production had barely coped with the losses in France up until the spring of 1917, when a massive expansion plan was introduced. Soon, production rose rapidly, with nearly four times as many aircraft being produced each month over the summer, although problems in engine production still slowed the over all process.)[241] This squadron was to be a designated fighter unit, the first in the theatre, and was rapidly followed by permission to raise a new observation squadron as well. No. 113 Squadron would be raised on the same terms – local pilots but aircraft from the UK – but with observation aircraft instead. Shortages in aircraft meant that the third requested squadron would have to be postponed until early 1918.

But even with this breakthrough, progress was slow. By the outbreak of the 3rd Battle of Gaza at the end of October 1917, No. 113 Squadron had just five 'of the latest' aircraft – RE8s – and was still predominantly equipped with the older BE2es. No. 111 Squadron fared a little better, although it had accumulated the hodge-podge of obsolete fighters already in theatre. These included five Vickers Bullets, three D.H.2s, two Bristol M1cs, and a single Bristol Scout. However, they also had the most important aircraft on either side: six Bristol F2b Fighters. Although called fighters and indeed fast and highly manoeuvrable, these two-seater aircraft, equipped with a forward firing gun as well as one for the observer, could also be used for reconnaissance and bombing work. They were by far the most capable aircraft in the theatre. The first F2b patrol was mounted on 7 October, and by the end of the month they had claimed two enemy aircraft shot down. More importantly, they could dominate the airspace over the British lines, and give Allenby the freedom to move his forces and deploy decoy sites without fear of discovery.[242]

To reflect the new capabilities of the RFC, on 5 October the Middle East Brigade was reorganised. The EEF elements were separated out to form the new Palestine Brigade, while the

Middle East Brigade was redesignated HQ RFC Middle East.
The new brigade was still under Salmond, but now was divided
into two wings. The Fifth (Corps) Wing, under Lieutenant
Colonel A.C. Boddam-Whetham, consisted of No. 14 Squadron
(BE2es) and No. 113 Squadron (BE2es and RE8s). As corps
squadrons these were to undertake artillery-spotting, 'contact
patrols' (monitoring and making contact with forward units on
the ground) and tactical reconnaissance operations. Meanwhile,
Fortieth (Army) Wing, under Lieutenant Colonel Amyas 'Biffy'
Borton, consisted of No. 111 Squadron (various – see above)
and No. 1 Squadron Australian Flying Corps (usually referred
to by the British as No. 67 Squadron to avoid confusion with
their own No. 1 Squadron, and equipped with a mix of BE2cs,
BE2es, RE8s, BE12as, and a Martynside). As army squadrons
these would be free to operate across the whole front, providing longer-range and strategic reconnaissance, escorts for corps
squadrons, and interceptors to chase off enemy aircraft. The brigade also included No. 21 Kite Balloon Company (consisting of
Nos 49 and 50 Sections) and a system of aircraft parks to provide
spares and repairs.[243] There would also be an expanded system
of some fifty-three wireless stations to improve communications
between the ground and the air.[244]

The reorganisation of the air forces reflected a reorganisation
that had already occurred on the ground. As had been suggested
by Murray earlier in the year, the Eastern Frontier Force was
abolished, and the EEF was formally restructured into several
corps to simplify the command structure. On 3 August 1917 it
was announced that three new corps were to be created, and that
the administrative and physical changes should begin immediately. The new structure was to be:

Desert Mounted Corps (based on the Desert Column)
(Lieutenant General Sir Harry Chauvel):
A&NZ Mounted Division
Australian Mounted Division

Yeomanry Mounted Division
Imperial Camel Corps Brigade

XX Corps (Lieutenant General Sir Philip Chetwode):
10th (Irish) Division
53rd (Welsh) Division
60th (London) Division
74th (Yeomanry) Division
Four brigades of heavy artillery

XXI Corps (Lieutenant General Edward Bulfin):
52nd (Lowland) Division
54th (East Anglian) Division
75th Division
Three brigades of heavy artillery

The 7th Mounted Brigade was kept back as an army unit, under the direct control of Allenby, as was a new Composite Force, consisting of the French and Italian contingents, the 20th Indian Imperial Service Infantry Brigade, and the 1st Battalion, British West Indian Regiment. The new structure was to come into effect on 12 August, 1917, the same day on which the new General Headquarters, EEF, was to become operational near Khan Yunis. This new GHQ would directly control the three corps in the field, while a rump headquarters would remain in Cairo to oversee Martial Law and other administrative and logistical issues. This move had been contemplated by Murray in May, but had been dismissed as it would, 'Completely upset the military and political machine in Egypt and would be most unfortunate from every point of view'.[245]

The move certainly did upset the situation in Egypt (see Chapter 6), but it also greatly improved the military situation in Palestine and came to symbolise the new, aggressive policy of the army.

10

PLANS

WHILE THE EGYPTIAN Expeditionary Force was undergoing reinforcement, reform and redirection, so were the Ottoman forces
opposing them. Throughout 1917 great changes were afoot,
although it would take many months to bring them into effect,
and as much, perhaps even more, discussion and dissent as to
what to do with the forces gathered. Just as the British senior
commanders were split between the Easterners and Westerners,
so the Ottoman high command would be split between those
intent on retaking lost ground, and those who wanted to concentrate on not losing any more.

After the 2nd Battle of Gaza, the Fourth (OT) Army
included the 3rd, 16th and 53rd (OT) Infantry Divisions, and
the 3rd (OT) Cavalry Division, spread along the lines between
Gaza and Beersheba. All of these forces were under strength.
The 3rd (OT) Cavalry Division consisted of only two cavalry
regiments (each the equivalent to a British brigade) although
as it was based in Beersheba it also had infantry units attached
to help man the town's defences while the cavalry conducted
longer patrols. All of the units also suffered from shortages of
men. The 16th (OT) Infantry Division, for example, had left

Constantinople in September 1916 with some 11,100 officers and men. After seeing action in the 2nd Battle of Gaza and spending the summer on the front lines, by October 1917 the division could muster just over 5,000 officers and men.[246] This was fairly typical, with battle casualties, desertions, and, by far the most draining factor, disease leaving most units at around 50 per cent of their authorised strength. Even units far from any fighting suffered similar rates. When the 24th (OT) Infantry Division was posted to Palestine from the Dardanelles later in the year, it left with 10,000 men but arrived with just 4,600. Some 19 per cent of the division had been listed as sick during the journey, and another 24 per cent had gone missing, with just 3 per cent being accounted for by sanctioned leave.[247] In an army that struggled to feed and clothe its soldiers or care for its sick, and where home leave was a rarity, the confusion of the movement of a division (which might also bring a soldier close to his home for the first time in years) could be the ideal time to desert, or at least take an extended absence without leave.

Through 1917, reinforcements poured into Syria, and later Palestine, to form the *Yildirim Ordular Grubunu*, or 'Thunderbolt Army Group'.* The exact origins of this force are a little obscure; the idea seems to have been around since late 1916, but the spring of 1917 brought the means, motive and opportunity for the plan to become reality. The core of the *Yildirim* was provided by the Germans (who knew it as Army Group F), under Field Marshal Erich von Falkenhayn. Prussian War Minister at the outbreak of war, von Falkenhayn had been appointed Chief of the General Staff of the German Army soon afterwards. In this role he had been the mastermind behind the bloody fiasco at Verdun, which had been intended to bleed the French armies dry, and had instead cost the Germans as many casualties themselves. After

---

* *Yildirim* is often translated as 'lightning', but the word in Turkish also has the connotation of violence and doing harm, so 'thunderbolt' is a more apt translation.

this, he had been appointed to command the German Ninth Army in Romania, where he had quickly taken Bucharest. Now he was being sent to conduct a similar role in the Middle East, where his initial objective was to be Baghdad.

With von Falkenhayn came a German staff, to which a handful of Ottoman officers were bolted on, and a central cadre of German and Austrian troops. This force would be known as 'Pasha II', coming after the small 'Pasha Force' that had arrived in May 1916. Pasha II consisted of three infantry battalions (No. 701 from Pasha I, and Nos 702 and 703 from Germany), and a mass of support units including machine-gun companies, a range of artillery units of different types and calibres, medical units, signals and wireless units, some very large transport units, and five new *Flieger Abteilung*, FA301 to FA305.[248] These new squadrons, each with a strength of eight aircraft (about half that of their British and Australian opponents), were equipped mostly with AEG C.IV two-seat reconnaissance aircraft (which could also carry a small bomb-load) but each also had a pair of Albatros D.III fighters, which were cutting edge at the time of despatch.[249]

These forces were useful in that they formed the support and logistical framework of an army corps, made up of units that were frequently lacking in the Ottoman services, but equally it was very light on actual fighting troops. The Ottomans seem to have been expecting several divisions of front-line infantry, but when these did not appear, they had to provide the troops themselves. The force was also extremely inexperienced when it came to the conditions they would face in Syria and Mesopotamia, and in working with the Ottomans. General Liman von Sanders, head of the German Military Mission to Constantinople, would later complain bitterly that neither he nor any of his staff had been involved in the formation of *Yildirim*, nor had their advice been asked to what equipment would be needed, what conditions would be faced, or whether special allowances needed to be made due to the nature of the theatre. Even the attachment of a handful of Ottoman staff officers to the headquarters did little to ease the problems that the force met as it travelled across the Ottoman Empire, ranging from simple language problems to misunderstandings as to how the local supply or command systems worked, to failure to anticipate the logistical problems that would be faced moving such a force around. The Ottoman railway and road system was still far below the standards that the Germans had expected, leading to long delays, while problems in recruiting drivers, drovers and other staff locally to help with the transport meant that large numbers of Germans had to be taken from their combat units to oversee the lines of communications instead; von Sanders claims that more of the Germans and Austrians were eventually used in this role than were used in the fighting units.[250]

Even as *Yildirim* began to gather at Aleppo, debate raged as to how to deploy them. The original plan had been to send them to Mesopotamia, to push back the British Army and retake Baghdad. This was the plan on which Enver Pasha, the Minister of War, was still intent. However, as *Yildirim* began to gather in May 1917, dissent grew. The forces were supposed to gather in the upper Euphrates, but Djemal Pasha successfully lobbied for them to be concentrated around Aleppo instead. This gave them better communications and also placed them in a more central position within the empire. From there, they could be sent to reinforce the fronts in southern Palestine, Mesopotamia, the Caucasus or even Syria should the British or French make a landing on the coast. As divisions began to gather, a series of conferences were convened in Constantinople to work out which of these fronts the force should be deployed to. Enver was still intent on Baghdad, while Djemal wanted to retain them in Syria to counter the growing British forces opposite Gaza (although he was worried about the *Yildirim* supplanting himself as the leading power in the region), using them as an imperial reserve and also a pool to allow him to rotate the divisions on the front line, who he currently could not relieve in any way.[251] Meanwhile, von Falkenhayn surprised many by switching from being pro-Mesopotamia to instead wanting to counter-attack across the Sinai.

The main reason for this debate was that *Yildirim* would be the Ottoman Empire's last reserve. The collapse of the Russian Army, the successes in Romania, and a general thinning of the Ottoman coastal defences in Anatolia and the Dardanelles allowed a massive concentration of forces to take place. Eventually, nearly eighteen divisions would be involved, out of an overall strength of some forty-five combat divisions fielded by the Ottomans. Not all of these divisions remained with the *Yildirim*, and many would not arrive until the end of 1917 or even the spring of 1918, but it was still clear that, once gathered, the empire would have very little more to spare. So far the empire had lost over half a million men killed, captured or missing, and around 750,000 wounded. On the other side of the ledger, around 100,000 young men per year reached the age of conscription, although this was reduced to only 90,000 by 1917 as parts of the empire in the Caucasus and Arabia were lost to the enemy. The forces that would eventually form the *Yildirim* would report shortages of some 70,000 men from their authorised strength, and yet receive just 27,000 reinforcements by the end of the year.[252]

Other reinforcements flowed in, in the form of complete divisions from all across the empire, albeit invariably as under-strength as those already in Palestine. It was a slow process, the 7th (OT) Infantry Division for example left Constantinople on 14 January 1917, but did not start to reach the railhead at Beersheba until 7 May, with the last units arriving only on 14 June. Other units had much further to travel; over the summer the 14th (OT) Infantry Division arrived from the Dardanelles, the 20th (OT) from Galicia (where Poland, Russia and Hungary meet), 26th (OT) from Romania, and the 48th (OT) and 53rd (OT) Infantry Divisions from the Caucasus. Two of the arrivals did not stay very long. In early October the 50th (OT) Infantry Division, which had arrived from Macedonia, was despatched on to the 6th (OT) Army in Mesopotamia, and the 59th (OT) Infantry Division, which had come from Aydin, on the Aegean coast of Anatolia, was broken up to be used to reinforce other divisions in the area. More arrived in the autumn, some only days or weeks before the expected British attack broke; the 19th (OT) Infantry Division arrived in late October from Galicia. Others still were even later; the 1st (OT) Infantry Division arrived from the Caucasus in December 1917, while the 42nd (OT) Infantry Division from the Dardanelles and the 2nd (Caucasus) Cavalry Division did not arrive until early 1918. Even some of the German units, such as the *Flieger Abteilung*, whose presence was supposed to form the core of the *Yildirim*, did not arrive until October or November.

The transport situation was a significant hindrance to the gathering of the forces for *Yildirim*. It took time to bring men and equipment across the patchwork of poor roads and incomplete railways that bound the empire together. The logistical situation was further damaged on 6 September, when a massive explosion ripped through the Haider Pasha (Haydarpaşa) railway station in Constantinople. The harbour, railway yards and warehouses at the station suffered considerable damage, while not only was valuable rolling stock lost, but also a considerable amount of supplies, mostly brought all the way from Germany and destined for *Yildirim*. It would be a severe blow in an empire with a small industrial base and limited resources.[253] The German air units were still moving through the station at the time. Several crated aircraft were destroyed and more damaged, and some of the ground crew injured. In addition to those caught in the explosion, more aircraft were damaged or lost in other transport accidents, or simply on one of the five occasions when the crates had to be transferred from rail cars to lorries or back again, or even between railways of different gauges. In all, eight of the fifty-six new aircraft were completely wrecked in the move.[254]

In September the Baghdad plan was abandoned, and with it looking as if he had prevailed and that the *Yildirim* would become

a central imperial reserve, Djemal took up an invitation to visit
Germany and the Western Front. While there he received news
that, in fact, *Yildirim* would be used on the southern Palestine
front, initially as reinforcements, and later as a force to counter-
attack across the Sinai. To this end, the forces in southern Palestine
were to be reorganised, and his own command reduced. The HQ
of the 4th (OT) Army was de-activated on 26 September 1917,
and Djemal's staff moved from Jerusalem north to Damascus.
Djemal now went from being military commander and virtual
ruler of Syria and Palestine, to being the Commander of the
Armies of Syria and Western Arabia. These consisted of the
Hedjaz Expeditionary Force, and of XII (OT) Corps, covering
the coastal areas of Syria from Jaffa north, the area east of the
Jordan, and the lines of communications for *Yildirim*.[255] This
latter task gave him responsibility for the logistical support
of *Yildirim*, and control of their supply and communication lines
back to Aleppo; north of Aleppo they became the responsibility
of the German Military Mission in Constantinople.

A few days after the dissolution of the 4th (OT) Army, the
8th (OT) Army was stood up in southern Palestine, commanding all of the units along the Gaza–Beersheba line. Command
was given to Friedrich Freiherr Kress von Kressenstein, the
German officer who had been fighting in the Sinai since 1915.
At the same time, the 7th (OT) Army was established at Aleppo,
with the intention of moving south as soon as possible to take
over the Beersheba end of the line. Command was given to
Mustafa Kemal Pasha, the hero of Gallipoli who later would
be instrumental in the formation of (and President of) the
Turkish Republic. Kemal (who would not be granted his more
familiar name – Atatürk, 'Father of the Turks' – until 1934)
had grave reservations about his new posting, and expressed
doubts over the offensive plan to attack Egypt, the ability to
supply the force, and the increasing influence of the Germans
throughout the Ottoman military. He expressed these directly
to Enver Pasha and within weeks resigned from his command,

being replaced by Fevzi Pasha.[256] Both of the new armies, and the 6th (OT) Army in Mesopotamia, came under the direct control of *Yildirim*, whose headquarters moved from Aleppo to Jerusalem. The commander, von Falkenhayn, remained for the moment in Aleppo, fearing to be caught on the road and removed from his staff and communications when the expected British offensive began.[257]

While these big movements and changes were taking place, smaller-scale reforms were also being made. Over the summer training was carried out with the latest weapons and techniques at all levels, with companies, battalions and regiments drilling together to improve efficiency and coordination. In particular, machine-gun companies were formed and trained for each infantry battalion, significantly enhancing their firepower in an area where Ottoman forces had traditionally been lacking. In September, an army-wide reform also saw assault units, based on the German 'stormtrooper' model, being formed within each division. Made up from the fittest and most aggressive young men, they were trained to take the spearhead in attacks, and received better equipment and rations. The *Yildirim* and the 4th (OT) Army both formed complete battalions of these troops.[258]

By late October, ten Ottoman divisions were in place along the Gaza–Beersheba line, although some of them just barely. The 7th (OT) Army had moved into the eastern end of the line through the month, and on 28 October 1917 officially took over that portion of the line. The III (OT) Corps transferred to the 7th (OT) Army and remained at Beersheba with the 3rd (OT) Cavalry Division and the 27th (OT) Infantry Division. This latter division consisted of nearly 80 per cent Arabs, making it unreliable in the eyes of the senior Ottoman and German commanders. Kress von Kressenstein classed it as 'badly trained, badly organised, and composed of Arabs who had to be watched'.[259] To the west was the 16th (OT) Infantry Division, holding the redoubts along the line as far as opposite Shellal, while the 24th (OT) Division was in reserve behind the lines.

The western half of the line was still held by Kress von Kressenstein's 8th (OT) Army. He believed that the coming British attack would fall on Gaza, based on his understanding of the logistics and capabilities of the British forces, and the information being fed to him by British intelligence (see below). Therefore, XXII (OT) Corps, consisting of the 3rd and 53rd (OT) Infantry Divisions, were heavily emplaced in the trenches around Gaza. The latter unit was fresh and new to the line, replacing the 7th (OT) Infantry Division that had been on the line all summer, but was now withdrawn (as part of the 4th (OT) Army) to the coastal area north of Gaza, where the British were expected to make an amphibious landing. To the east of XXII (OT) Corps was XX (OT) Corps, with the 26th and 54th (OT) Infantry Divisions. The 19th (OT) Infantry Division was just arriving in the army area, and was being placed in reserve. These dispositions meant that the western end of the line was held in much greater strength than the eastern end.[260] Between them, the two armies fielded a force of around 33,000 infantry (British intelligence estimated 40,000), plus 1,400 cavalry and 260 field guns.[261]

For the British, this was fortunate, as the plan now being put together by Allenby and his staffs envisaged only diversionary attacks against Gaza, while the main breakthrough was made at Beersheba, before turning west and north-west to roll up the Ottoman line. This plan had been formulated by Lieutenant General Sir Philip Chetwode when he was commander of Eastern Force, aided by his Chief of Staff, Sir Guy Dawnay. In a paper put before General Murray on 21 June 1917, they proposed that the defences around Gaza were too strong for any attack with the resources currently available (or reasonably expected to be available) to have any success. An attack to the east of Gaza would also run into strong enemy positions, and leave the attacker open to counter-attack from the eastern half of the defences. An attack on the eastern end of the line, particularly at Hareira and Tel el Sharia, however, would not only pierce the line, probably forcing the Beersheba garrison to retreat rather than be cut off, and allow the British to threaten the supply lines to Gaza and so possibly inducing them to retire as well, but would also secure the attacking force good sources of water. This still left the problem of having the resources to follow up this success properly. Chetwode and Dawnay were of the opinion that some divisions would need to be stripped of their transport in order to allow others the freedom of movement that would be needed to chase the Ottoman Army and keep it retreating, rather than allowing it to simply take up position in the defensive line that was even now being prepared along the Wadi Hesi. It was also recommended that any advance be made before October, when the rainy season would begin and the roads turn to mud.[262]

This plan was based on the opposing sides having roughly equal numbers, although reinforcements on both sides made Chetwode's calculations obsolete. The Ottoman strengths are stated above, while the EEF had grown to around 80,000 infantry and 15,000 cavalry, although garrison and lines of communications commitments cut these figures back to about 60,000 infantry and 12,000 cavalry usable for the coming offensive.[263] This was a far lower ratio than the three-to-one attacker-to-defender ratio usually taken as standard in military operations to give a reasonable chance of success. Certainly, it meant that any direct attack on Gaza was out of the question, and on his arrival Allenby took the Chetwode plan and used it as the foundations of his own, although it was far from a simple copy.

For one thing, it soon became obvious that the September deadline that Allenby had talked about on first arrival was impractical, and the date was pushed back into October. This did of course put it into the rainy season, with all of the problems of mud and floods that that entailed. As the rain fell on the Judean Mountains, which ran down the western bank of the Jordan Valley and the Dead Sea, and flowed out to the sea, the usually dry wadis were likely to become difficult or even impossible to pass, with flash-floods causing additional dangers. Large parts of the coastal plains would become marshland as they became inundated with water. This created many problems, large and small, from the transport and movement of the army, to the welfare of the soldiers. Plans had to be made to issue the men with extra blankets, cardigans and greatcoats before the offensive, and to arrange for the supply of khaki serge uniforms to replace their thin khaki drill tunics and shorts as soon as possible after it began, as protection from the winter weather.[264]

A larger change came in identifying Beersheba as an important, even vital, objective to be seized directly rather than just threatened into submission. As the plans evolved the water at Beersheba grew in importance, and it became obvious that the town had to be taken on the first day of the offensive so as not to give the Ottomans time to destroy them. To take it meant deploying a larger force than previously envisaged on that flank, straining the accessible water supplies. Therefore it became doubly important to take the town on the first day, in order to supply the men of the attacking force.[265] The supply of water would become an all-pervading obsession for the planners, and rightly so. Even a single brigade required 20,000 gallons (91,000 litres) of water per day, not including the 9,000 gallons (41,000 litres) required for their camel transport train.[266] To keep the army fighting fit and able to advance, water had to be the overriding concern.

By 15 August 1917 Allenby was able to place a provisional plan before his corps commanders. By then the importance of Beersheba was recognised, and that town had become the primary objective on the first day of the attack. While XXI Corps demonstrated against Gaza (where an artillery bombardment by the army and from the navy off-shore would have been grasping Ottoman attention for some days), XX Corps and most of the Desert Mounted Corps (DMC) (supplemented by transport vehicles and animals stripped from XXI Corps) would sweep massive troop movements needed took place in the weeks before the battle:

> Canteens, cook-houses, horse lines, temporary shelters, in fact anything that would indicate the presence of the army, where left standing to deceive the enemy; while to prevent aircraft observation from detecting any change in areas, incoming troops took over bivouacs vacated by others, and the use of any new ground was strictly forbidden.[272]

Rigorous aerial patrolling also sought to keep enemy reconnaissance aircraft away, but inevitably such large-scale preparations were impossible to hide completely. Since August, the railway across the Sinai had been steadily converted into double-track, proceeding at a rate of up to a mile a day. By the end of October, it had reached Bir el Mazar, about halfway along its 140-mile length. Branch lines of the railway had been built out to Qamle, Shellal, Kharm and across the Wadi Ghazze to the east, while smaller railways had been built to fill in various gaps. New pipelines had also been laid to the eastern ends of the front line.[273]

Such preparations could not be kept entirely secret. Some were in fact blatant. Major The Lord Hampton of the QOWH recorded how, on 2 October 1917:

> A large number of Officers of the Nth Infantry Division were anxious to examine the country bordering the Wadi Saba, a tributary of the Ghuzze, and more particularly the Turkish trench systems South West of Beersheba. It fell to the lot of my Squadron, among others, to provide protection and act generally in the capacity of Messrs. Cook & Son. It was a curious sight. As far as the eye could see the hills were dotted with Khaki figures carrying large scale maps and getting ever closer to the white chalk lines which marked the enemy's defences. The Turks sat in rows in or around their trenches and watched the proceedings with considerable interest, but, much to my

relief, attempted little retaliation. Some wit observed that
they did not shoot because they mistook the operations for a
whole scale desertion of the British Army waving white flags
in token of surrender.[274]

By mid October, according to Hüsnü, the Ottomans knew that
something was afoot, that large bodies of troops were on the
move, and that at least some of the camps opposite them were
empty. However, many of the scraps of information coming to
them only confirmed that a large offensive was brewing, without giving any real indication as to where the main attack would
fall. Such accurate information as they did have was well mixed
in with British disinformation and deception.

1. Hussein Bey al-Husseini, Mayor of Jerusalem.

2. Sergeants Fred Hurcomb and James Sedgewick, 2/19th London Regiment, photographed overlooking Jerusalem shortly after the surrender.

3. British prisoners captured during the disastrous 1st Battle of Gaza.

4. British Yeomen posed with one of the ill-fated tanks used during the 2nd Battle of Gaza. (By kind permission Trustees of the QOWH)

5. The 3rd (OT) Cavalry Division ride out of Beersheba to attack the British flank during the 2nd Battle of Gaza. One Ottoman officer, Rafael de Nogales, called this ride 'one of the most cherished memories of my four years beneath the Crescent'.

6. British trenches in the coastal zone opposite Gaza. Trenches were hard to dig in the sand and had to be strongly buttressed to stop them caving in. At least they avoided the mud of the Western Front.

7. A British sniper and his spotter watching the Ottoman lines opposite. Both sides kept up a brisk sniper duel throughout the summer of 1917.

8. British troops in a nullah (dried stream) off the Wadi Ghazze, converted into a trench for the dry summer months.

9. Members of the 5th Australian Light Horse Regiment lay in wait in one of the endless ambushes and skirmishes on the eastern flank of the army during the summer of 1917.

10. British Yeomen, probably from the Norfolk Yeomanry, rest under a temporary shelter during one of the constant patrols on the eastern end of the line.

11. A gun from the Hong Kong and Singapore Mountain Battery at practice. This unit were know as 'Bing Boys' after the noise made by their short-barrelled guns, which were designed to be dismantled and carried on mules.

12. Yeomen inspect a horse. The months in the desert had a serious effect on the health of the army's animals, with overwork, poor fodder, lack of water and the ingestion of large quantities of sand all taking a toll.

13. A member of the Norfolk Yeomanry posing with men of the Camel Transport Corps. These Egyptian civilians were absolutely crucial to keeping the forward units of the army supplied.

14. Pupils at the School of Cookery at Ismailia, August 1917, showing the mix of nationalities in the EEF. Good food preparation skills in such an unhygienic environment and with fairly basic and repetitive ingredients were vital for maintaining morale and health among the troops.

15. Ottoman lancers patrolling south of Beersheba. Although equipped with lances they usually fought on foot with rifles, as the skirmish line out in front of them is here.

16. Field Marshal Erich von Falkenhayn and Djemal Pasha (either side of the little girl, centre) at Jerusalem railway station.

17. A column of troops from an Austrian mountain artillery unit, marching past the Citadel in Jerusalem, heading south on the road to Bethlehem.

18. Oberleutnant Gerhard Felmy, the star pilot of FA300, in the cockpit of his Rumpler C.1.

19. Albatros D.IIIs, new arrivals with the *Yildirim* force, at the aerodrome at Huj. Each of the German squadrons in Palestine was mainly equipped with reconnaissance aircraft, but also had two of these fighters.

20. Ottoman trenches in the Hureira Redoubt system, showing the wide open ground that gave the defenders an excellent field of fire. Even with the relative lack of barbed wire, such positions could be formidable.

21. An Ottoman machine-gun detachment in the improvised defences at Sharia. The closest group is using a range-finder to help the machine gunners aim correctly. Without these devices, judging distances in such a bland landscape could be difficult.

22. Men of the 5th Mounted Brigade resting during the pursuit north. The exhaustion of both man and horses is obvious. The standing horse has had most of the kit that would usually hang from the saddle removed. (By kind permission Trustees of the QOWH)

23. Sergeants Hurcomb and Sedgewick pose with Hussein Bey al-Husseini and his party, 9 December 1917.

24. No. 11 Platoon, C Company, 1/5th Welsh Regiment (Lieutenant W.A. Woods commanding) stand as the first British guards on the Jaffa Gate, 9 December 1917.

25. Australian Light Horsemen, presumably from the 10th ALH, waiting in the streets of Jerusalem to take part in the official entry to the city.

11

BEERSHEBA

THE FINAL PREPARATIONS for the attack on Beersheba began in the middle of October 1917. The last branch lines of the railways running east were laid as quickly and as late as possible, while supply dumps and hospitals were also delayed until the last possible moment. On 22 October, Allenby issued his final orders. It had been thought that a week would suffice for moving the divisions involved, but this was extended to ten days. Troops would only move at night, and an average speed of 1mph had to be allowed for, given the difficulties of navigating in the dark across ground that was broken with wadis and nullahs, and offered little in the way of definite landmarks. Some brigade columns ended up using a system of setting up lamps at intervals, between which the troops would march.[275] The two cavalry divisions aimed deep into the desert south of Beersheba – the Australian Mounted Division to Khalasa and the A&NZ Mounted Division to Bir Asluj. Both divisions, like the infantry that moved through positions closer to the front lines south-west of Beersheba, moved in stages as brigades, so as not to over-tax the water supplies at any one place. In preparation for the offensive, nine officers and 117 other ranks were left behind by each infantry battalion, to form a cadre to either provide reinforcements, or for the battalion to be re-formed around if casualties were catastrophic.[276]

Engineers worked hard to develop these water sources as rapidly as possible, and supplemented some of them by connecting them to the pipeline system. The springs at Shellal were connected to the pipeline, so that water came to it all the way from the Sweet Water Canal outside Cairo, while the pipe head and springs had equipment installed that could fill some 2,000 'fanatis' (large, metal jerrycan-like containers which could be carried, one on each side, by camels) with 25,000 gallons per hour. Supply dumps were also rapidly thrown up. It was intended to place dumps containing everything the army would need for the first week of the offensive as close to the front lines as possible, and along its entire length. XXI Corps, holding the line opposite Gaza, would need these supplies just as desperately as the more isolated Desert Mounted and XX Corps, despite being nearer the railway system. To give the two eastern corps as much support as possible, XXI Corps' transport was stripped away and sent to their aid, leaving the corps essentially immobile from 8 October. Three motor transport companies totalling some 130–140 vehicles were also brought up from Cairo, despite their limited use in the rough desert terrain,* while 134 of the more useful Holt's tractors were also used. These heavy caterpillar-tracked vehicles were more adept at crossing rough ground, although they did it slowly and noisily, and were useful for hauling ammunition in bulk.

Camel companies would form the backbone of the mobile supply system. Some 32,000 were deployed with the EEF. For now, XX Corps had 20,000 of them – 8,000 attached directly to the divisions to carry their own stores when they moved, and 12,000 under the direction of the Corps HQ for forming supply convoys. XXI Corps and the Desert Mounted Corps each had

---

* The standard tyres on army lorries were designed to last 10,000 miles. In Palestine, they generally lasted less than 2,000 miles.

6,000 camels for their own use, to carry food, water and ammu-nition.[277] Eventually, of the four infantry divisions of XX Corps (10th, 53rd, 60th and 74th), three had three echelons of trans-port, and the fourth had two, while the Desert Mounted Corps also had three. Each echelon carried a day's worth of supplies for each division, and the three echelons would, in theory, create a continuous chain of convoys moving between the advancing divisions and their supply dumps.[278]

This activity could not and did not go unnoticed, and in the early hours of 27 October the Ottomans pushed out a large recon-naissance west of Beersheba. This operation was actually carried out in considerable force – the 125th (OT) Regiment of the 16th (OT) Division towards the ridge of El Buggar, and elements of the 3rd (OT) Cavalry Division and 27th (OT) Infantry Division slightly to the east.[279] It struck against an extended piquet-line of British cavalry provided by the 8th Mounted Brigade, screening the movements of the 53rd (Welsh) Division, and strung out in a line along El Buggar ridge and then across several hills known as Points 720, 630 and 510. The right of the line was held by the 1st County of London (Middlesex) Yeomanry, the left by the 3rd County of London Yeomanry, with the City of London Yeomanry in reserve behind. The line was 19km (12 miles) long, and held by isolated posts of one or two troops (thirty to sixty men) at key points. The advancing Ottoman formations broke over these scattered posts at 4.15 a.m. on 27 October, supported in places with artillery fire. On Point 720 Major Alexander Lafone, commanding 'B' Squadron, 1st County of London Yeomanry, had only two of his troops with him, but still managed to hold off several charges by the Ottomans throughout the morning.

At 10.10 a.m. he managed to send a final message to his head-quarters that: 'My casualties are heavy. Twelve stretcher-bearers required. I shall hold on to the last as I cannot get my wounded away.' In fact, he managed to move most of his wounded – which was most of his men – down into trenches behind the crest of the hill, covering their retreat with the remaining three unwounded

men. Soon after 11 a.m., another wave of Ottomans attacked
and, seeing the hopelessness of the situation, Lafone ordered
his remaining men to fall back, apparently stepping out into the
open to meet the charge on his own. The post, and Lafone, fell.
He would receive a posthumous Victoria Cross for his 'conspicuous bravery, leadership and self-sacrifice'.[280]

Attempts by the brigade reserves to relieve the various posts
failed, although they did, with artillery support from the Hants
Battery RHA, stem the Ottoman advance. Late in the day the 3rd
ALH Brigade and 158th Brigade arrived to counter-attack and the
line of outposts was reoccupied. Both sides would claim inflated
enemy numbers and casualties, but the 8th Mounted Brigade suffered ten officers and sixty-nine other ranks killed or wounded
(against '200' claimed by the Ottomans); of these, 'B' Squadron,
1st County of London Yeomanry suffered two officers and
eight other ranks killed, ten wounded and eight missing. The
Ottomans recorded one officer and nine men killed, and around
forty wounded, but had failed in their aim of clarifying the numbers and intent of the forces moving across their front.[281] While
an attack on Beersheba still remained the likely answer, the true
question – whether this was to be the main British thrust or
merely the diversion – was as unanswered as before.

On the same day, a massive British bombardment of the Gaza
defences began.

To prepare for the coming attack, the III (OT) Corps commander, Colonel Ismat Bey, did all that he could to defend his post.
Beersheba was a new town, although on very ancient foundations.
It was the site of the Wells of Abraham, the very reason why it was
being fought over and the source of its name. Sometimes rendered
as Bir Es Saba, Bir Saba, or some variation on those spellings, the
name meant 'The Seven Wells', and the source of the water was the
Wadi Saba, which runs down from the north-east to a point 3.2km
(2 miles) east of the town, where it joins several smaller wadis near
the mound of Tel Saba. It then runs west, past the southern edge
of Beersheba. In recent centuries it had been a small village existing

on trade with the nomadic Bedouin tribes of the Negev desert to the south, but at the turn of the twentieth century the Ottomans decided to develop it into an administrative centre for the Negev region. A railway, a governor's residence (now the Negev Art Museum), a mosque and other building had been built as a nucleus for the new town, and parks were laid out around them. This central area was widely spaced out, and the houses and commercial premises that grew around them were also well dispersed. By August 1916, when Swedish explorer Sven Hadin visited the town as Djemal Pasha's guest, it had become something of a model town, albeit still on the inhospitable side:

> Until the war broke out, Bir es-Seba – or 'The Seven Wells' – was a miserable hole; now it has suddenly become an important base ... When the worst heat was over, the colonel and the government surveyor, Dr Schmucher, took me on a tour of the town, which is springing forth out of the desert at an American pace. We visited various buildings on the base, the electric stations, the factories and workshops, the printing office, the bazaar, the hotel, the parks and gardens – which of course have not yet grown much – and the ice factory – the most beneficial establishment in this heat. Then we visited the agricultural school, the motor-driven pumping plants, the immense reservoirs, at which water is distributed to camels, horses, asses, and mules. Finally we visited the hospital, in which 400 sick were lying at the time, cared for by Austrian physicians and nurses. Bir es-Seba's climate, while not exactly unhealthy, is very unpleasant. The region is very windy, the desert sandy, the soil broken up because of the heavy traffic, and no vegetation offers protection from the suffocating dust clouds that roll from all sides into the burning hot streets.[282]

Ismat Bey threw out forward defences around 3–4km from the centre of the town in an arc running from the south to the west, covering the most likely lines of approach for the British.

He added further defences at Tel Saba, which dominated the approaches from the otherwise flat east and south-east. All of these defences had been seen and plotted by British reconnaissance, although a smaller crescent of trenches, closer in and to the south of the town just below the Wadi Saba, had not. To man these positions, Ismat Bey had ten battalions of infantry (seven from the 27th (OT) Infantry Division and three from the 16th (OT) Infantry Division), two cavalry regiments from the 3rd (OT) Cavalry Division, a reserve of one infantry battalion and one cavalry regiment, and an assortment of support troops – engineers, searchlights, signallers and a mobile bakery. This gave a total fighting strength (i.e. riflemen and cavalry sabres, as opposed to supporting clerks, cooks, herdsmen, etc.) of somewhere fewer than 5,000 men. For heavy weapons, he had just five batteries of four field guns each, although between his various regiments and battalions he could muster some fifty-six machine guns.[283] To provide enough troops to man his defences, he was forced to deploy his cavalry as infantry rather than maintaining them as a mobile reserve, a decision that would be heavily criticised by Kress von Kressenstein later. For his own part, the German was still convinced that there was not enough water to sustain a serious British attack on Beersheba.[284]

The British had found the water, though, and by dawn on 30 October all was ready. At Bir Asluj (where the water supply was shorter than expected), 38km (24 miles) south of Beersheba was the A&NZ Mounted Division and the headquarters of the Desert Mounted Corps. At Khalasa, 48km (30 miles) south-east of Beersheba, was the Australian Mounted Division, while the Yeomanry Mounted Division was detached to Shellal, covering the gap between XX and XXI Corps. The 7th Mounted Brigade, still independent and under Allenby's direct control, was at Bir El Esani. At dusk on 30 October, having drunk their fill, the two Mounted Divisions would strike out on long flanking marches to the east of Beersheba; the A&NZ Mounted Division would be east and north-east of the town for the attack, and the Australian Mounted Division to the south-east. The 7th Mounted Brigade would remain to the south, ready to support the main infantry assault.

This assault would be launched by the 60th and 74th Divisions. The former spent the night at Abu Ghalyun, and the latter at Khan Khasif, which still placed them some 16 or 19km (10 or 12 miles) from their starting points for the following day. The 60th Division would attack Beersheba from the south, and the 74th from the south-east. The 53rd Division was slightly further west, applying pressure to the Gaza–Beersheba road, while the Imperial Camel Corps Brigade (with two battalions of the 158th Brigade, 53rd Division) covered the gap between them and the 74th Division. The 10th Division was held back in reserve. Between the cavalry and infantry divisions, the British fighting strength was over 40,000 men.

Charles Hennessey of the 2/15th London Regiment (also known as the 2nd Civil Service Rifles) was briefed by his commanding officer at the assembly point:

From this we learned exactly how the various British Divisions were disposed along the front from Gaza on the extreme left, to where we were on the extreme right. We were also shown a number of aerial photos of the Turkish trenches, and were told to make a particular study of the ones it was 'C' Company's business to deal with.

Following this cosy chat we were each issued with 2 Mills Bombs, an extra bandolier of ammunition, and a couple of aeroplane flares. It now appeared that the Battalion was on the extreme right of the British line; that the only troops on our right were a few squadrons of London Yeomanry; and, as we had already been told, that our Company was to form the first wave of the attack on Beersheba.

One night only was spent at the Assembly Point, and the following evening 'C' Company moved off to take up a position in a 'wadi', which we learned was to be our jumping off point. Our soda water bottles had been filled with tea and rum the day before, and dire were the penalties threatened if we drank any of it if permission hadn't been given. The march to our 'wadi' began after dark and word was passed that there was to be no smoking, and no talking or other noise, in case the Turks should hear us. What a hope! Of course Johnny Turk could hear us coming. The loud clanking of our equipment could have been heard for miles.[285]

At dusk on 30 October, the desert seemed to come alive as tens of thousands of men, horses and vehicles rose out of their daytime cover and began the advance on Beersheba. Captain Ashton of the Royal Welsh Fusiliers was with the 53rd Division:

The noise of tractors bringing up guns was overpowering, as if the whole British Army was on the move, and sounded like the roar of London traffic from a little way off. The whole plain behind us hummed with mechanical noises, and I marvelled that the enemy in their trenches could not hear it. They afterwards told us they were taken by surprise, but it is indeed hard to believe.[286]

The night was bitterly cold, but marching kept the men warm. When the units began to reach their allotted positions in the early hours the real suffering began. Hennessey:

Around midnight we filed into a shallow wadi and were told to make ourselves comfortable till dawn. It soon became very cold, and we missed our greatcoats which had been left behind in our packs. We were also short of our tunics as we'd been told we should be carrying out the attack in our shirt sleeves. There certainly seemed a lot of people who were determined to make the war as difficult for us as possible. Taking it all round it was a dreary time waiting in the dark and cold for the arrival of dawn.[287]

For Gunner J.W. Gough of the Royal Field Artillery, waiting was also the hardest part:

> 3 a.m.: We have now been in our position for an hour or so, it is very cold hands quite numb. Laying tel. wires etc. here. Bty is opening fire on enemy at 7 am. 6.15 a.m.: Bty ready for action & lined on target – only awaiting orders from Hdqrs. All the men are tired & hungry after travelling and digging etc. Hostile planes are about, we're not spotted – yet. I am detailed to repeat orders from B.C. to B.L. by megaphone. I'd gladly accept a cup of tea or anything warm before we 'raise the curtain' – with I trust, a splendid 'debut' for Johnnie Turk.[288]

The curtain was to be raised by the 60th Division. In front of the Ottoman line to the south of Beersheba stood a hill, known at the time as Point 1069, although it was later renamed Point 1070.[*] Point 1069 gave good views over the Ottomans lines, the British positions, and the surrounding landscape. It had to be taken before the general attack could go forward, and responsibility for this fell on General Shea, commanding 60th Division. He was given free rein as to judging when the preliminary bombardment had cut the wire, and so when to send his men in. This was not an easy call to make. The guns designated for the barrage on Point 1069 opened fire at 5.55 a.m. Over a hundred guns[**] concentrated on a 4,500yd front, and after an hour so much dust had been raised by the explosions that nobody could tell what the state of the wire was. The barrage was suspended for half an hour or more to let the dust

---

[*] Points or Hills were named for their height in feet. Clearly, after capture Point 1069 proved to be, on closer inspection, a foot taller than previously assumed.

[**] Consisting of seventy-six 18-pounders, twenty 4.5in howitzers, four 3.7in howitzers, eight 60-pounders, eight 6in howitzers, and some 4.5in howitzers designated for counter-battery fire as and when the Ottoman artillery revealed their positions.

settle, but even then the view was unclear. In the end Brigadier
General De Costa, commanding 181st Brigade, who would be
making the assault, requested and received permission from Shea
to resume the bombardment while he moved his force forward
behind its cover. An intensification of the barrage was planned
for 8.20 a.m., to last ten minutes, by which time his brigade were
only 460m (500yds) from their objectives on the crest of the point.
Wire-cutting parties went forward under the cover of the barrage, which was landing in some places just 27m (30yds) ahead of
them, and made gaps or widened existing holes. At 8.30 a.m. the
2/22nd London Regiment stormed the point. The following day,
Colonel A.D. 'Bosky' Borton, commanding the 2/22nd, wrote
home to his father, with slight variation on the official reports:

> The eyes of many were on us, and we 'did them proud' ... We
> worked our way up to about 500 yds. of the enemy and lay
> 'doggo' while our Artillery tried to cut gaps in the wire. This
> however they could not do as well as each shell raised such
> an awful dust that observation was impossible and we had
> to lie up for two hours under a very heavy fire in the open.
> It was darned trying, but the men were too wonderful. Our
> casualties during this time was pretty high – about 15%. The
> Brigadier then got a message out to me to know whether we
> could go without the gaps being cut?
>
> It was the one thing that I had been hoping for, as I felt
> that no was wire was going to stop us. I was very lucky, as
> owing to my having had to shove all my 4 companies into the
> line, I was able to hand over my Battalion HQ to my Adjutant
> and go with the men. I'd got a flag with the Queen's badge
> on it, in my pocket, and ... I tied it to my walking stick and
> away we went. I've never felt so damned proud in my life.
> The Flag was a surprise to the men and tickled them to death!
> We got in practically without loss, we cut the wire 25 yards
> behind our own barrage. This of course meant a few hits from
> our own guns, but not a soul in the trenches dared show his

head, and the moment the guns lifted we were into them with
bomb and bayonet and scuppered the whole garrison.[289]

As Borton led his men on, the 2/24th Londons swung around
the flank and cut the Point off from the Ottoman forces to
the north. The 2/23rd Londons then came up to support the
2/22nd and extend their line, while the 2/21st remained behind
in reserve. Once the Londoners burst through the wire it was
all over in a matter of minutes, with ninety prisoners and Point
1069 being taken.[290]

The way was now clear for the 60th and 74th Divisions to
advance on the main Ottoman line. The 74th had already
marched as close to the Ottoman lines as possible, suffering from
artillery and long-range machine-gun fire as they did so. Their
path lay across a series of low rises, and as the columns crossed
the crest of each they stood out stark against the skyline as easy
targets. This fire pushed the right-hand unit, 231st Brigade, further right, and the left-hand unit, 230th Brigade, had to extend
their own line to cover the growing gap between them. Despite
these problems, by 10.40 a.m. the 231st Brigade had advanced
to within 460m (500yds) of the Ottoman lines, while 230th
Brigade was held at around 820m (900yds) out. Meanwhile,
60th Division paused, and had breakfast.

With guns having been hauled up onto the point to support the
attack, the barrage was restarted. Again, it fell to Shea to decide
when the wire was suitably cut for the two divisions to advance,
and at 11.40 a.m. he consulted General Girdwood, the commander
of 74th Division. Girdwood's view of the Ottoman wire was also
obscured by dust, but he assured Shea that his men would find a way
regardless. Shea passed this up the chain of command to Chetwode,
who authorised the attack to start at 12.15 p.m. William Hendry of
the 2/14th London Regiment (London Scottish) recalled:

Then an order came to make a meal, in which we soon con-
sumed our bottle of rum, as it was a cold night. We then said

good-bye to the desert. Our machine gunners took up their covering positions, then our guns started to bark, pouring shells on a hill on our left which had to be taken before we could advance. Suddenly a rocket burst in the air, which was the signal that the hill had been captured, and over the top of the hill we went, with the din of our machine gun bullets and shells whizzing over head. We dropped down like lightning into the wadi below and up again we went hard for the Turk's trenches. The barbed wire was well cut by our shells and all we found was a few killed and wounded. According to a doctor we captured the men had flown along the trenches to be taken prisoners by the trousered regiment, as they did not want to be captured by the skirted devils as called us, they were given to understand we took no prisoners. Well we advanced to a position as arranged and soon got to work with picks and shovels digging in, as bullets were still coming at us from the direction of Beersheba.[291]

By 1 p.m., the 60th Division (less the 2/22nd Londons, digging in on Point 1069) had taken all of their objectives, about a mile and a half beyond the Ottoman trenches. The 74th Division had been delayed by having to send forward wire-cutting parties, but were able to declare their own objectives achieved only moments later. Acting Corporal John Collins of the 25th Battalion, Royal Welsh Fusiliers took a leading role in the attack, and was one of the first to enter the Ottoman trenches and engage the enemy hand to hand. During the 74th Division's long march under fire he had repeatedly risked himself to rescue the wounded and bring them back under cover, and after the final assault he led a Lewis gun section out beyond the objective, giving covering fire for his unit as it consolidated its position and reorganised their scattered men. For his 'conspicuous bravery, resource and leadership' throughout the day, he was awarded the Victoria Cross.[292]

Over all, resistance had been lighter than expected. Although well sited, the Ottoman lines were thinly held, and once the

British infantry had closed to bayonet range the 67th and 81st (OT) Infantry Regiments had been unable to resist the weight of numbers thrown against them. As the final assault started, as many Ottoman units as possible were withdrawn in good order back towards the town, and for the moment no British pursuit was mounted. After their night march and morning's action, the troops badly needed to rest, quite apart from the need to re-form themselves after the advance. On top of this, it had been decided that the Desert Mounted Corps should be the ones to actually take the town, as they would be in greater need of the water. In fact, only the 230th Brigade of the 74th Division would see any further action, at dusk as they advanced north to cut the Beersheba to Tel el Fara road. At 9.40 p.m. the divisional commanders received news that the town had fallen into British hands at 7.40 p.m.[293]

While the infantry had been coming on from the south-west, the cavalry had attacked from the east. Theirs had been a long ride to get into position, and Lieutenant Briscoe Moore of the New Zealand Mounted Rifles found that:

> The early morning hours of darkness are the most trying, for then vitality is at its lowest and fatigued bodies ache all over. Then comes the first lightening of the eastern sky, and the new day dawns with a cheering influence, which is increased as the next halt gives the opportunity for a hurried 'boil-up' of tea; after which things seem not so bad after all to the dust-smothered and unshaven warriors.[294]

The A&NZ Mounted Division had advanced to the north-east of Beersheba. The New Zealand Mounted Rifles (NZMR) Brigade had turned towards the eastern side of the town, with the 1st ALH Brigade slightly behind them in reserve. Meanwhile, the 2nd ALH Brigade carried on north and pushed back the 3rd (OT) Cavalry Division, capturing the Ottoman post on Tel el Sakaty at noon, and from there cut the Hebron road by 1 p.m. This road would later also be cut much further north, about 32km (20 miles) north-east of Beersheba, by a small but heavily armed party of about seventy cameliers under the command of Lieutenant Colonel Stewart Newcombe of the Royal Engineers. Newcombe had already established a reputation for daring independent action with the Sharifian forces in Arabia, and on the night before the attack he had led his force out of Bir Asluj as far north as they could reach. Armed with ten heavy machine guns and a number of Lewis guns, his men established themselves across the Hebron road late on 31 October and proceeded to create as much noise and destruction as possible, attacking passing convoys and cutting the telegraph lines. He had hoped to attract local tribesmen to rise up and aid him, but was disappointed in this. Even still, his force held out until 2 November, created much confusion (giving the Ottomans the impression that the British intended to advance on Hebron) and drew off small but significant Ottoman forces to deal with him. Eventually the force was overwhelmed after taking 50 per cent casualties. Newcombe was taken to Constantinople as a prisoner, although he would rapidly escape with the aid of a French lady whom he later married, and lived free in the city for the best part of a year. This amazing character deserves to be better known.[295]

The A&NZ Division then began to advance in towards Beersheba at shortly before 9 a.m., and the NZMR Brigade and the 3rd Australian Light Horse Brigade (attached from the Australian Mounted Division) were told off to attack the dominating height of Tel el Saba. Around 300m (1,000ft) high at the time,* the tel sat at the convergence of two wadis, and these would provide the key to taking the position (as well as a source for a small amount of water for the horses). They provided the only decent cover in the area and led directly to the tel, but

---

* The tel has been extensively excavated since then and is much lower now than in 1917. However, there is an observation platform on top of the tel that gives a clear impression of how this hill dominated the areas to the east of Beersheba.

even so, it would prove a tough nut to crack. A battalion of the 48th (OT) Infantry Regiment was well dug in, with machine-gun and artillery support, and excellent fields of fire. The Auckland Regiment NZMR was first into action, supported by the Somerset Battery RHA. Their 11th Squadron rode along the wadi bed to about a mile from the tel before dismounting and beginning to advance on foot, coming under heavy machine-gun fire from the tel, and from a smaller hill slightly to the east of it. The other two squadrons – the 3rd and 4th – managed to close to about 800m (875yds) from the tel before being forced to dismount in the wadi. The Canterbury Regiment NZMR came up on their right flank, while the Somerset Battery opened fire from around 3.2km (2 miles) away, at which range their fire was too inaccurate to be very effective. The 3rd ALH Brigade advanced on their left, and at 10 a.m. the 1st ALH Brigade was also committed to the attack. An hour later the Inverness Battery RHA added their fire to the bombardment, and under the cover of this the Somerset Battery advanced, halving their own range and improving their accuracy. This battery was being directed by the commander of the Auckland Regiment, and the regimental history records that, after this move:

> No time was lost in correcting the range of the guns, a sig-naller with flags passing on the messages given to him orally by the Auckland colonel. It was only a matter of minutes before several changes in the range were flagged back, and the shells were bursting right over the machine-gun emplace-ments of the enemy. 'That's the stuff to give 'em,' ejaculated Lieutenant-Colonel McCarroll as he saw the goodly sight.
>
> Immediately this remark was sent back as a message by Lieutenant Hatrick, who doubtless had his tongue in his cheek as he did so. After the fight the battery commander, an Imperial* officer, inquired who sent this message. 'I could not

---

* 'Imperial' meant British, as opposed to the 'Colonial' troops from elsewhere.

find it in my book of signals,' he said, 'but I would like to say that we understood it perfectly, don't you know.'[296]

As the bombardment gained effectiveness, the attack moved closer in short dashes under galling machine-gun fire. New Zealand and Australian troopers converged on the tel from the north, east and south, and at 2.40 p.m. the smaller hill was captured, along with sixty Ottoman soldiers and two machine guns that were turned onto the tel. With this additional covering fire, the Aucklands rose for a final dash. Briscoe Moore recorded:

> The line then commenced to move forward, first one part advancing covered by the fire of the others, then another section. The ground, being more or less broken, afforded fairly good cover, but the Turkish artillery made good shooting and put over many good bursts of shrapnel which whipped the ground amongst the advancing New Zealanders into myriad spurts of dust. The engagement thus developed until the attacking line was perhaps two or three hundred yards from the Turks, when heavy fire was exchanged from both sides. Then the New Zealanders charged with fixed bayonets, pushing the attack home with great determination as they mounted the rising ground towards the enemy. The sight of the cold steel coming upon them was evidently too much for the morale of the Turks, for their fire died down as our panting men approached their trenches, and those that did not bolt soon surrendered. Thus was another victory added to the record of the New Zealand Mounted Rifle Brigade.[297]

The Ottoman forces had already begun to withdraw towards the town as the final assault swept over the tel at 3 p.m., but even so seventy prisoners and two machine guns were captured. The way now lay clear for the advance into Beersheba itself.[298]

However, time was beginning to become an issue. The remains of the Ottoman forces were consolidating in the town, and were in a position to easily blow the wells should either wing of the British attack resume its advance. Meanwhile, dusk was approaching, only two hours away. The next move had to be not only decisive, but also swift, and Chauvel turned to his last uncommitted cavalry formation, the Australian Mounted Division under Major General Henry Hodgson. A brief consultation followed. The 5th Mounted Brigade was probably best suited to make a mounted charge into the town; they were equipped with swords and trained for fighting from the saddle. However, they were several miles away, and with time of the essence it was decided to use Brigadier General William Grant's 4th ALH Brigade instead. Although unsaddled and dispersed, they were close at hand and well rested having seen no action yet during the day. Although no water had been found for the horses, some feed had been issued to them. At 3.45 p.m., Grant ordered his men saddle up and form up, and called his senior officers together for a briefing. They would have to cross several miles of open ground, swept by artillery and machine-gun fire, and then tackle a crescent-shaped system of trenches just south of the Wadi Saba. This system consisted of several lines of trenches, but thankfully had no barbed wire protecting them.

At 4.30 p.m. his forces were ready. The 4th ALH Regiment (Lieutenant Colonel Murray Bourchier) were on the right, with the 12th ALH Regiment (Lieutenant Colonel Donald Cameron) on the left. Each was drawn up in three lines, each of a single squadron, with their headquarters, signallers and ambulances behind. Within each line, each trooper was spaced at about 4 or 5m (4 or 5yds) from his neighbours, so that a single burst of machine-gun fire or shell would not cause too many casualties. The gaps between the squadrons was 300m (330yds), giving plenty of time for the riders coming up behind to swerve around any fallen men or horses in front of them. Behind the two leading regiments, the 11th ALH Regiment was held in reserve. The 5th and 7th Mounted Brigades were also ordered to come up with all haste to support the attack, while the Notts Battery RHA and 'A' Battery HAC provided covering fire.

As the advance started, two German aircraft swept out of the sky to bomb and strafe the advancing ranks, but with little effect. Instead, the advancing squadrons, beginning at the walk, sped up into a trot. Artillery, long-range machine-gun and rifle fire was now falling among them, but the advance remained steady and sedate, making sure that the formations remained together for maximum impact. Closer to the enemy, they broke into a canter, and finally a gallop for the last few hundred metres. The fire of all calibres was heavy and intensive now, but the Australians had two advantages: the dust thrown up by their horses' hooves, and the speed of their advance. As panic and urgency gripped the Ottoman defenders, many apparently forgot to adjust the sights of their weapons. These had been set high initially for the long-range fire, but as the troopers got closer many forgot to lower their sights, sending their bullets and shells high over the Australians' heads. According to one study, most of the weapons recovered after the charge still had their sights set at 800m (875yds).[299] However, enough accurate fire was being laid down, and the horsemen faced additional dangers from steep-sided wadis, rifle-pits and trenches, all of which could easily disable a horse. Sergeant Charles Doherty charged with the 12th ALH:

> As the long line with the 12th on the left swung into position, the rattle from enemy musketry gradually increased in volume ... After progressing about three quarters of a mile our pace became terrific – we were galloping towards a strongly held, crescent shaped redoubt of greater length than our own line. In face of this intense fire, which now included frequent salvos from field artillery, the now maddened horses, straining their hearts to bursting point, had to cross cavernous wadies whose precipitous banks seemed to defy our progress. The crescent redoubt – like a long, sinuous, smoking serpent – was taking a fearful toll of men and horses, but the line

remained unwavering and resolute. As we neared the trenches
that were belching forth death, horse and rider steeled themselves for the plunge over excavated pitfalls and through that
tearing rain of lead.[300]

Trooper J. 'Chook' Fowler, in one of the following lines, captured the confusion of the charge:

The level country near the trenches was deep in dust. This
was one of the worst features of the Palestine Front, for six
months each year without rain. The horses in front stirred up
the dust and we could see only a few yards, our eyes almost
filled with dust, and filling the mouth.

The artillery fire had been heavy for a while. Many shells
passed over our heads, and then the machine-gun and rifle fire
became fierce as we came in closer to the trenches some of the
Turks must have incorrectly ranged the sights on their rifles, as
many bullets went overhead ... The machine-gun fire was now
very heavy. I felt something hit my haversack and trousers and
later, on inspection, I found a hole through my haversack and
two holes in my trousers. One bullet left a black mark along
my thigh. Some horses and riders were now falling near me.
All my five senses were working overtime, and a 'sixth sense'
came into action; call it the 'sense of survival' or common
sense. This said, 'If you want to survive, keep moving, keep
moving,' etc. So I urged my horse along, and it wasn't hard to
do so he was as anxious as I was to get past those trenches
... No horseman ever crouched closer to his mount than I did.
Suddenly through the dust, I saw the trenches, very wide with
sand bags in front; I doubt if my horse could have jumped
them with the load he was carrying, and after galloping two
miles. The trench was full of Turks with rifle and fixed bayonets, and hand grenades. I heard many grenades crash and
ping-g-g-g-g over the noise of rifle and machine-gun fire.
About 20 yards to my left, I could just see as a blur through

the dust some horses and men of the 12th Regiment passing through a narrow opening in the trenches. I turned my horse and raced along that trench. I had a bird's eye view of the Turks below me throwing hand grenades etc. but in a flash we were through with nothing between us and Beersheba, and the sound of machine guns and grenades behind.[301]

The 4th ALH met the thicker sections of trenches and became embroiled in clearing them, using their bayonets as swords or dismounting to clear the trenches hand-to-hand. It was hard, grim work but many of the Ottoman defenders were stunned by the suddenness and brutality of the attack. The 12th ALH met with less resistance and fewer trenches; parts of their leading squadron dismounted to clear those they encountered while the two following squadrons sped on into the town. At 4 p.m. Ismat Bey had ordered a general withdrawal of the forces in Beersheba, and the effect of the Australians, even if now in small, scattered groups, erupting through the streets was immense. Ismat Bey barely escaped, while most of his staff and the papers in his headquarters were captured.[302] The Australians rounded up over a thousand prisoners, and captured nine field guns and three machine guns. The 11th ALH, coming up behind, carried on through the town and pushed the last Ottomans out of the northern parts.[303] Ismat Bey was only able to stop the retreat and begin re-forming his men some 8 or 9.5km (5 or 6 miles) north of Beersheba, although it took days to properly re-establish his corps.[304]

Beersheba had fallen. A few demolition charges had been set off by the Ottomans, but the wells were taken largely intact, but unfortunately proved not to as prolific as thought. Barely enough was found to water the mounted divisions, and over the next two days the cavalry and infantry carried out small, limited attacks north and east of the town to secure further sources.[305] The infantry had to remain reliant on water convoys from the rear. In the town, the work to clear up after the battle began. Patrick Hamilton helped to collect and treat the wounded:

In the operating tent our medical officers worked steadily and almost in silence. Continuous skilled surgery hour after hour. Anaesthetics, pain killing injections, swabs, sutures, tubes in gaping wounds, antiseptic dressings, expert bandaging. The medical orderlies did a fine job assisting.

Stretcher bearers were standing by for the change-over. Two on either side lift the stretcher clear of the stands, and replace with the next patient all within two minutes. The pace never slackened!

Here, out in the field at night, surgical work of the first order was performed. This was the 4th Light Horse Field Ambulance at work! About 2 a.m., after six hours of dedicated work by all hands, the last of our 45 wounded was put through. All patients by now were bedded down under canvas and made as comfortable as possible. Most slept through sheer exhaustion or under drugs. We arranged shifts and lay down on the hard ground fully clothed for a few hours' rest.[306]

In total, over 1,500 prisoners had been taken. During its charge on the town, the 4th ALH Brigade had suffered surprisingly light casualties – two officers and twenty-nine men killed, and four officers and twenty-eight men wounded. The 60th Division had suffered three officers and sixty-seven men killed, and thirteen officers and 358 men wounded.[307] On the Ottoman side, the III (OT) Corps had been almost destroyed, although they had no reason to feel ashamed. While accusations and recriminations flew between the corps and Kress von Kressenstein, with the fact that the corps had a high proportion of Arab troops being often cited as a reason for its 'poor' performance, they had in fact behaved admirably. The Ottoman lines had held against great odds and heavy attacks through most of the day, longer than the British had thought they would. It was only the late, desperate charge of the 4th ALH Brigade that had finally shattered their lines.

With Beersheba taken, attention now turned to the western end of the line, and the great fortress town of Gaza.

12

BREAKTHROUGH

BY THE END of the first day of the offensive, the British had broken into the Ottoman lines, but they had not broken through them. Although the defences at Beersheba had been overwhelmed, there were still large bodies of Ottoman troops to the north, barring any further advance in that direction. It is true that these forces were in some cases in disarray, had taken heavy losses, and had suffered a blow to their morale, but they were re-forming themselves fast. Despite communications and control issues due not only to the fall of Beersheba, but also the various reorganisations that had taken place in the last few days before the attack, regiments and battalions were being rushed across to cover the Hebron road, running north out of Beersheba. Some of these units were 'scratch' forces formed from various depots – troops assigned to training or guard duties, now being stripped out and formed into ad hoc battalions – but others from the 8th (OT) Army reserves, including the 19th (OT) Infantry Division. Kress von Kressenstein's main concern was that the British would simply continue north, up the road that passed through Hebron and on to Jerusalem. The noise and confusion caused by Newcombe's force helped to convince him that this was a serious proposition.

However, the British had other ideas. To move directly up the Hebron road would certainly offer the shortest route to Jerusalem as the crow flies, but it was far from an ideal option. A few miles north of Beersheba the Judean Mountains began: a jumbled mass of steep-sided hills that could only be traversed with great difficulty. An army could not advance along a single road, but any units moving along either side of that road would be slowed to a crawl. Infantry, who usually marched at 3mph in open ground, would find themselves advancing several miles up and down mountain sides to achieve a single mile on the map, while anything with wheels, hooves or (in the case of camels) pads would be slowed even further. Wagons and artillery pieces would have to be manhandled all the way. At the same time, the ever-increasing flanks of the army would be vulnerable to attack from either the east or the west, not least from the several corps of Ottoman troops still holding the Gaza line.

For the offensive to have any serious chance of success, the rest of the Gaza–Beersheba line would need to be cleared out first. The Ottoman defenders would need to be driven out of their formidable prepared defences, and pushed north into the open. There an already defeated and hopefully disorganised and demoralised enemy could be driven away from their headquarters, communications networks, supply dumps and logistical systems. They could be harried and chased into chaos, as long as enough pressure was kept on them to prevent them from forming any new defensive lines. Once the British were clear of the Gaza–Beersheba defences, they could keep pushing north up the coastal plain, which offered not only the easiest (and fastest) ground to traverse, but also the quickest routes to the campaign's two key objectives. By advancing up the coast the British could capture the port at Jaffa, thus allowing them to use their naval superiority to bring supplies directly into their forward areas by ship, rather than relying on a lengthy and precarious system based on the railway and then wagons and camels. Once on a level with Jaffa, the army could also swing to the right, and advance up the main road to Jerusalem. While still slow going, the distance to be traversed through the mountains at this point was much shorter than would be the case if advancing from Beersheba.

All of this depended upon the breaking of the defences at Gaza and along the road to Beersheba. This was far from a given; the defences were made up of many separate, independent systems, and (in particular around Gaza) formidable in their own right. On the inland flank, the position at Beersheba could be exploited to push along and behind the lines, bypassing many of the great redoubts along the road and forcing the Ottomans to pull back and defend themselves from an unexpected angle. Gaza would not be so easy. Two previous attempts to take the town had failed, and the trench systems to the south and southeast had only become stronger since. Instead of advancing straight into the mouth of the defences, aiming at the crucial high ground around Ali Muntar, a different approach would be taken. This time, the main axis of advance would run up the coast, along the beach between Gaza and the sea. While still heavily entrenched, this should provide an easier route for the British to get through the lines and then loop around behind the town, forcing the garrison to either withdraw or be cut off from the rest of their army.

As a preliminary to this, a massive bombardment opened on Gaza on 27 October 1917. A force of sixty-eight guns or howitzers was split into three parts; one for the general bombardment, and two (dividing the battlefield in half between them) for specific counter-battery work, destroying Ottoman artillery. The barrage intensified on 29 October when a flotilla of Royal and French Navy ships off-shore joined in.* The largest guns that the Royal

---

* This force included the cruiser HMS *Grafton*, the French coastal defence ship *Requin*, the monitors HMS *Raglan*, *M.15*, *M. 29*, *M.31* and *M.32*, two British and five French destroyers, two motor gunboats, three seaplane carriers and a range of trawlers, launches and drifters. Some were used to screen the force from submarines rather than shelling Gaza, and not all were present at once, as ships returned to Port Said to refuel and take on more ammunition.

Artillery could provide were 60-pounder (5in) and 6in field guns, and 6in and 8in howitzers. The cruisers and monitors off-shore provided, apart from numerous comparable or lighter guns from their secondary armament, a range of 9.2in, 10.8in, and even 14in guns, significantly increasing the weight of the shelling. Indeed, this would be the largest British bombardment staged outside of the Western Front, and even by Western Front standards it was formidable.[308] An unidentified sailor on one of the British destroyers, HMS *Comet*, would recall the awesome effects of the shelling:

> I have been trying to think of a suitable simile to describe this bombardment but can't, the best I can do is to have two similes, one for the view & the other for the sound. The sound is the easier, so take that first. A heavy brewer's dray drawn by a rattling old steam roller going at 50 miles an hour over a cobbled paved road is my best description. This does not describe the actual noise so much as the continuity of it. A thunderstorm (i.e. rolls of thunders) best describes the sound … The view. Suppose the 5 odd miles of coast was a giant piano the keys of which when struck gave out a flash of light instead of a note of music. Imagine that, then further imagine two gods were playing one of Beethoven's sonatas & you get some idea. In other words there was one continuous roll of thunder & one continuous flash of light from the guns.
>
> This morning I experienced quite the most unique & awe inspiring experience of my life. On shore the old piano was going full blaze, a barrage fire to cover the advance … I said the shock of our guns was enormous, you shall judge for yourself. The panel of the port door of the charthouse was blown right out & over the side. The clock, seemingly clamped on to the wall was utterly jiggered up, plaster, nuts, odds & ends such as loose bits of woodwork lay in a chaotic debris about the floor, the bookcase (also clamped to the wall) came down & one window & three electric bulbs were smashed – all by the concussion.[309]

The gunfire was not a continuous effort; to fire non-stop for six days would over-heat and burn out the guns (and indeed the crews). Instead, a fire plan dictated when and where each battery fired, and how many shells. Enemy gun batteries, supply dumps, headquarters, roads and trenches had all been plotted by aerial reconnaissance and received their doses of shell. The wire in front of the trenches was systematically destroyed, and then occasionally revisited to hamper Ottoman efforts to repair it. Gas shells were also fired at enemy batteries, but as with their use in the 2nd Battle of Gaza, it seems that they had almost no effect and the Ottomans may not even have been aware of their use.[310]

Allenby had originally planned the ground assault on Gaza to start around twenty-four or forty-eight hours before the renewal of the attack in the east, on Sharia. This was set in the immediate aftermath of the fall of Beersheba for 3 or 4 November, and so the date of 2 November was chosen. It quickly became apparent that the wells in Beersheba were not as plentiful as had been hoped, and while a small amount of ground water left over from a recent thunderstorm helped to supplement the supply, it would take longer than thought to establish an adequate and regular flow of water. Therefore, the Sharia operation was postponed, but it was decided to go ahead with the Gaza plan anyway. Preparations had already been made, apart from the bombardment. Troops had been practicing on full-scale mock-ups of the Ottoman trench systems, and nightly raids had been made against advanced Ottoman posts. During the afternoon on 1 November, companies of the Egyptian Labour Corps were formed up and marched down to the shore at Deir el Belah, within sight of the Ottoman defenders, and were loaded onto trawlers and launches, attempting to reinforce the deception that the British were going to make an amphibious landing north of Gaza. After dark the Egyptians were disembarked again, although the small ships remained and occasionally showed lights during the night to give the impression of activity.[311] Meanwhile troops were prepared for the assault by being issued extra equipment, and marching to their concentration points. Sergeant W. Town MM, a veteran of the 1st Battle of Gaza, was with the 1/5th Essex Regiment:

> On the morning of 1 November, we were busy getting ready for the evening 'entertainment'. Bombs were issued, Lewis guns overhauled, and extra good grub served out. A Communion Service was held in the afternoon, and was well attended ... We halted just by Sheikh Ajiln and lay down to rest, for we were laden with all sorts of articles, picks, shovels, Lewis gun magazines, bombs etc. We talked to each other in whispers, why I cannot say, because we were well behind the line, and the guns were making a terrific row.[312]

The first phase of the ground assault began at just before 11 p.m. on 1 November by the 156th Brigade of the 52nd (Lowland) Division, on loan to the 54th (East Anglian) Division who were to be the main attacking force. The 1/7th Scottish Rifles, supported by two companies of the 1/8th, crept into no-man's-land opposite Umbrella Hill, which jutted out of the Ottoman lines to the south and from which they could direct fire onto the flanks of attacks to either side. The troops were spotted as they gathered, and received machine-gun and rifle fire until a British barrage descended on the Hill at 11 p.m. At ten past, the artillery lifted and the Scots swarmed over the Hill and rapidly evicted the garrison from the 138th (OT) Infantry Regiment. A heavy Ottoman counter-barrage caused heavier casualties among the Scots than the assault had, but no attempt was made to retake the outpost. Thanks to the raids over the previous few nights, this was assumed to be another such probe that would withdraw of its own accord. Instead, the Scots dug in, having secured the flank of the main attack. Further to the east, the 75th Division, and beyond them the composite force of French, Italian, Indian and West Indian troops made smaller diversionary attacks.

The main attack was to run up the beach to the west of Gaza. This stretch of open ground lay below the hill-top town between

it and the sea, and was only thinly defended. The front line consisted of three small redoubts – Beach Post, Cricket Redoubt
and the Sea Post – joined by trenches, a second line of trenches
behind, and fairly clear ground back to Gun Hill and a further
trench system, beyond which was the small village of Sheikh
Hasan on the coast. Once Sheikh Hasan was taken, there was one
more trench – Lion Trench – between them and open ground,
and a clear path to the Ottoman rear. A further series of trench
systems ran at ninety degrees to these, along the western side of
the town on high ground overlooking the beach. At the south-
west corner was El Arish Redoubt, with Burj Trench to the
north of it and running into Zowaiid Trench, which itself ran
into Rafah Trench. The sand was deep and soft, making it slow
ground to cross. On the other hand, it also meant that the British
bombardment had been unusually effective, and many of the
trenches had at least partially collapsed under the concussions.

The attack would be made by 54th (East Anglian) Division on
a front of about 3.2km (2 miles). The start time was set for 3 a.m.,
which was a compromise based on the conditions faced. The darkness would help cover the advance, which would be slow over
the soft sand, as well as being long; no-man's-land was just under
a kilometre (1,100yds) wide at this point. On the other hand,
it was only just past the full moon, so there should be enough
light to navigate by. Two brigades would make the first assault.
The first wave of the 163rd Brigade would angle across towards
the El Arish Redoubt (which would also be attacked from the
east by the 156th Brigade) and Burj Trench, before the following wave moved through them and pushed further into the Gaza
defences, with their final objectives around 460m (500yds) behind
the Ottoman front lines. On their left, the 161st Brigade would
have a longer haul, sweeping up Beach and Sea Posts and Cricket
Redoubt, before continuing on to come up on the northern side
of 163rd Brigade to take Zowaiid and Rafah Trenches. These
attacks would be supported by six tanks (with two in reserve).
The tanks would be used in closer cooperation than during the

2nd Battle, but still as individuals rather than in their most effective formations of small teams. Behind the two leading brigades, 162nd Brigade would come up, passing directly up the beach to take Gun Hill and Sheikh Hasan. Typical of the flexibility that Allenby weaved into all of his plans, behind them would be the Imperial Service Cavalry Brigade – three regiments of Indian lancers – who would be ready to exploit any breaches in the Ottoman lines, albeit in a limited fashion. A single brigade was unlikely to be enough to turn an Ottoman retreat into a rout, but they could certainly help cause fear and confusion by attacking the rear areas.

The Ottoman bombardment provoked by the attack on Umbrella Hill died down just as the main assault forces were forming up, and so it did not impede the operation at all. A heavy British barrage replaced it as the two leading brigades surged ahead, but both ran into problems immediately. Heavy cloud blocked the moon and starlight, while the bombardments had thrown up dust, sand and smoke in vast billows. Visibility was greatly reduced, and most of the advancing units were either delayed or lost their way. The first wave of the 163rd and 156th Brigades successfully took El Arish Redoubt and Burj Trench, supported by two tanks which were quickly either disabled or knocked out. The following wave, though, became disorientated and scattered. Few men made it through to their objectives, and these were soon pushed back by counter-attacks from the 163rd (OT) Infantry Regiment, while Ottoman artillery fire also pounded the captured positions. The 161st Brigade successfully overwhelmed the 79th (OT) Infantry Regiment detachments in the Beach and Sea Posts, Sergeant Town recalling how:

> At that moment the signals came to 'Advance!'. Then it seemed that an absolute inferno was let loose … so loud was the uproar that we were unable to hear the bursting of Johnny's shells, or the whistle of their bullets as they opened fire on us …
>
> The order was given to charge, and we set up a yell with such wind as we had left, and charged through the wreckage

of 'Johnny's' wire ... Well, we piled into the trenches, and set
to work to clear away any Johnnies left. L/Cpl S— discovered
a dug-out full of Turks, who fired at him; to quote his own
words, he at once 'let drive' with some Mills No. V Bombs, a
sure cure for Turks. Two more he bayoneted, as they tried to
escape. I found myself in a communications trench, which led
into a deep hollow, and there were quite a few Turks dodging
about that hollow. Needless to say, I also 'let drive' with my
rifle, and it was quite exciting for a time.

However, they had to bypass Cricket Redoubt until tank support could be brought forward. Then this brigade too became
confused and disjointed as they advanced north-east against the
main Gaza defences. The battalions detailed to take Zowaiid
and Rafah Trenches somehow swapped places without realising
it. The units fragmented in the confusion of battle, and command and control began to break down.* Still, the next phase
of the operation went ahead as planned, with the 162nd Brigade
moving directly up the beach behind them. After a brief struggle, Gun Hill fell and by 6 a.m. the brigade was ready to attack
Sheikh Hasan. A fifteen-minute barrage cleared a path and the
settlement fell to the brigade. Just the Lion Trench now lay
between the EEF and open ground, and at 7.30 a.m. this too was
taken by a company of the 1/4th Northamptonshire Regiment.
However, by now the Ottomans had started to bring up their
reserves, with the 20th and 21st (OT) Infantry Regiments of
the 7th (OT) Infantry Division pushing south to shore-up the
Gaza defences. By 8 a.m. the single company of British troops
had been pushed back to Sheikh Hasan, and by 9 a.m. a series
of counter-attacks were being staged all along the front. The
British artillery had not had either the range or a clear view to
support the position at Lion Trench, but now heavy barrages

---

* Lieutenant Colonel T. Gibbon gives an excellent account of attempting to
control his battalion in these circumstances in *With the 1/5th Essex in the East*.

could be placed to break up advancing Ottoman formations. All along the line the British went to ground in whatever cover they could find, often in trenches that were badly damaged and partially collapsed. Over the following day, night and into 3 November the Ottoman counter-attacks, and limited British attempts to expand their toe-hold on the city, continued. The initial assault troops were still on the front line and taking the brunt of the fighting. Sergeant Town:

> 'Abdul' got excited, and his machine guns started ripping the sand bags on the trench to pieces. We had to lie flat because the trench was very shallow, having been almost obliterated by our artillery ... Shortly afterwards we had to withdraw from our part in the communications trench, it having become untenable. We got out by wriggling and squirming along, dragging the Lewis gun and magazines with us. We managed to find a fairly comfortable part of the trench, and settled down again. Thirst was an awful drawback. For the first forty-eight hours we had only what water we had brought in our bottles, and the men were in a state of semi-stupor by the time we got the glad news that several petrol tins of water were being sent up at night ...
>
> Johnny tried to counter-attack three times, but the monitors lying close in to the shore had him 'taped' with their search-lights, and broke up his attacks before they could develop. The night passed fairly quietly, except for constant artillery fire from both sides, and rifle and machine-gun fire from the left sector ... We had no blankets or great-coats, just our thin khaki drill tunics and shorts, and the nights were perishingly cold.

By the end of 4 November both sides were exhausted, and the fighting petered out, although local Ottoman counter-attacks continued for two more days. British loses had been heavy – over 360 men killed, nearly 2,000 wounded and nearly 400 missing, against nearly 450 prisoners taken – and Gaza was still substantially in Ottoman hands. However, the fighting had drawn in the Ottoman reserves in this sector, and further depleted the overall Ottoman reserve pool. This left the Ottoman forces in the east under-strength for the counter-attack they were planning to retake Beersheba.

In the hills north of Beersheba, the re-formed III (OT) Corps was gathering. The 19th (OT) Infantry Division formed the core of the force, with elements of the 16th and 27th (OT) Infantry Divisions (the rest of which were formed in a screen running through Sharia), and the 3rd (OT) Cavalry Division on the far eastern flank. The RFC spotted and plotted the gathering of these forces from 2 November, but their exact intentions remained unclear. Allenby worried that they were meant to create a threat on his flank, forcing him to divert troops into the Judean foothills where they would become increasingly sucked into the rugged, tangled and waterless hills.[313] Another possibility was that the Ottomans would strike south towards Beersheba, recapturing the valuable water supplies. This counter-attack option seems to have been the actual intention of the Ottomans, but confusion as to the situation reigned within their own ranks, too.[314] By the time that they began to form a coherent force, this area and most of the formations had been under the command of the 7th (OT) Army for about a week, but Kress von Kressenstein, commander of the 8th (OT) Army, was still issuing them orders.[315] (The Ottoman command problems would be further exacerbated when Falkenhayn finally decided to join his headquarters in Jerusalem, leaving Aleppo on the morning of 4 November. After spending the night in Damascus, he reached Jerusalem on the evening of 5 November, having been out of touch with his staff and senior commanders for the best part of two days.)[316] From Allenby's point of view, whatever the intentions of the enemy, a solid line had to be formed and held to the north of Beersheba; one that would neither be lured into an advance in the direction of Hebron, nor allow the Ottomans to threaten Beersheba. This task was given to

53rd (Welsh) Division, supported by cavalry on their right flank
and parts of the 74th Division on their left.

On 2 November, the 53rd Division were dug in around Abu
Jerwal, about 13km (8 miles) north of Beersheba. From here, the
plan was to swing to the west as part of the general British advance
towards the Sharia positions, while the A&NZ Mounted Division
screened the area to the north. However, to block the Ottomans
more effectively, the infantry would need to advance 4.8 or
6.5km (3 or 4 miles) to the north, further into the hills and more
in line with the cavalry piquets. The move began on 3 November,
with the division marching over harsh terrain that made every
mile on the map expand into several on the ground. They met
the Ottoman forces dug in on a line of hills that formed a ridge
around Khuweilfeh. These hills commanded the local area, and
53rd Division immediately began to attack several points of the
line in an attempt to push the Ottomans back and use the ridge as
their own defensive line. The 7th Mounted and 2nd ALH Brigades
meanwhile occupied a second commanding height, Ras el Naqb,
nearly 4.8km (3 miles) to the east, to protect their flank. During
the afternoon these two brigades were forced to withdraw to water
their horses, but were replaced by the 5th Mounted Brigade of the
Australian Mounted Division. The gap between Ras el Naqb and
the 53rd Division was screened by the Imperial Camel Corps.

There followed a scrappy and confused battle spread over
several days, with the jumbled terrain and lack of decent maps
making the course of events hard to trace at the time as well as
now. Conditions in the hills were grim for the infantry, whose
water still needed to be brought up from Beersheba, 18 or 19km
(11 or 12 miles) to the south. On the night of 4/5 November, the
resupply convoys became lost, and the food, artillery shells and,
most importantly, water, in them was many hours late in arriving at the front. One Welsh officer recalled:

> Hard days these. Very little water, never enough for a wash;
> bully beef and biscuits unvaried, no mails ... We wore 'tin

hats,' and the intense heat of the sun on them made our heads
feel like poached eggs ... We had about three pints [of water]
for forty-eight hours, which included a long march up the
stifling, winding ravines of the Judean foothills, followed by
incessant fighting, the temperature, thanks to the Khamsin,
which prevailed, being that of August. It was real hell. A lot
of men went nearly mad with thirst.[317]

After a concerted effort on 6 November, 158th Brigade took
the main hill in the chain, usually known as Khuweilfeh Hill
or Tel Khuweilfeh. They lost it again shortly afterwards to an
Ottoman counter-attack, but retook it again and then held it
against five more attacks. During this bitter fighting Captain
John Fox Russell RAMC (attached 1/6 RWF), who had already
been awarded the Military Cross for saving the wounded under
fire at the 1st Battle of Gaza, was killed doing the same here.
He was awarded a posthumous Victoria Cross. In all, the brigade
lost thirty-six officers and 584 men killed or wounded.[318] In
the early hours of the following morning the Ottoman forces
began to withdraw, although skirmishing continued until the
10 November. However, by now any chance of the Ottomans
restoring the situation by retaking Beersheba had now been lost.

Shortly before dawn on 6 November, the delayed break-out
from Beersheba had begun. Water had been the problem; even
with the Beersheba wells at full estimated production, the army
would have had to have spent several days on short rations, but
the amount available had been over-estimated, while the coming
of the furnace-blast of the *khamsin* wind had increased demand.
More time had been needed to secure other local wells, and
even then some the Australian Mounted Division had needed
to be sent back to Kharm to water their horses. Over the night
of 5/6 November the army finally moved into position. The
Yeomanry Mounted Division had swapped places with the
Australian Mounted Division, moving up from Shellal to support the flank of the 53rd (Welsh) Division fighting around

Khuweilfeh while the other division had withdrawn to Shellal to cover the 15-mile gap between XX and XXI Corps. The remaining three infantry divisions of XX Corps then drew up in a north–south line, some 13 or 16km (8 or 10 miles) north-west of Beersheba and facing west towards Sharia. Furthest north was the 74th (Yeomanry) Division, with the 60th (London) Division on their left flank, and then the 10th (Irish) Division at the southern end of the line.

To their west stood the main Ottoman defensive systems along the Gaza–Beersheba road, and the defences at the Sharia logistics hub. A railway ran south through Sharia and on down to the main defensive line before turning east. To the east of this railway the Ottoman defences were fairly thin and scattered, a 5.5km (3.5-mile) long line of trenches and positions, not connected into any coherent system and without barbed wire. Most faced south, and had been sited with the assumption that an attack would come from that direction. While they could support each other against anyone advancing from the south, they could easily be picked off individually by an attack from the east. Beyond the railway the defences were much more formidable. Three large trench systems had been built on a line running north-west to south-east and covering a front of 6.4km (4 miles). Just west of the railway was the Kauwukah System, with the Rushdi System to its north-west, and then the Hureira Redoubt north-west of that. These were far more serious defences, with layers of inter-connected and mutually supporting trenches and strong-points, each protected by aprons of barbed wire. However, again they were mainly constructed in the expectation that the attack would come from the south.

At 5 a.m. on 6 November, 74th Division began its attack, crossing 3.5km (about 2 miles) of open ground before reaching the first enemy trenches. The assault was fast moving over broken ground, and they soon outran their supporting artillery, while increasingly coming under fire from Ottoman guns around Sharia. Even so, by 8.30 a.m. the division had

advanced approximately halfway along the line, although it
then had to pause to re-form its units, which had become scattered and mixed up in the rapid advance through the tangled
trenches. Once proper control had been re-established, the
advance resumed and by 1.30 p.m. the whole line as far as the
railway was in British hands. Now it was the turn of the 60th
and 10th Divisions, who had been shadowing the 74th to the
south. Their artillery had already begun a bombardment on the
barbed wire of the Kauwukah System, and at around 12.15 p.m.
the assault began, much to the inconvenience of some. Private
C.R. Verner of the 2/21st London Regiment recalled:

> This was unfortunate, because we had just started investi-
> gating our rations – eating them was difficult because of the
> intolerable thirst – and we had no time to put them away
> again. We fell in, extended to five paces, and doubled off over
> the crest of the hill.
>
> All the Lewis Gun ammunition was dumped some way
> back, which made things easier for us, but we must have been
> an odd looking crowd because we were carrying tins of bully,
> tins of jam, biscuits and slabs of crushed dates in our arms.
> Our rifles were slung.[319]

This was harder going against deeper and more complex
defences, but even so by 2 p.m. the Kauwukah System was in
Irish and London hands, and the Rushdi System fell by 3.30 p.m.
Orders now came for the 60th Division to turn north, ready to
advance on Sharia Station, where warehouses, a hospital and
other buildings were clustered. Then the division was to move
beyond, crossing the Wadi Sharia and assaulting the final objective, the height of Tel esh Sharia which dominated the area.[320]

Tel esh Sharia was supposed to fall by the end of the day, but
by the time the 60th Division had reorientated itself there was
only an hour of daylight left. Even so, the advance began, and
ran immediately into heavy Ottoman fire. Verner:

So far we had caught no shell fire worth speaking of ... but directly we moved from the railway embankment we were spotted and the fun began. A sudden burst of shrapnel right on top of us drove us headlong to cover, which was luckily near in the shape of a steep dip in the ground ... and then for about fifteen minutes the Turkish batteries worked at high pressure and the air shrieked with shrapnel.

Shell after shell cracked just above us, but the aforesaid dip proved wonderful cover. The shrapnel drove up clouds of sand just behind us, and hissed a few feet above our backs. I took one mighty thump on the back which proved to be a stone.[321]

The fighting continued after dark, becoming increasingly confused and disjointed. British troops advanced to within 460m (500yds) of the station, but at around 7 p.m. one of the warehouses, full of ammunition, began to explode. The troops were rapidly pulled back away from the danger as the fire and explosions spread to other buildings. Progress along that route was now blocked, and so the advance was halted and orders issued to resume the advance at 3.30 a.m. on 7 November.

This gave the Ottomans the chance to commit their last reserves, a scratch force, known as the Zuheilika Group, of around a thousand men gathered from divisions all along the front. This was pushed in to positions around Tel esh Sharia, supporting the 48th (OT) Infantry Regiment. Meanwhile, Kress von Kressenstein had finally accepted the inevitable and had ordered the start of the evacuation of Gaza, moving the artillery back first, although at the same time he began preparations to use the troops from Gaza in a counter-attack to the north-east of the city.[322] However, any such plans were immediately upset as the British resumed their attack.

The original starting time of 3.30 a.m. was put back to 5.30 a.m. as it took longer to move the attacking brigades into position. They were moving over broken and unfamiliar ground in the dark, and a general lack of landmarks impeded progress. At dawn the artillery began a covering barrage, to which the Ottomans replied in kind. Colonel 'Bosky' Borton of the 2/22nd London Regiment experienced this barrage somewhat closer than most, after inadvertently moving too far north during the night:

> There was no time to reconnoitre and we started in the pitch dark, over the most difficult country you can imagine, deep nullah after deep nullah. Everyone lost touch and it became so hopeless I halted until the moon rose (2 a.m.) when I found that my direction was right – I had only got one Company and no sign of any other Battalions. I decided however to push on and walked slap into the Turk in force. The first I knew was 5 Machine Guns opening on me at about 100 yards. It did not take me long to realise that this was no job for one Company, so I fell back slowly and just before dawn ran into my other 3 Companies and again went forward and shoved the Turk back.
>
> As the light grew better I found we were in a devilish awkward fix – we were swept by machine-gun fire from both flanks, and behind their artillery put down a barrage on top of us and if it had not been that the light was so bad – would have been wiped out in a matter of minutes. It was impossible to stay where we were, and hopeless to go back, so to go forward was the only thing to do –
>
> And we went –
>
> One of the men had a football. How it came there goodness knows. Anyway we kicked off and rushed the first guns, dribbling the ball with us. I take it the Turk thought we were dangerous lunatics, but we had stopped for nothing, not even to shoot and the bayonet had its day. For 3,000 yds.[2.7km] we swept up everything finally capturing a field battery and its entire gun crews – The Battery fired the last round at us at 25 yards.[323]

For his actions in leading his men from the front at Sharia, and at Beersheba, Borton received the Victoria Cross.

26. Thick cacti hedges were a considerable obstacle to the attacking British, Australian and New Zealand troops during all three battles outside Gaza. Similar, although by all accounts less dense, hedges are still used in the area today.

27. The view from the top of Tel El Jemmi looking towards Gaza. This hill dominates the area, making it an obvious place to set up an headquarters, as well as a good landmark for troops to navigate by.

28. The Wadi Ghazze today, near Tel el Fara.

29. The memorial and grave marker for the men of the Egyptian Labour Corps who died during the campaign, just outside the walls of the Old City, Jerusalem. Shockingly, the names of these invaluable men were not recorded.

30. The springs and pools at Bir Asluj, the jump-off point for the Australian & New Zealand Mounted Division for their part in the attack on Beersheba, 38km (24 miles) to the north.

31. The Ottoman Governor's residence in the centre of the 'old town' in Beersheba, now the Negev Museum of Art.

32. The view from the top of Tel Saba, looking south. It is clear how the tel dominates these approaches to Beersheba.

33. The Commonwealth War Graves Commission cemetery at Beersheba, on the edge of the 'old town' and near the old railway station.

34. The graves of some of the Lighthorsemen killed in the charge at Beersheba.

35. The striking memorial to the charge of the Australian Light Horse, in the Park of the Australian Soldier in Beersheba.

36. The memorial to the Ottoman soldiers who died at Beersheba, next to the restored railway station (the train behind dates from the 1940s). The bust to the right is of Mustapha Kemal, 'Atatürk', who briefly commanded the 7th (OT) Army before the 3rd Battle of Gaza, and would assume command again in 1918.

37. The ANZAC Memorial on Sheikh Abbas, overlooking Gaza. The design is intended to be reminiscent of the letter 'A', and of a charging horse.

38. The Augusta Victoria Hospital on the Mount of Olives. This was the local German headquarters and hospital, and it was later occupied by the British for the same uses. It later became the headquarters of the British Mandate in Palestine.

39. The view south from Bethlehem. What was a small village in 1917 is now a sprawling town. Few of the buildings shown would have existed when the British advanced on it from the south, and instead the Ottoman defenders had broad, open fields of fire.

40. The mosque at Nabi Samwil, rebuilt in the 1920s after being destroyed by Ottoman artillery. The rest of the village was destroyed in the late 1960s and the ruins of the Crusader castle and Hellenic-period village underneath exposed.

41. The 60th Division Memorial in Jerusalem (also known as the 'Allenby Memorial'), on the site where Mayor Husseini finally surrendered the city.

42. The Jaffa Gate, through which Allenby entered Jerusalem. The large gap to the left had been knocked through the walls to allow Kaiser Wilhelm II to enter in 1898.

43. The steps of the Citadel, Jerusalem, from which Allenby read his declaration of Martial Law, 11 December 1917.

44. The memorial in Jerusalem to the Hindu and Sikh soldiers killed in the campaign, and whose ashes are scattered on the site. A similar memorial wall to the Muslim soldiers who were killed stands directly opposite.

45. The memorial opposite Jerusalem War Cemetery commemorating the Australian Imperial Force's part in the Egypt, Palestine and Syrian campaigns, 1915–18.

46. The Jerusalem War Cemetery and Memorial to the Missing, on Mount Scopus, Jerusalem. The wall at the back records the names of all those killed in the Sinai and Palestine who have no known graves.

47. A company signalling section with the tools of their trade – flags and mirrors. These were still the most reliable methods for long-range communication available, and obviously set definite limits on what messages could be sent, how far, and when.

48. A camouflaged artillery position south of Gaza, May 1917.

Elsewhere, other Londoners were also coming under heavy artillery fire as they advanced. William Hendry of the 2/14th (London Scottish):

Away we went from our cover, quite in day light. They instantly spotted us, about a mile away. We got into artillery formation (commonly known as blobs) and quickly advanced through a din of splitting shrapnel. It was a splendid sight to look back and see all the blobs moving steadily forward, with shrapnel bursting over-head, and as if nothing was happening, and the German gunners which the Turks had, desperately trying to stop our advance by firing hundreds of shells into the air. It was really astonishing the number of shells that burst right above us, and caused so few casualties … We were getting near the front of the hill now, when I noticed blood on my tunic and found my chin bleeding. I dropped into a crack in the ground, broke my iodine bottle and well spread it over my chin, putting a bandage on. While I was doing this the bullets were raining down on the ground around, but only my legs were exposed. I jumped up quickly and ran on to catch up the company, when I suddenly felt a sharp pain in my arm and blood was trickling into my hand, but I did not stop this time and caught my platoon at the foot of the hill. Up we went firing at any slight object ahead. Our machine gunners got going also and covered our advance firing from the flank. When we arrived at the top we found the Turks had fled from their trenches, which we occupied firing hard at the retreating Turks.[324]

The Londoners swept through the station, across the wadi and over the Tel, the last Ottoman defenders falling back before them. The 60th Division established a new line north of the Tel, and the fighting died down apart from the occasional exchanges of shell-fire. It was a chance to rest for the infantry, and their supporting artillery. Gunner J.W. Gough wrote in his diary:

Nov. 7th Open fire on Turkish trenches about six, fired about
250 rounds, Johnnie falls back, we cease firing. There are
only occasional bursts about now – miles from our position.
I suppose it will mean another advance for us. I hope we can
squeeze a little rest before hand it is now 52 hours since I slept
last, a wash wouldn't do the troops any harm.[325]

Some relief came with the arrival of water. Private Verner:

> We were somewhat cheered during the afternoon by the
> announcement of the fall of Gaza, but the great sensation was
> caused by the appearance of camels on the crest of the hill
> behind … and we knew that water was coming. The Turks
> saw them too and tried to stop them with a barrage, but after
> the NCO in charge had stopped panic amongst the camel
> drivers with his fists we saw them (the camels) winding their
> way down to the railway cutting to a point where water could
> be issued in safety.
>
> We restrained ourselves with difficulty from charging
> down on the camels and helping ourselves, and presently
> an order arrived that one man from the Lewis Gun team
> should bring the water-bottles of the rest. This man was me. I
> started off with a good load, and my pace was accelerated by a
> machine gun while crossing the open ground.
>
> I found a sergeant major having great difficulty in keeping
> order among the crowds of thirst-maddened men around the
> Fantassies … [Back at my position] I handed around the bot-
> tles … and as long as I live I shall never forget that drink.[326]

A little while earlier the 10th Division had also resumed its
advance, taking the Hareira Redoubt soon after dawn.[327] Earlier
still, in the early hours XXI Corps had resumed the attack on
Gaza, rapidly discovering that the defences had been abandoned
and pushing on, into the ruined town. At 7 a.m. on 7 November,
Ali Muntar was occupied.[328] For the assaulting troops, it was

an immense relief not to have to face these still-formidable defences. Captain Harry Milson of the 1/5th Somerset Light Infantry recorded:

> Accordingly we were on the move again just as it was dawn. A wonderful sight greeted us, we were abreast of Gaza close on our left, the country was interlaced with trenches and dense cactus hedges, also bushes and trees grew plentifully, all affording excellent cover, especially for machine guns, but not a shot was fired at us and we advanced, unopposed, finding a vast quantity of ammunition and bombs left in the trenches.[329]

The British had obtained their breakthrough. Most of the Ottoman front line had now been taken, apart from the Beer, Atawine and Tank trench systems just east of Gaza. These would all fall on the following day, 8 November, as the 10th and 75th Divisions closed the gap between the two British corps, although not before the bulk of the Ottoman garrisons had slipped away to rejoin the main force. Apart from the far right, where the 53rd Division was still embroiled around Khuweilfeh, the Ottomans were out in the open and in retreat. With the loss of Sharia, a gap had opened between the 7th (OT) and 8th (OT) Armies, who had also lost communications with each other, only re-establishing links on 9 November.[330] There were no more reserves to push in to stem the British advance. On 8 November, Kress von Kressenstein had to report to Falkenhayn that the Ottomans were 'incapable of offensive movements'.[331] Any chance of stopping the British now depended on the endurance and courage of the poorly fed, badly equipped and generally exhausted *mehmetçik* who had already faced a week of combat.

13

PURSUIT

WITH THE OTTOMAN Army forced from the heavy defences it had
been preparing for six months or more and out in the open,
General Allenby's campaign was just starting. The emphasis
now switched fully to XXI Corps in the coastal region, and the
retreating 8th (OT) Army. The 7th (OT) Army had the refuge
of the Judean Mountains to fall back into, and would be able
to find endless strong positions in which to dig in and defend.
The 8th (OT) Army had far fewer such natural positions to
exploit, while pushing them north offered several important
strategic advantages. Having the sea, controlled by the Royal
Navy, on their flank would allow a certain amount of supplies
to be landed; this would not be much, as ship's boats would
have to ferry the supplies in through the surf onto the beach,
but every little would ease what would become an increasingly
taut logistical chain. Eventually, the coast would also lead to
Jaffa. Although the harbour there was little more than a sheltered anchorage, without quays where a ship could tie up to
unload directly onto land, the calm waters would allow the
faster and safer use of boats. Advancing up the coast would also
allow the British to outflank many of the 7th (OT) Army's lines

of defence, and offer a shorter route through the mountains towards Jerusalem from the west.

Ideally, Allenby wanted not just to pursue, but to cut off and destroy as much of the 8th (OT) Army's surviving forces as possible. The cavalry divisions now gathered around Sharia were placed ready to launch north-westward, behind the bulk of the retreating Ottomans. If they struck as near the head of the retreating army as possible, where the defeated troops would still be in some disarray, they could cut through and block the path north. This would allow the infantry just north of Gaza to spring north, overwhelm the relatively well-ordered Ottoman rearguard, and destroy or capture the forces before them. El Medjel, a village around 24km (15 miles) further up the coast from Gaza, had been identified as the best place to mount such a interception, but it became clear on 7 November, while the cavalry were still waiting for the infantry to complete the breakthrough at Sharia, that such a move would not be possible. The Ottomans were falling back too fast, the British forces were too exhausted to undertake a rapid advance, and the water supplies between Sharia and El Medjel simply would not support the numbers of cavalry needed. Still, on that day the three Mounted Divisions of the Desert Mounted Corps were ordered to proceed in that general direction at their best pace, although the New Zealand Mounted Rifle Brigade (from the A&NZ Mounted Division) was ordered to take up position with the 53rd (Welsh) Division north of Beersheba. At the same time, the Yeomanry Mounted Division, which had been on the eastern flank, was still switching from one side of the offensive to the other, and would lag a day behind the other two divisions.[332]

As the cavalry moved to cut the Ottomans off, the 52nd (Lowland) Division pushed forward to keep the retreating enemy moving. Eleven kilometres (7 miles) north of Gaza was the Wadi Hesi, a major watercourse along the northern bank of which the Ottomans had already prepared some basic defences. Rapid action was needed to stop the Ottoman rearguard strengthening this line, and at dusk on 7 November the 157th Brigade managed to establish a bridgehead across the Wadi near its mouth. The 155th Brigade followed overnight, and preparations were made to attack to the east at dawn, where, about 5.6km (3.5 miles) inland, a tall ridge ran north-south along the main Gaza–Jaffa road. Ottoman forces were already in position along this, known to the British as 'Sausage Ridge', and needed to be evicted in order to clear the path for the rest of the army. This ridge proved to be longer, higher and indeed a kilometre (three-quarters of a mile) further east than it appeared on the divisions' maps, and some delays were encountered in finding it and organising the attack by the two brigades, which went in on the morning of 8 November. Hard fighting continued until well after dusk, with the ridge changing hands at least four times until, at around 9 p.m., it finally fell to the Lowlanders.[333]

To the south-east, 60th (London) Division, supported by the Desert Mounted Corps, was also keeping the pressure on the retreating enemy. The infantry were tired from their previous days' fighting, and were given the relatively limited objective of pushing on to Huj, where there was an Ottoman airfield and, more importantly, a large supply dump. Through the morning of 8 November the infantry brigades took a succession of ridges held by Ottoman rearguard forces. Some were routed easily while others, supported by concentrations of artillery, proved more costly to shift.[334] Shortly after midday the 179th Brigade took the village of El Maharata, nearly 4.8km (3 miles) south of Huj, despite heavy artillery fire, and were forced to pause to reorganise their ranks. During this lull, General Shea, commanding 60th Division, arrived and personally drove north of the village to investigate the next area of advance. He found columns of *mehmetçik* straggling back towards another ridge, where a battery of field artillery was establishing its guns. Some machines guns were also being set up in support, and anywhere from several hundred to several thousand infantry were behind the ridgeline. Shea also discovered the equivalent of three squadrons of cavalry from the 5th Mounted Brigade – one and a half squadrons each from the Warwickshire Yeomanry and the Queen's Own Worcestershire Hussars (QOWH), totalling 190 men and under the command of Lieutenant Colonel Hugh Gray-Cheape of the Warwicks. The commander of the Worcesters, Lieutenant Colonel Williams, had already ridden to find the 3rd ALH Brigade to enlist their support in assaulting the ridge. However, the cavalry of the DMC were well spread out, and it would take time to find and gather mounted support. Instead, Shea ordered Gray-Cheape to charge the ridge at once.[335]

The enemy positions lay nearly a mile away across a broad, open valley. However, Gray-Cheape led his force in a wide arc to the east, using natural cover to mask their approach for as long as possible. Unfortunately, this ran his troops into the fire of two more batteries which had been hidden from view, one of mountain guns and one of 6in howitzers. The force quickly split into three separate charges, each targeting a different battery. Gray-Cheape led two troops to the Warwicks to overrun and seize the howitzers, and Major 'Toby' Albright led 'A' Squadron QOWH directly at the closer mountain guns. Trooper Harry 'Pat' Crombie, recalled following Albright:

> A shell exploded in the mouth of the gun temporarily blinding me, when I could see there was nothing between me and the gun, which was about six feet from me. Sitting under it was the gunner pointing a pistol at me, I punctured his neck with my sword and went on, following Sergeant Allen and followed by Dicky Dunn, when a shell burst overhead, my mare jumped and turned. Then I saw Dicky and his horse lying on the ground, Dicky's wrist was shattered by a piece of shrapnel and his horse's back was broken by another piece, there were some Turks with a machine gun beside us, they did not move, so I got Dicky onto my mare and headed back to where the survivors were gathered.[336]

The yeomen would tear through the gun line, losing half their number killed (including the highly popular Albright) or

wounded, before swinging to the left under Major Bill Wiggin
to rejoin the attack on the main battery. This force, with
'B' Squadron of the Warwicks under Captain Rudolf Valintine
and two troops of 'C' Squadron QOWH under Lieutenant
J.W. Edwards, had charged directly across a narrow valley,
briefly falling out of the direct line of fire as they crossed the
bottom and climbed the far side. At the top they passed through
a thin skirmish line of infantry, and faced 200m (220yds) of open
ground before reaching the guns. Captain Oskar Teichman,
medical officer of the QOWH, was lagging slightly behind:

> The Worcester and Warwick Squadrons, already thinned
> out by casualties, swept on, and topping a rise, charged
> through the infantry screen and were lost from view.
> Suddenly the terrific din of shrieking and exploding shells
> ceased, and we knew that the end had come.[337]

The final stretch of ground saw the British formations shattered
by the artillery and machine-gun fire, and all order melted away.
Lieutenant W. Mercer recalled how:

> A whole heap of men and horses went down 20 or 30 yards
> from the muzzles, the Squadron broke into a few scattered
> horsemen at the guns then seem to melt away completely;
> for a time I thought I was the only man alive.[338]

The survivors swept through the guns, hacking at the gunners,
many of whom took shelter below their guns or limbers, and
ran into machine-gun and rifle fire from the supporting troops
behind. Sergeant J. Hayden of the Warwickshire Yeomanry:

> We came into range of their guns which sounded like a roar
> of thunder, they seemed to have turned every gun they had
> onto us at one moment. Men and horses were pitch-polling
> on either side of me, I expected my time was coming every

second. The dust was so thick we could not see the horse in front of us ... By this time our squadron only numbered 25 unhurt ... I was shot, it caught me in the face, within 30 yards of the guns, I thought to myself I am only hit slightly as I could still see out of both eyes, but after a few minutes my left eye stopped up with blood. We were 10 or 12 [left] by now and carried on without a check ... I galloped round the guns like Lord Nelson with one eye blocked up ... As we surrounded their guns there were Turks under each gun with all hands up, quite clear from the reach of my sword and all surrendered. I was then making for a bit of cover, and had only cantered about 30 yards from the guns when a machine-gun opened fire on me from the left rear, shooting my horse through the head and neck, as he dropped he fell across my leg and foot, pinning me down.[339]

Hayden and many others were lucky in that the shock of the charge had an effect on the Ottoman troops behind the guns out of proportion to the remaining numbers of yeomen. Most fled, and the few machine guns that remained were quickly overrun and the weapons turned to encourage the Ottoman retreat.

The cost had been high; of 190 officers and men, thirty-six were killed and fifty-seven wounded, while 110 horses had been killed or had to be destroyed. However, the potential cost to the infantry if they had advanced against these positions once they had been properly prepared was much higher still. The shock of the action also cleared the way to Huj, as the demoralised Ottoman forces fell back in disarray, destroying the valuable supply dumps as they went. By dusk, the 60th Division had advanced several miles north of the village.

The divisions of XX Corps – the 10th, 53rd, 60th and 74th – were now reaching the end of ten days' hard marching and fighting, and, as predicted in the original planning, were becoming exhausted. A period of rest, or at least the army's interpretation of what constituted rest, now began for them. In real terms this meant only limited and necessary movement, while troops repaired and attended to their kit and equipment and made themselves combat ready once again. But troops would also be assigned extra tasks. Working parties would aid the Royal Engineers (RE) in building or repairing roads and bridges. Others would help the specialists of the RE, Army Service Corps, Army Ordnance Corps and Royal Army Medical Corps in bringing up and sorting supplies (although units still often subsisted on short rations of both food and water themselves), and the clearing up of the battlefields. Equipment had to be recovered if reusable or destroyed if not, and munitions made safe. Perhaps most importantly, bodies from both sides would be located, recorded and buried. The 1/5th Essex even spent two days combing the area around Green Hill, searching for, and finding, men killed during the 1st Battle of Gaza, eight months before.[340] As well as human bodies, the bodies of animals also had to be disposed of for the sake of sanitation. One officer of the 2/20th London Regiment recorded that from his unit's rest camp:

> We get some lovely views from the hills. The flies here are worse than ever, and we cannot eat without eating a few. There is also a plentiful supply of dead horses, which does not add greatly to the charm of the place! We are doing our best to bury them, though it is very hard work, and sometimes almost calls for the use of gas helmets.[341]

However, the scale of the task was great, and the army had other priorities. Acting Sergeant James Scott of the 2nd (London) Sanitary Company RAMC arrived in Gaza in late November, and 'had to walk into the town which we found deserted, many houses wrecked, dead donkeys lying in the streets' before moving north into the more recent battlefield. Even a month after the fighting he found that:

> We had to immediately get to work cleaning up, burying and burning dead camels and donkeys. We had to re-bury a lot of

dead human bodies which had been hastily buried and a few
isolated ones which had not been buried. The camp site evacuated by the Turks was very dirty and filthy. Sheep skins and
old clothing were all over the place full of fleas etc. A large
store of grain had been set on fire and was a glowing mass.[342]

The pause also allowed the field ambulances and casualty clearing stations (CCS) regain some semblance of order. Due to the
distances involved in evacuating casualties from the front all the
way back to the field hospitals south of the Wadi Ghazze, and
then back to Egypt, an ad hoc system had been set up to deal with
the problem. Field ambulances with the forward troops were
supposed to patch up the wounded to the extent that they were
out of immediate danger and able to travel, before passing them
back to a CCS for further treatment. However, the speed of the
movement of the different divisions and the numbers of men
needing treatment (up to 11 November, over 8,000 wounded
were processed along with a roughly equal number of sick),
meant that most field ambulances were unable to clear their
waiting rooms before their parent brigades needed to move.
Rump units had to be left behind to finish processing and then
evacuate the wounded, and eventually these detachments began
to double as rest stations, where the wounded could pause on
their long, uncomfortable journeys back to a CCS. This had the
knock-on effect of leaving the field ambulances under-manned
at the front and even less able to cope with the influx of casualties, and the pause in operations allowed them to clear the
backlog and reunite their units.[343]

Another effect of the pause was to allow the divisions of
XX Corps to restock their supplies, as keeping a continuous and
sufficient flow of material into units that were moving and fighting was already proving problematic. There simply were not
enough camels to go around, while motor transport continued
to suffer severely, becoming either frequently bogged down in
the marshy coastal regions, or worn out on the rougher country

in land. As an example of the harshness of the ground, motor lorry tyres designed and tested to last 16,000km (10,000 miles) frequently wore out after less than 3,200km (2,000 miles) of use in Palestine.[344] From the start many units were on short rations of both food and water, although even so vast amounts needed moving. Including the extensive logistical system, the EEF had some 250,000 British (less than half of which were front-line troops, the rest being involved in the lines of supply and communications), 100,000 Egyptian and 18,000 Indian personnel to feed, plus the smaller French and Italian contingents, plus around 150,000 animals.[345] At least small amounts of food and water could be obtained locally by most units, and if the situation was bad enough then authorisation could be given for the use of the emergency ration that each man carried in his pack. Ammunition was more critical, though, and some 250 tons of it was sent forward from the vast dumps accumulated near the old front lines every day. As the army moved north, ammunition was increasingly transported by sea and landed on the beaches to keep adequate supplies flowing to front-line units.[346] Very slowly through the early winter the Ottoman railway system was put back into use. However, the Ottoman and British lines were of different gauges, preventing them from being joined together, while few engines and little rolling stock had been left behind.

This left the burden of supplying the army laying mostly on the backs of the camels, and the shoulders of the Egyptian Labour Corps and Camel Transport Corps. Organised into 'trains' of different sizes, these ran in a near-continuous chain from the rear areas to the corps dumps, from which divisional trains collected their quota. It was a round-the-clock effort, with convoys travelling by day and night over unfamiliar and often poorly mapped ground, their directions usually not more than a simple compass bearing. Indeed, some directions were less even than that: on 10 November 1917 the staff captain of the 157th Brigade was preparing a camel train from the central

52nd Division dump near the mouth of the Wadi Hesi when he received the instructions that his brigade was now as Esdud, 'fifteen miles up [the coast], three miles inland'. He found his unit, but only after marching all night and much of the next morning, collapsing with fatigue on arrival.[347]

Such movements were based on either knowing where the destination unit should be (or would be by the time the camel train arrived), or on selecting a point on the map and arranging for men and animals from the units to be supplied to rendezvous with the camels there. Both approaches could go seriously awry if the planned movements of front-line units were delayed or changed. The postponement of the final assault on Sharia almost led at least two camel trains into disaster, as they approached the town on the night of 6 November, by which time the station was supposed to be in British hands. One train, carrying supplies for the 10th Royal East Kent Regiment (The Buffs) penetrated 3.2km (2 miles) into the Ottoman lines in the darkness, and only real-ised their mistake after capturing a wandering *mehmetçik*. By some miracle, they managed to extricate themselves without being discovered.[348] The other was the cavalry ammunition column which was supposed to set up a dump for the Desert Mounted Corps units to refresh their supplies from. It had set off on the morning of 6 November, and was scheduled to reach Sharia in the late morning of the next day. As it was, it arrived a little early, and soon after dawn was seen proceeding past the leading units of 60th Division as they moved in on the enemy. They stopped in time, preventing what would have been a severe blow to the cavalry divisions if the Ottomans had captured or destroyed the train, possibly even putting a halt to further operations until more ammunition could be brought up.[349] As it was, they then became lost on the way home, and were unable to catch up with their corps headquarters for another twelve days, finally reappearing at Junction Station on 19 November.[350] These are two extreme cases, but examples abound where troops had to wait, hungry and thirsty, for hours while camel trains that had gotten lost or been delayed (including by the units not being where they should have been) finally located them.

Logistics remained the defining feature for the rest of the advance. On 9 November the DMC was supposed to carry on their advance, but only the A&NZ Mounted Division was in a position to move. Both the Australian Mounted Division and the newly arrived Yeomanry Division needed to spend the day in watering their horses. The following day all three cavalry divisions were on the move, heading north, as were the 52nd (Lowland) and 75th Divisions, despite the rising of another *khamsin* to again make the day's march even harder. The 54th (East Anglian) Division remained at Gaza still, and now passed all of its transport across to keep the more northerly divisions moving. The Ottoman forces were still managing to keep one step ahead of the British, and as the next major objective came in sight it became increasingly important to keep the pressure up.

Junction Station now lay only 16–24km (10–15 miles) from the most advanced British positions. This aptly named depot was on the Ottoman railway system, at the point where the main line from Syria split into two, heading south towards Gaza and Beersheba and also east towards Jerusalem. Taking it would not only potentially deny the Ottomans the valuable supplies held there, but also cut the principal line of communications between the 7th and 8th (OT) Armies. Once the line at Junction Station was cut, the next closest railway that ran east-west was at Nablus, around 65km (40 miles) further north. The roads in the Judean Mountains were mostly barely worthy of the name, and were often unmade animal tracks at best. Once the railway line was cut, the garrison of Jerusalem and the defending army around it would be reliant on supplies being brought to them by camel or mule from the railway at Nablus, or a slightly longer distance from the line at Amman, across the Jordan Valley.

The Ottomans knew the importance of the station too, and had begun to re-form the 8th (OT) Army on a long, sweeping line to the west, south-west and south of it. Approximately

15,000 men had been dug in along a series of strong, well-sited positions, using hill or ridge-top villages, many of which were surrounded by dense cactus hedges or other natural barriers. Other, smaller forces were dug in on equally well-chosen sites to keep slowing the British advance down as they continued north, giving the new defensive line more time to prepare. On 11 November, rearguards had to be dealt with, in cost of time and lives, along the banks of the Nahr Sukereir, and on the high ground at Burkah. The former were ousted by the 1st ALH Brigade, and the latter by the Scottish infantry of 156th Brigade, 52nd Division. These in particular had a rough time of it, taking the positions around Burkah and on the nearby Brown Hill. The 4th Royal Scots Fusiliers (RSF), already depleted by casualties and sickness, suffered very heavily taking and then losing Brown Hill. Near dusk, the 2/3rd Gurkha Rifles, from the neighbouring 74th Division, passed by the battalion head-quarters. Lieutenant Colonel Mitchell appealed to them for aid. According to the regimental history:

> An invitation to fight was a temptation that the Gurkhas never tried to resist, and they promptly despatched two com-panies to aid the Royal Scots.[351]

Unfortunately, when the Gurkhas reached the Scots, it was dis-covered that none of their officers spoke English. Only because one of the RSF's remaining officers, Captain Bolton, had been in the Indian Civil Service and knew some of the native languages could even very basic communications be established, and in the end the Gurkhas and the remaining sixty or seventy Scotsmen coordinated their final, successful assault on the hill after dark with a mixture of sign language and a shared offensive spirit.[352]

On 12 November, von Falkenhayn unleashed his counter-attack into the British eastern flank and rear. As the advance on the coast proceeded much faster than the advance through the moun-tains, the British flank became increasingly open and vulnerable, although Allenby saw this as a calculated risk. The Australian Mounted Division was screening this area, spread into small sub-units over a 19km front, when the 8th (OT) Army launched four divisions down the railway line from El Tine. The 54th (OT) Infantry Division on the right and the 53rd (OT) Infantry Division in the centre ran into British and Australian cavalry units pushing north in the opposite direction. The 28th and 16th (OT) Infantry Divisions, on the left and in reserve respectively, met less resistance. Although impressive on paper, the Ottoman attacking force was only around 5,000 men in number, with all units being greatly reduced by the previous fighting and marching. They were also very tired from their earlier moves, and the long night marches to bring them into place. Witnesses on both sides agreed that the *mehmetçik* attacked without their usual spirit and dogged courage. Even so, the outlying troops and squadrons of Lighthorsemen and Yeomen fell back before the superior numbers. The Royal Gloucestershire Hussars were most exposed, north of the railway station at Balin, and the QOWH and Warwickshire Yeomanry rushed to help their brigade-mates. All three regiments were then forced to fall back as Ottoman infantry curled around their flanks. Balin was abandoned, much to the alarm of the brigade field ambulance, who no one had informed of the move, and who were forced to run or gallop to safety as the Ottomans poured in just a few hundred metres away.[353]

Eventually, a new line was stabilised some 4.8–6.5km (3–4 miles) back from where the division had begun, and with good use of machine-gun strongpoints and supporting rifle-men, the Ottoman advance was stopped. For their part, the Ottoman forces began to dig in along their new line at dusk. The Australian Mounted Division had only lost around fifty men, although most of these were from the 5th Mounted Brigade. Already under-strength from the previous fighting, including the charge at Huj, this brigade would shortly afterwards be withdrawn from the division and replaced by the 7th Mounted Brigade.[354]

The Ottoman counter-attack had not distracted Allenby in any way from his overall plan or diverted any troops, and preparations had continued for the attack on the Junction Station defences. The 75th Division was to attack the southern-most group of defences, piercing the main lines at Mesmiye El Gharbiye, and then advancing north-east. This would bring them across at an angle north of El Tine, threatening to cut off the four Ottoman divisions that had attacked the Australian Mounted Division and (with an attack by the latter) force them to retreat. Both divisions would then advance on Junction Station from the south-west. Meanwhile, the 52nd Division would attack from the west and north-west, sweeping up the outposts at Beshshit before tackling the strong positions around Qatre and El Maghar. The Yeomanry Mounted Division would be on their left, swinging around the Ottomans' northern flank, while the A&NZ Mounted Division screened the army's open left flank. The plan, drawn up by Major General Bulfin of XXI Corps, had no set timetable beyond the start time and showed a flexible and adaptable approach, and Allenby approved it without change before leaving Bulfin to implement the plan while he kept himself engaged with the bigger picture across the whole front.[355]

The attack began on 13 November, and it proved a long, hard day. The 75th Division faced solid resistance at Mesmiye El Gharbiye, crossing open ground before assaulting the village, which was on a ridge and surrounded by thick cactus hedges. It fell at around noon to 233rd Brigade, although snipers remained an active distraction in the thick hedgerows until late in the afternoon. The advance then continued across a series of ridges, each taking time to clear, until the left-hand brigade was held up by long-range fire from the Ottoman positions at Qatre. On the right, the 234th Brigade had faced stiff resistance around Mesmiye esh Sherqiye, but with support from the Australian Mounted Division had finally taken the village near dusk. The brigade then began to advance up the railway line from El Tine towards Junction Station.[356]

The 52nd (Lowland) and Yeomanry Mounted Divisions had also faced hard fighting on the left flank. Beshshit had fallen easily to 155th Brigade in the morning, which then advanced on the villages of Qatre and El Maghar. These sat on top of a ridge either side of a steep defile where the Wadi Qatra ran between them. To the north of the defile, El Maghar was at the southern end of a long, fairly low but steep ridge that ran off to the north-east. Along this ridge, and at Qatre just to the south, were the remains of the 3rd and 7th (OT) Infantry Divisions, perhaps 3,000 men, well dug in and with the two villages as bastions. The two villages were already in strong positions and well-ringed with cactus, while the area immediately west of the ridges was flat and wide open. Now trenches and machine-gun posts were added to make them into formidable redoubts.

The 155th Brigade began their attack soon after 11 a.m., crossing over 2.7km (3,000yds) of open ground before even reaching the ridge. The Ottoman positions were too well sited, and the defenders too determined. At 1 p.m. the divisional commander, Major General Hill, called off the attack. He instead conferred with his artillery commanders, and visited the commander of the Yeomanry Mounted Division on his left, Major General Barrow. Between them it was agreed that a short, intense bombardment would be laid down at 3.30 p.m., during which the infantry and cavalry would both advance on Qatre and El Maghar. The Yeomanry Mounted Division had already advanced in a broad sweep on 52nd Division's flank, taking the village of Yibna and coming up on Wadi Janus, which the Wadi Qatre joined after emerging from the defile and turning north. The 6th Mounted Brigade was already poised on the Wadi Janus and had reconnoitred as far as possible the ground between themselves and the enemy-held ridge. The 22nd Mounted Brigade was coming up on their left, and would also provide support. As the Wadi Janus ran north and the ridge veered north-east, the 6th Mounted Brigade would have over 3.7km (2.3 miles) to cover, the last 900m (0.5 miles) or so up the steep slope, while the 22nd Mounted Brigade would have even further to go.

The attack would therefore go in mounted, at the gallop, the whole way.

At 3 p.m., the cavalry began their advance, trotting out of the Wadi Janus in open, artillery order. The Queen's Own Dorset Yeomanry rode on the left while the Royal Buckinghamshire Hussars wason the right, closest to El Maghar, and each was in three lines of a squadron each. Behind, the Berkshire Yeomanry was in reserve. The lines quickly spurred into a canter, crossing the open ground between the wadi and the ridge as quickly as possible, while over their heads the guns of the Royal Horse Artillery and the brigade's machine-gun sections gave covering fire. It was a long way to ride, and over rough terrain. Cohesion began to be lost, and the formation was well dispersed by the time it struggled up to the crest of the ridge. The Bucks Hussars arrived first, charging their blown horses over the lip of the ridge and in among the Ottoman trenches. Lieutenant Cyrus Perkins recalled:

> As we neared the ridge swords were drawn and very soon we were breasting the rise with their gun blasts feeling like pillows hitting one's face. Then in seconds they were all around us, some shooting, some scrambling out of slit trenches and some sensibly falling flat on their faces. It had taken us, I suppose, a bit over five minutes.
>
> Blown and galloping horses are hard to handle one handed while you have a sword in the other – so hindered by the clutter of rifle butt and other equipment troopers found it nearly impossible to get at a low dodging Turk ... By then, those of us who had got there still mounted were among a seething mob – literally like mounted policemen in a football crowd – shouting at them to surrender.[357]

As more troopers rode over the crest, or dismounted to charge over on foot, the Ottoman force north of El Maghar village fell back in disarray. The Dorset Yeomanry, with further to ride, arrived moments later and added to the rout. The 6th Mounted Brigade lost sixteen men killed and 114 wounded in the charge, while 265 horses were killed or injured. However, they had broken through the main Ottoman defensive line, and several hundred prisoners and a dozen machine guns were captured.

The infantry attack on El Maghar and Qatre began as the cavalry had started their advance, the brigade commander, Brigadier General John Pollock-McCall, himself snatching 'up a rifle and bayonet, shouted to the Borderers to follow him, and dashed out into the open'.[358] The men of the 4th and 5th King's Own Scottish Borderers who had taken cover around the Wadi Janus/Wadi Qatre surged forward with him, taking advantage of the lull in Ottoman fire as the defenders of El Maghar turned their rifles and machine guns onto the yeomanry. The infantry also charged up the hill and poured into the Ottoman positions, slowly clearing out the enemy at bayonet point among the cacti and the houses, before emerging from the far side of the village to link up with the cavalry. Meanwhile, the 5th RSF assaulted Qatre under cover of a fifteen-minute artillery bombardment, and by 4 p.m. that village too was in British hands.[359]

While the infantry were clearing their way through the villages, another cavalry attack had occurred on the left flank of the 6th Mounted Brigade. The 22nd Mounted Brigade had advanced on this northern flank about half an hour after the first charge. They had also rapidly crossed the open ground and then ridden up and over the ridge, but resistance here had been lighter and the yeomen had carried on, becoming increasingly disorganised and scattered; they had passed over the ridge and carried on to Aqir, about 4.8km (3 miles) north-east of El Maghar, and the site of the headquarters for the XXII (OT) Corps. Here a small party of yeomen from 'A' Squadron, East Riding Yeomanry, under Major J.F.M. Robinson had taken the village and cut the main road that ran through it. Unfortunately, they were too few in number to hold the village in such isolation, and they and the rest of the 22nd Mounted Brigade were forced to withdraw. The

6th Mounted Brigade and 155th Brigade were in no fit state to move forward and support them, being preoccupied with re-forming their own ranks, collecting their casualties (the infantry had suffered eighty-four killed and nearly 400 wounded), and rounding up over a thousand Ottoman prisoners. No advance on Junction Station could be made from that direction that evening, but the Ottoman defensive line had been decisively broken.[360]

To the south, though, the 234th Brigade was still advancing up the railway line towards Junction Station, with orders to seize it if possible, but at the very least infiltrate a demolition party to blow a bridge to the north of the junction, to prevent any more rolling stock or supplies being rescued by the retreating Ottomans. After fighting several confused skirmishes with stray Ottoman units, the brigade finally halted in the early hours to await for daylight. When the demolition party was called forward, it was discovered that the pack horse carrying the charges had panicked and bolted during one of the brief fights, and could not be found, so that plan had to be abandoned. This allowed at least one more train to escape Junction Station heading north before dawn; it contained Kress von Kressenstein, commander of what was left of the 8th (OT) Army.[361]

At dawn a detachment from the 12th Light Armoured Car Battery caught up with 234th Brigade, and, with the support of two of their armoured cars, patrols pushed forward into the depots and warehouses around the junction. The Ottomans had left in a hurry, and much valuable material had been left behind unscathed. Food and equipment that the Ottomans could scarce afford to lose was left neatly packed in the warehouses, although of greater value to both sides were the two locomotives and sixty wagons, which the British could put to use on the railway back down to Gaza. The most crucial capture was beyond doubt the steam-driven pumping station, in full working order, that tapped deep underground water sources. In effect, this gave the British the ability to pump clean water rapidly from an almost limitless source.[362]

14

INTO THE JUDEAN MOUNTAINS

WITH THE FALL of Junction Station on 14 November 1917, Allenby had several options open to him. While he had left General Bulfin to conduct the operation, his attention had been on the wider and longer-term prospects for the campaign. He was again receiving mixed signals from London, being told by Robertson that the War Cabinet wanted him to press forward and 'exploit to the utmost' his recent successes, while at the same time being warned that no reinforcements would be forthcoming, and indeed that some of Allenby's divisions might even need to be withdrawn to Europe in early 1918. The differing voices of the 'Easterners' and the 'Westerners' could easily be discerned in these hedged missives.[363] In truth he was now at both a literal and a metaphorical crossroads.

The EEF was now pushing across the Jaffa–Jerusalem road, which was the only even vaguely modern road running east to west through the mountains to Jerusalem. Allenby could continue north, further pursuing the now shattered 8th (OT) Army. Reports from the front as well as long-range reconnaissance from the Royal Flying Corps (who were busy keeping ground commanders informed of enemy positions and movement, as well as directing artillery and bombing and strafing columns to add to the chaos on the roads) showed that the 8th (OT) Army was in disarray. Hüsseyin Hüsnü Emir, on the army's staff, admitted as much, and that:

> It was feared that the whole army had been broken up. The effective strength of the troops with the army was greatly reduced and companies contained only ten to fifteen men … The superior forces of the enemy were making a slow and methodical advance and nothing could be done to stop him.[364]

By keeping to the advance up the coastal plain, Allenby could almost immediately capture Jaffa, giving him a secure forward supply base, and then keep chasing the Ottomans until his own troops were too exhausted to follow. However, beyond the capture of Jaffa – now less then 16km (10 miles) from the forward units of the A&NZ Mounted Division – there was little of strategic importance to be gained. Instead, he could turn right at the crossroads, and begin his advance on Jerusalem. This would achieve the aim of forcing the 7th (OT) Army also to retreat, pulling north to avoid being cut off, and thus putting an end to the threat to his open inland flank. However, the timing was difficult. His current forces – 52nd (Lowland) Division, 75th Division and the three cavalry divisions of the Desert Mounted Corps – were greatly reduced in numbers from casualties and illness, and were approaching exhaustion. He had already begun to call up the 54th (East Anglian) Division from Gaza, and prepare the divisions of XX Corps for another advance, but such moves would take days if not weeks. The rainy season was about to begin in earnest, and the torrential downpours promised would no doubt make operating in the mountains extremely difficult. Was it better to make what advances he could while it was still dry, or to wait for not only the rain but for fresh troops to face those challenges? Waiting would also of course give the Ottomans more time to prepare, and at the moment the 7th (OT) Army's forces on this flank were still in retreat and disarray after being pushed back from around Balin by the loss of Junction Station.

Allenby decided to move on Jerusalem immediately. By keeping up the pressure and maintaining his focus on his original objective, he judged he had more to gain than potentially lose. However, it was first necessary to clear a little elbow room to the north, and the A&NZ Mounted Division continued to advance; by dusk on 15 November the 1st ALH Brigade had taken Ramleh and Ludd, where Ottoman supply dumps and an airfield were captured, and by dusk on 16 November the NZMR Brigade had taken Jaffa without resistance: the rest of the Desert Mounted Corps, meanwhile, moved fast to keep pressure on the Ottomans of the retreating 7th (OT) Army on the right. The Australian Mounted Division closed on the main Jaffa–Jerusalem road, and pressed towards the narrow, 4-mile-long defile near Latron (Latrun), a pinch-point where the Ottomans could easily dominate the road with relatively small forces. They had already destroyed or damaged parts of the road to slow the British advance, and the cavalry struggled to move directly across country, up and down mountainsides. The Yeomanry Division came up on their left, working along the Vale of Ajalon on even rougher tracks and through the steep jumbles of mountains, valleys and ravines on either side.

The cavalry divisions had been used simply because they were nearby and available. On the open plains to the south and west, the mobility of the cavalry had been useful both on a local scale, speedily crossing the open ground at Huj and El Maghar, for example, as well as part of the larger campaign, such as switching divisions and brigades between the flanks as the main axis of advance changed from the area north of Beersheba to the coastal region. However, in the mountains the cavalry's main advantages were negated, or even became hindrances. Horses struggled to cope with the steep, rough slopes, removing the cavalry's mobility, while at the same time they continued to require significant logistical support to bring up enough fodder and water. In action, each unit (already weaker than the infantry equivalents, and weaker still after weeks of campaigning) then lost a quarter of their remaining number to hold and lead the horses.[365]

The infantry of the 52nd and 75th Divisions, meanwhile, were given an opportunity for a short rest while the 54th Division caught up. A long fortnight's march and several stiff fights had worn them down, especially when the heavy weight of their rifles and packs, lack of water and poor rations were taken into account. Captain James R Mackie, 2/4th Somerset Light Infantry, took the opportunity to write home:

> 16 November 1917: I have not written to you for a fortnight but I am sure you will forgive me when you hear the reason. During the last fortnight we have hardly had an hour's rest, we have had nothing to eat but bully beef & biscuit & very little of that & we have suffered terribly from thirst. In addition we have been into action, and I believe did very well indeed, and as a result we arrived here to-day (not far from Jerusalem) in a state of complete exhaustion.

> 17th: I took my boots off to-day for the first time for five days and managed to secure a quart of water to wash in. Three of us have already bathed all over in it and they are still washing socks in it.[366]

All of the troops enjoyed not only the rest, but also the opportunity that the pause gave to the corps supply lines to catch up a little. Relative luxuries, such as tobacco, were warmly welcomed by the troops, while some began to receive around this time their first issues of fresh bread and vegetables in three weeks; a pleasant change from the ubiquitous tins of bully beef, and hard slabs of biscuit.[367]

After a day of rest, the advance resumed on 18 November. The newly arrived 54th Division now joined the A&NZ

Mounted Division in screening the northern flank above Jaffa. The 75th Division was to advance astride the Jaffa–Jerusalem road, with the 52nd Division to the north on their left flank. The Yeomanry Division was on the advancing force's left flank, while the Australian Mounted Division was down on their right flank. However, after managing to force the Ottomans out of Latron by manoeuvring around them on 18 November, two of that division's brigades were withdrawn on the following day, leaving only the newly returned 5th Mounted Brigade to support the 75th Division. These three divisions and attached brigade were to advance up their respective routes to a point west of Jerusalem, and then turn in unison to the north-east. They were to swing north of the Holy City, cutting, or at least threatening, the road to Nablus, and forcing the Ottoman forces around Jerusalem to either withdraw or surrender. No fighting was to take place within 9.5km (6 miles) of Jerusalem, to ensure no damage was done to religious or historical sites.[368]

Having formed up, the two infantry divisions entered the Judean Mountains on 19 November, at the same moment as winter finally arrived. While thunderstorms and showers had been increasingly common over the previous few weeks, these had in a strange way been almost a relief to the troops after months of being baked in the desert. Sergeant S. Hatton of the Middlesex Yeomanry recalled how once:

> During the night a heavy thunderstorm arose and just lying down in the open as we were, it was really a treat to be drenched. We had not seen rain since leaving Salonika, and I remember yet the joy of the renewed sweet coolness in the air, and the rich smell of the wet earth, after the protracted heat and dust, and that terrible khamsin wind. I awoke, cold, soaked, and found the earth slippery with mud, but it was good to have a change of discomfort.[369]

Now, the hard, steady winter rains started in earnest. The vast majority of the troops were still equipped in light, cotton drill uniforms, without greatcoats and with just one blanket if they were lucky. Most of the infantry still wore shorts. They found they had no protection from the rain, and became soaked even as they marched into the higher altitudes of the mountains, where temperatures plummeted.

The rain also made the roads treacherous – either washing down mountainsides to make the rocks slippery underfoot, or simply turning the dust and soil to mud to bog travellers down. Not just the front-line troops suffered from this; on the first day of the rains the 1/5th Essex gave aid to a bogged-down staff car, which turned out to contain both General Allenby and Sir Reginald Wingate, the High Commissioner of Egypt. The battalion's commander was later able to record with pride that both senior officers were more than willing to put their shoulders into the job of freeing the car alongside his men.[370]

The roads marked on the maps were soon discovered to be rather optimistic projections. The Romans had built several roads stretching through the mountains, and although still used they had received precious little maintenance since then. Apart from deliberate damage by the Ottomans, roads were degraded and even partially destroyed by centuries of use, bad weather, and rock falls. An officer in the 5th Highland Light Infantry opined that:

> If ever a road disgraced its name is was this Roman Road of the maps. Here was no purposeful track, broad, smooth and white, keeping its way straight through every obstacle. It bent and twisted and turned. Often it crept underneath a great rock and lost itself. Fifty yards further on one would find it, shy and retiring, slipping down the face of a slab of rock, always with the deceitful promise that over the next hill it would be better behaved.[371]

Despite all of the obstacles, progress across the whole front was relatively good for the first day, and resistance was light. Small Ottoman rearguards put up determined fights from strong positions. Trenches were usually impossible to dig in the mountains, but both sides became adept at building stone-walled positions, known as 'sangars'. Even a small detachment, with rifles or machine guns, could hide among the rocks and dominate an entire valley, inflicting a steady trickle of casualties as the advancing troops struggled to locate and then dislodge the defenders. Despite their small numbers, these scattered outposts caused disproportionate problems for the British.

Only on 20 November did the British begin to encounter the main Ottoman defensive positions around Jerusalem. The 75th Division took the ridge at Saris in the afternoon after a stiff fight, and were then held up by the defenders of Kuryet el Enab ridge behind it. No progress could be made until late in the afternoon, when a fog suddenly encompassed the battlefield, allowing the British to advance unseen and take the well-sited machine-gun posts with bayonet charges. To the north, the Yeomanry Mounted Division was close to its ultimate objective – the Nablus road – but repeatedly failed to shift the Ottoman defenders on imposing Zeitun Ridge. The original plan called for them to cut the Nablus road that evening, but with front-line numbers reduced to around 1,200 men, and with only very light artillery support from the Hong Kong and Singapore Mountain Battery, the division simply could not muster the strength and fire-power to break through.[372]

The poor roads and bad weather inhibited the support that the infantry and cavalry at the front needed. Although work had begun to repair and even improve the roads, wheeled transport was still almost impossible to move, and pack animals struggled. The ration convoys for the 52nd Division did not arrive until after dark, and those for the 75th Division not until noon the following day, and the men spent a miserable, cold and wet night with just their emergency 'iron' rations to sustain them.

On the southern flank, conditions were even bad enough to suppress inter-service rivalry to the extent that Lord Hampton, whose squadron of the QOWH had been helping the artillery traverse the roads, accepted an invitation to 'dine' with the battery's officers. He soon found himself:

> Sat down in a pool of mud to one of the best meals of the campaign. They are wonderful fellows, Gunners. On this occasion they produced a ham, some cold fowl, bread and good hot tea, and it is wonderful what hot tea alone will do for one on a cold night. I have long been of the opinion that, as a profession, tea planting ranks almost with Medicine in the benefits conferred upon a grateful and suffering humanity.[373]

However, few were as lucky. Further north, Sergeant Hatton recalled:

> During this night it rained a gentle drizzle and, without cover of any kind, we were soon soaked, a condition which, added to the cold, rendered sleep impossible and life in general thoroughly wretched and miserable. Moreover, now out of touch with any transport we were on half-rations of 'bully' and biscuits; meagre fare to tired, cold and hungry men … We continued our march next morning, but the road now ceased to exist, and it became a mere goat track across which at intervals lay huge boulders often four and five feet in diameter. We attempted to lead our horses in single file, but progress was dreadfully slow. Our boots were cut to pieces on the rough stones, but with aching and bleeding feet we blundered on up the goat track to Beit el Fokka.[374]

On 21 November, while the yeomanry continued unsuccessfully to assault Zeitun Ridge, the infantry began their swing north-east. They were by now closer to Jerusalem then had been initially intended, and ran hard into the main Ottoman defensive line around the city. The most important action of the day began late in the afternoon, when troops from 75th Division assaulted the heights at Nabi Samwil, only a few miles west of Jerusalem. Sitting at the end of a ridge, this high, conical hill dominates the western approaches to the Holy City. Supposedly the last resting place of the Prophet Samuel, it is holy to Christians, Muslims and Jews, and during the Crusades a castle had been built on the summit; it was here that Richard the Lionheart was supposed to have decided to turn back from his attempt to 'liberate' Jerusalem in 1192. Now a mosque and a small village sat on the remains of the castle, while the steep sides had been terraced to a certain extent, as generations of villagers had attempted to create flat growing land on the hill's slopes. Rising some 150m (500ft) above the surrounding area and overlooking the convergence of several valleys below, any forces on Nabi Samwil would be able to fire on any movement on the roads to Jerusalem below.

The assault on this vital height began at around 5.15 p.m., and was undertaken by two battalions of the 233rd Brigade – the 3/3rd Gurkhas and 2/4th Hampshire Regiment – and two from the 234th Brigade – the 123rd Outram's Rifles and 1/4th Duke of Cornwall's Light Infantry (DCLI). All four battalions were under-strength, with the whole force numbering around 1,100 men.[375] Even so, their rapid advance up the hillside was effective, and after fighting hand to hand in the village, the summit fell to the British and Indian troops after dark. However, the Ottomans remained well dug-in on the eastern faces of the hill, and during the following day mounted an almost continuous series of counter-attacks, with heavy artillery support. Brutal close-quarters fighting raged all day in the village and around the mosque, where the British and Indian wounded were taken for shelter. At one point that building was all but surrounded, until a Gurkha counter-attack with bayonet and kukri rolled the Ottoman forces back down the steep slopes of the hill, followed by a shower of rocks. Several times the hill nearly fell, and only the timely arrival of reinforcements near dusk halted the final Ottoman assault. The 1/7th and 1/8th Scottish Rifles, who had been marching since 5.30 a.m., began to arrive near the hill at 2.30 p.m., and struggled to the top at nearly 6 p.m. They were in time to push the Ottomans at bayonet-point back through Nabi Samwil and relieve the troops in the mosque, which had again been surrounded. By that time, the original four battalions had suffered 567 men killed, wounded or missing in the day's fighting, or around 50 per cent casualties. The 3/3rd Gurkhas alone had suffered 216 casualties, and could muster just one officer and sixteen men fit for action. The Scottish relieving force had themselves suffered 200 casualties. Only after dark could the wounded begin to be evacuated down into the valley for proper care.[376]

While the fighting had raged on Nabi Samwil on 22 November, a further battle had been fought only a short distance to the north, around the hill of El Jib. On the northern side of Nabi Samwil runs a broad valley, from east to west, providing easy going compared to the ridges and slopes either side. The army wanted to use this valley for a rapid advance, but in the centre sat the conical hill of El Jib. Like Nabi Samwil, the sides were terraced and a village sat on top, although this hill was much lower, only rising around 30m (100ft) about the surrounding valley to a height of about 790m (2,600ft) above sea level. Even so, the steep sides and wide open ground around the hill made it easily defensible. Any attacker would have to cover some 1.8km (2,000yds) of open ground to reach the bottom of the slope. On 22 November the attack had stalled under heavy fire, and the next day a fresh attempt was made by the 75th Division. The 1/5th Somerset Light Infantry and the 2/3rd Gurkha Rifles advanced from the south-west, while the 1/5th Devonshire Regiment attacked from the west. However, heavy fire not only from El Jib, but also from the Ottomans still clinging to the eastern slopes of Nabi Samwil, caught the advancing troops in a cross fire, causing heavy casualties. A few men of the Somersets reached the hill, and even

climbed it and entered the village, but all were killed or captured. The rest of the three battalions were forced into cover,
and remained so until after dark. Only then could they collect their wounded and pull back, having to leave most of their
dead behind. Between them, they had lost 372 men killed,
wounded or captured.[377]

The British had managed to bring up some artillery to this
area during the day, by almost doubling the gun teams up to ten
horses. In all, six 18-pounders and four 4.5in howitzers were
dragged up during the day, but they arrived too late to have
any effect on the attack. They were used the following day,
24 November, as 75th Division, already badly reduced in numbers by casualties, handed the task over to 52nd Division. The
155th Brigade attacked El Jib, while 156th Brigade attempted to
sweep the Ottomans off the reverse slopes of Nabi Samwil. The
attacks began just after noon, and after one hour 155th Brigade
was pinned down, and within two hours so was 156th Brigade.
The 157th Brigade, waiting to move between the two other brigades and advance up the valley, could only wait impotently. At
4 p.m. the attack was renewed, but within ten minutes it was
called off completely. The 52nd Division had lost 630 men for
no gain, 256 of them from 156th Brigade, which had only been
1,400 men strong to begin with.[378]

To their north, the Yeomanry Mounted Division had already
been told to cease offensive actions the previous day (the same
day on which they received permission to send their horses back
to the coastal plain, having requested this on 20 November).
On the plains, the New Zealand Mounted Rifles Brigade,
with the 1/4th and 1/6th Essex Regiment from 161st Brigade,
had mounted a small attack across the Nahr el Auja, north of
Jaffa, intended to draw off Ottoman reserves and prevent them
from moving troops from this now-quiet part of the line in to
the mountains. Orders had gone out from General Bulfin just
after midnight on 24 November, and the attack had gone in
at 10 a.m. after some incredibly fast staff work and planning.

While some Australian Light Horse demonstrated further in land, the NZMR Brigade had crossed the river at its mouth, sweeping north-east, and covering the crossing of the infantry 3.2km (2 miles) inland at Jerishe. Both operations had been successful and met little resistance, and two pontoon bridges were quickly thrown across the river behind them. All of the units began digging in, but they were widely spaced and when the 3rd and 7th (OT) Infantry Divisions began a counter-attack before dawn on 25 November, the outlying cavalry posts were quickly forced back, and so later in the morning were the infantry. By dusk, the whole force was back south of the river, having escaped extremely lightly, and the Ottomans made no move to try and pursue them.[379]

General Bulfin now ordered all attacks to cease, and reported that his depleted divisions could go no further. On 25 November, Allenby ordered that XX Corps should be brought up to relieve XXI Corps, who were to return to the coast to rest and refit. In fact, Allenby had anticipated this need several days before, and the 60th Division had already begun to arrive that day to relieve the 75th Division, although the 10th (Irish) and 74th Divisions were still four or five days' march away. The advance on Jerusalem was, for now, halted. It had been a gamble by Allenby, and one that had substantially paid off. His troops had cleared a path deep into the Judean Mountains, to within a few miles of Jerusalem (in fact, from Nabi Samwil, literally within sight of the Holy City). They had faced and cleared some determined pockets of Ottoman rearguards on the way, and if the advance had been put off for even a few more days, these would have been all the more formidable. The advance had also allowed work to begin immediately on repairing the existing roads and building new ones, greatly improving the supply lines for the fresh troops who would be coming up to make the final attack against the Ottoman defenders.

However, while Allenby and his army may have wanted to pause operations, von Falkenhayn had other plans. The British were granted 26 November in peace, but on 27 November a series of Ottoman counter-attacks were launched along the whole line. This line was now essentially two straight lines; one south to north facing Jerusalem, with the 60th (London) Division having taken over from the 75th Division and, by dusk on 27 November, the 52nd Division too. North of the Londoners, the Yeomanry Mounted Division held on, still waiting for relief and now reduced to around 800 men holding a line of scattered posts more than 6.5km (4 miles) long. Their left flank turned back at its tip, starting to run back north-westwards towards the coast. Next in line was the 54th (Lowland) Division, also running north-westwards, but due to poor coordination and confusion caused by inaccurate maps, a gap some 8km (5 miles) wide had been left undefended between the two divisions. This already dangerous situation was made even more so by the fact that the main supply road for the yeomanry ran parallel to and only just behind this gap.[380]

The Ottoman counter-attacks landed all along this line, although problems in communications and their own poor maps meant that little coordination could be achieved. The most serious attack on the first day of the Ottoman offensive fell on the Yeomanry Mounted Division in the early afternoon, when the 24th (OT) Infantry Division, supported by elements of the 3rd (OT) Cavalry Division, swept over Zeitun Ridge. The 6th Mounted Brigade took the brunt, with a troop of the City of London Yeomanry on City Hill being pushed back, although an outpost of the Berkshire Yeomanry of three officers and sixty men held out at Sheikh Abu ez Zeitun. By dusk they were reduced to twenty-eight officers and men, and reinforcements were sent in of two troops, one each from the Berkshire Yeomanry and the Buckinghamshire Hussars, totalling around fifty men. However, the next dawn the position was revealed to be hopeless, and the garrison was withdrawn as the 22nd Mounted Brigade, on their left, was pushed back by the 19th (OT) Infantry and 3rd (OT) Cavalry Divisions.

Meanwhile, relief was on its way; the 7th Mounted Brigade and Australian Mounted Division were both under orders to move up and take over from the yeomanry, but when news of the fresh attacks arrived both formations began a night march to arrive as soon as possible. Such was the nature of the country, the 7th Mounted Brigade appears to have passed within 600m (660yds) of the 19th (OT) Infantry Division in the dark, with neither noticing the other. By now it was also apparent just how large the gap was between the yeomanry and the 54th Division, and the nearest infantry, the 52nd Division who were just pulling back from opposite Jerusalem, where immediately ordered to redeploy to cover the hole. Unfortunately the move was slightly too late, as Ottoman forces advanced into the gap, and the Smalls Arms Ammunition Section of the Yeomanry Divisional Ammunition Column was caught by surprise on the main road and virtually wiped out in the mid-morning of 28 November. The arrival and counter-attack of the 155th Brigade helped to block the hole, but significant forces had already slipped through over the previous day.[381]

Some of the Ottoman force that had made use of the gap attacked west, into the 54th Division. On 27 November at the German colony of Wilhelma, between El Yehudiye and El Tire, the 1/4th Northamptonshire Regiment stood firm as their flank was turned by the 16th (OT) Infantry Division, some posts literally holding on to the last man. (Elsewhere on the 54th Division front the 20th (OT) Infantry Division, fresh troops who had so far seen no fighting, were wasted as they floundered around failing to find any significant British forces to engage.) However, most ran directly into the 52nd Division, who dug in and held out tenaciously, despite their exhaustion. The line flowed backwards and forwards for some days, until a final Ottoman attack, utilising the 'stormtrooper' battalion of the 19th (OT) Infantry Division, almost broke the Australian Mounted Division line at El Burj on the night of 30 November to 1 December. The Ottoman stormtroopers used the latest Western Front tactics to infiltrate the line in small groups, 'bombing' their way forward by lobbing hand grenades into trenches, sangars and posts. Two companies of the 1/4th Royal Scots Fusiliers were rushed forward in the middle of the night to the top of a ridge to block the break through, and at dawn began to 'bomb' their own way forward, taking on the stormtroopers at their own game. At least some of the Scots seem to have taken the action more personally than usual, one being heard to shout (as he threw repeated grenades):

> They mairched us a hunner miles! (Tak' that, ya —!) An' we've been in five fechts! (Anither yin, ya —!) and they said we wur relieved! (Tak' that, ya —!) and we're oot oor beds anither nicht! (Swalla that, ya —!)[382]

One of the RSF officers, Second Lieutenant Stanley Boughey, led his bombing party with aggression and skill down the forward slope of the ridge, rolling back the Ottomans as they went. Near the bottom, he personally took the surrender of some twenty-five or thirty Ottoman troops, before being shot in the head. He died of his wounds three days later, but received a posthumous Victoria Cross for his bravery and skill. Most of the Ottoman stormtrooper battalion, the best equipped, best trained and fittest men in their division, were killed or captured in the attack.[383]

As the gap on the British northern flank was closed, so too was the increasingly dangerous gap that was developing as the Yeomanry Mounted Division was scattered and depleted. Elements of the 52nd and 74th Divisions and the Australian Mounted Division began to arrive on 28 November, and the following day the yeomanry were officially relieved. It was not a smooth process, as again vague or inaccurate maps hampered movements and the relief of particular posts. The 231st Brigade of the 74th Division got particularly scattered on the night of 29/30 November, as it moved forward to take up positions west of Foqa. In the dark, 'D' Company of the 25th Royal Welsh

Fusiliers under Major J.G. Rees managed to stumble into Foqa itself, arriving outside the village just before dawn. Faced with the options of either withdrawing and being caught in the first light of dawn in the open by the Ottoman garrison, or attempting to take the village by surprise and storm it, he chose the latter course. After a brief fire-fight, Rees' company of around eighty men took the surrender of the 450-strong Ottoman garrison, who had been caught mid-breakfast. He was then faced with the question of what to do with his prisoners, and eventually sent them back towards the rear with an escort of just twenty men. Along the way the column came under long-range fire from Ottoman positions, obviously mistaking them for British troops. Some of the prisoners were killed and others took the opportunity to escape, but just over 300 were brought safely into British lines. Unfortunately, the rest of Rees' company fared less well. Just after dawn they held off an Ottoman counter-attack, but at 8.30 a.m. were surrounded and were forced to break out back towards their own lines. This then created a gap that the attackers used to turn the flank of the 10th Shropshire Light Infantry, forcing them also to retreat. Although the line was later stabilised, the shoddy maps available made the British counter-attack on 1 December a difficult and confused affair, and although they could not retake Foqa they did manage to re-establish the front line.[384]

While the fighting had raged across the northern and north-eastern parts of the British line, repeated heavy attacks had also been made against Nabi Samwil. The Ottomans still held the reverse slopes of the hill, and infiltrated snipers and patrols into the village on top, while the crest of the hill was dangerously exposed to Ottoman artillery. The 2/17th and 2/19th London Regiment had taken over the positions on the hilltop on 25 November, and they came under heavy and prolonged artillery fire and repeated infantry attacks. Khalil Sakakini, a Christian Arab living in Jerusalem, could see the village from his house, and recorded in his diary:

Tuesday 27 Nov 17 … Heavy shelling continued until the morning hours from various directions. At 3 p.m. the shelling reached an unprecedented intensity. The shells fell like drops of rain on the mosque of An-Nebi Samwil and its surroundings, and at 4 p.m. the minaret fell down, after having withstood so remarkably. Later shells started coming down on the mountain from its beginning to its end, on its sides, at its feet, and in the wadis around it, until it resembled an erupting volcano. At sunset the shells exploded with blinding flashes. Later the shooting of the guns subsided, then stopped entirely and it became silent. God knows the number of dead and wounded on both sides. Undoubtedly it is enormous.[385]

For those on the hill the experience was indeed very grim. The 2/20th London Regiment replaced the 2/19th on the night of 28 November, and one of their officers described the scene in the village:

A roofless mass on the top of a hill standing in the moonlight. No minaret, and great holes in the walls. Scattered all around are dead Turks, dead Gurkhas, dead English, and dead animals; rifles and equipment all over the place; sniper's bullets cracking continually overhead; soldiers picking their way quietly along the sheltered corners of the debris, and, in places where there is no cover, running the gauntlet for ten, twenty, thirty, or forty yards in the open – silent groups of eager, alert men along a very artificial line in the village watching the windows and corners of houses, in some places only twenty yards away. Sometimes you crawl through the inky darkness of the inside of a ruined house and scramble over you know not what …[386]

The 2/20th then stood the brunt of the heaviest Ottoman attack, on 29 November, the artillery barrage for which started at 8.30 a.m.:

[On 29 November] the bombardment increased in fury
throughout the morning, and at 1.30 p.m. it became intensive
... Soon after 1.30 p.m. a large body of Turks made a rush
into the mosque, doubtless expecting to find our posts evacuated after the bombardment. Our men were all ready and
waiting ... Met by the full fury of Lewis guns, rifles, bombs,
and Stokes mortars, the Turks stood for a moment, drew
back, rallied, advanced, and then, in terrified disorder, rushed
back and vanished over the brow. Twice that afternoon the
enemy came to the assault, assisted by a continuous intensive
artillery barrage. He gained not an inch.[387]

Both sides suffered heavily; 'C' Company of the 2/20th in
particular took severe casualties, with one outpost completely
wiped out, and one platoon, already down to sixteen men (from
an official strength of fifty), was reduced to just two men. The
following day, the battalion was relieved by the 2/22nd, under
Colonel Borton VC.[388]

This was the last major Ottoman assault on Nabi Samwil, and
after 1 December all of the attacks along the line petered out.
Limited British counter-attacks were mounted, but after a failed
attempt to take Foqa on 3 December, General Chetwode (whose
XX Corps had officially taken over control from XXI Corps at
midday on 28 November) called a halt to any further local, limited offensive operations. Instead, the army was to prepare itself
en masse for the next attempt to take Jerusalem.[389]

15

JERUSALEM

THE NEW OFFENSIVE was to start on 8 December 1917. In the mean-time, the army prepared on all levels. The replacement of XXI Corps by XX Corps was completed and the line adjusted accordingly. The 74th (Yeomanry) Division took over the Nabi Samwil positions from 60th (London) Division, which shifted south. The dividing line between the two divisions now ran 3.2km (2 miles) south of Nabi Samwil, with the 60th below that line and the 74th Division above. To the north-west of the 74th Division the 10th (Irish) Division had now entered the line, and to their north-west the Australian Mounted Division filled the gap between them and the 54th (East Anglian) Division, and to their west the A&NZ Mounted Division carried the line on to the sea. The Yeomanry Mounted, 52nd (Lowland) and 75th Divisions were held in reserve behind the line on the coastal plain.

On the south-east of the line, the 53rd (Welsh) Division had been brought up from the Beersheba area, travelling north through the Judean Mountains along the main road to Hebron. On 1 December, No. 7 Light Car Patrol had successfully driven the length of the road from south of Bethlehem, down through Hebron and to Beersheba. They confirmed that it had been damaged or destroyed in places, and that there were no Ottoman forces beyond small patrols.[390] Coming the other way a few days later, the Welsh found this report to be accurate, and resistance was light. On 4 December they had reached Hebron, and Major General Mott entered the town to take formal possession. Among his guard was Corporal C.C.M. Millis (on his horse, Jim) from the corps cavalry regiment, the 2nd County of London (Westminster Dragoons) Yeomanry:

> On 4 December we made our official entry into Hebron with as much pomp & circumstance as we could muster. Considering the ghastly time we had endured with lack of water & food & continually on the march, the procession which was formed up to make the formal entry was quite impressive. The General headed the column & then followed in order his ADC, Staff Officers, then myself poshed up as well as I could under the circumstances & carrying for the first time in the formal entry of a capitulated town, the General's Pennant with lance. With tin hat at a rakish angle, sword, rifle & full equipment I found myself almost puffing with pride. So did 'Jim' who had been well groomed & whose saddlery had had a special clean for the occasion.[391]

The division was supposed to move into position on the southeastern flank of the 60th Division, just north of Bethlehem. In the event, the condition of the road and heavy rain slowed the advance and by 8 December they were still some miles south of their intended position.[392]

The other divisions were ready for the general advance to start, although by now the term was relative. Few units in the 60th and 74th Divisions (or the units they had replaced from the other two corps) would have been at more than 50 per cent strength, and the men were tired, cold, wet and hungry. At least these divisions had received some level of re-equipment during their time on the plain, receiving greatcoats and at least some items of thicker serge uniforms, and replacing some of their worn out equipment. The divisions of XXI and the Desert Mounted Corps were now going through the same process on the plains, receiving among other things new boots to replace those shredded on the rough mountain terrain, and socks and puttees to replace the ones used to bind the worn-out boots to hold them together.[393]

By 7 December, apart from the 53rd Division, all was ready, but that night a torrential downpour began. Despite this the attack began that evening. The 60th and 74th Divisions were to advance across a 4½-mile front running from a mile or more south of Nabi Samwil, down across the Jerusalem–Jaffa road, to just south of Ain Karim. Some miles south-east of Ain Karim the 53rd Division would attack north through Bethlehem, with the 10th Australian Light Horse Regiment doing their best to screen the large gap between the two attacks. The first unit to move out was the 179th Brigade of the 60th Division, who marched shortly after dusk on 7 December, crossing the Wadi Sarar. They were on the southernmost end of the line advancing from the west of Jerusalem, reflecting General Chetwode's reversal of the plan previously attempted by General Bulfin. Instead of swinging around to the north of Jerusalem, this time the army would swing up from the south-west, and Ain Karim was the first objective in this sweep. The 179th Brigade was in position and attacked that village at 2 a.m., taking it by 3.30 a.m. and then pushing out to the east and south-east to take the ridges beyond and secure the army's right flank. At 7.30 a.m. the brigade halted and consolidated their positions, unable to go further as their own right flank was dangerously in the air (despite the efforts of the 10th ALH) until the 53rd Division could catch up.[394]

The most serious resistance to this advance had been encountered by the 2/14th (London Scottish) Battalion, London Regiment, who swept around to the south of Ain Karim to take a part of the ridge behind known as Tumulus Hill. Soon after dawn, the battalion was pinned down by two machine guns behind a sangar. The Ottoman gunners were well placed to dominate the slope, while an enfilading fire also opened up from somewhere behind the battalion. Taking casualties, arrangements were being made to extract one company to attempt an attack on the flank, when Corporal Charles Train stood up and dashed forward, working his way around the sangar, firing rifle grenades and then shooting the German officer commanding the position before charging in to kill or capture the gunners. For his 'most conspicuous gallantry, dash and initiative' Corporal Train received the Victoria Cross.[395]

To the north of 179th Brigade, the 180th Brigade assaulted a series of redoubts and positions around Deir Yesin. The brigade had begun their march later, having less far to go, and crossing the Wadi Hannina after midnight, their attack began just before dawn. Within a few hours, the Ottoman strongpoints known as Heart and Liver Redoubts were taken and Deit Yesin occupied. There the advance was held up by fire from Ottoman positions in quarries on the far side of the village. The advance paused while artillery and machine-gun support was brought up and the brigade realigned. Shortly before 4 p.m., with heavy supporting fire, the brigade took the quarries at bayonet-point and secured their objectives.[396]

The 74th Division made shorter but just as successful advances on the left of the army. While the 231st Brigade stood firm on Nabi Samwil, the 230th Brigade, to their south, faced the difficult task of crossing the Wadi Buwai, which ran through a steep-sided ravine around 300m (1,000ft) deep. It took more than three hours to bring the brigade across, and their attack on the ridge above was twenty-five minutes late going in, although it was entirely successful. From there the advance became more difficult as enfilading fire from the Ottomans still on the lower slopes of Nabi Samwil bit into the brigade's flank. In late morning the village of Beit Iksa was reached and entered, although it took several hours to clear the village completely. On the right of 230th Brigade, the 229th Brigade had advanced on a narrow front along the northern verge of the Jaffa–Jerusalem road, and had experienced little resistance.[397]

In the south, the advance of the 53rd Division was hampered by communications problems with the rest of XX Corps, by the rain, and by the fact that their main objective was Bethlehem. General Mott was unwilling to risk damaging any of the holy sites in Bethlehem, despite coming under Ottoman rifle and artillery fire from the village. Instead of tackling this threat directly, throughout the afternoon elements of the division had swept around to the north of the village, forcing the garrison to withdraw. By evening the division had still not made direct contact with 60th Division.[398] Chetwode had meanwhile ordered the 60th and 74th Divisions to cease their advances in the mid-afternoon, partly to allow the 53rd Division to catch up, but also to allow the artillery and transport to come up as well, and to rest his men. After long night marches in the cold and rain, and a morning's fighting, his forces were in need of rest, as well as in need of closer artillery support and resupply of food and ammunition.[399]

At dawn on 9 December the army prepared to advance again, but the patrols sent out before dawn all along the front began to bring back the news that the enemy positions appeared to be deserted. More patrols followed, along with large numbers of scouting parties to reconnoitre the road ahead for battalions or batteries. One of these was led in person by Lieutenant Colonel H. Bayley DSO, commanding 303rd Brigade, Royal Field Artillery, who had been surveying the ground ahead of the 180th Brigade near the village of Lifta. Around 9 a.m. he paused near the Jaffa–Jerusalem road to 'enjoy the warm sunshine, the beautiful view, and the knowledge that we were again successfully advancing' when:

> I noticed movement and through my glasses I spotted a white flag with numbers of persons surrounding it and that a few were now coming towards me.

I was there alone with Armitage.* I told Armitage to go back and get a couple of fellows with rifles, if he could, while I would stop and interview the advancing persons. I beckoned the leading man and he came up to me. He spoke in French and said there were no Turks near; they had all gone; and that the Mayor of Jerusalem was at the white flag. I walked on and there he was, with three chairs in a row on the road. He was an Arab gentleman in European clothes and a Tarboosh. He said very quietly and in faultless English 'I am the Mayor of Jerusalem and I desire to surrender the city to the British General.'[400]

The defences to the south and west of Jerusalem had been abandoned by the Ottomans overnight, as had the city. Although rearguard units were taking up positions to the north and east, determined to cover the retreat, the withdrawing main force now had all of the appearances of a defeated army. Dr Steuber, Chief Medical Officer of forces on the Palestine front, was among the retreating mass:

The Jerusalem–Nablus road is good, but is today congested with troops and columns of the beaten and disintegrating 8th Turkish Army ... Here two brown Anatolians drag with them a mortally wounded comrade; the bloody, torn limbs hang loosely from the ripped rags. There lies a man behind a boulder, his head covered with a kaffiyeh, and rings with death. In between, Turkish officers on jaded, skeleton-like nags, stolid and outwardly untouched by the limitless misery all around. Suddenly, the motor-car stops: three camels lie down across the road, Turkish harem-women are on the camels' backs, their heads veiled, their naked legs dangling down. Only the driver's shrill siren makes them clear the road with a wild leap.

---

* Captain R. Armitage, commanding 'A' Battery of the 303rd Brigade RFA. Actually, both officers also had their orderlies with them to hold their horses.

A column of rickety carts is overtaken; a Red Crescent and a penetrating iodoform smell mark them as remnants of a field infirmary. Suddenly, loud shouts: a Turkish field battery blocks the road, and the horses, buffaloes and mules cannot go on. A herd pushes into it all, and soon the car crushes a long-eared goat ... The uninterrupted, piercing sound of the motor-car sirens, the shouts of men and animals, all this preys hypnotizingly on one's thinking and feeling, and deadens one so dreadfully, that in lucid intervals one asks oneself whether one still is a civilized being at all.[401]

At least the Ottoman forces were not being closely pressed. Caught by surprise, through the rest of the morning the British scrambled to advance and occupy the city but were in no position to mount any kind of pursuit. If the situation was a surprise, it was also a relief, as the British high command had been having the same concerns as General Mott over the possibility of fighting around and possibly damaging holy sites.

At 5.30 a.m. the 53rd Division was moving, passing Bethlehem and reaching the southern side of Jerusalem in mid-morning. By 11 a.m., one brigade was advancing a short way down the road to Jericho. The division came under fire from an Ottoman rearguard on the Mount of Olives and prepared to assault this ridge on the eastern side of Jerusalem at 4 p.m., but the attack was then postponed until the next day. Meanwhile, the 60th Division had swept around the northern side of the city, and had driven an Ottoman rearguard off Mount Scopus to the north-east at 2 p.m. At around the same time the left flank of the division had reach Shafat, around 3.2km (2 miles) north of the city, and there pushed a larger rearguard force out. The 74th Division also swung forward and towards the north, taking Beit Hannina.[402] Over the following three days little activity followed. The 60th and 74th Divisions rearranged their lines and patrolled the area in front of them but otherwise remained where they were. The 10th and 53rd Division made small, limited advances, the latter occupying the now abandoned Mount of Olives and Bethany to the north-east.[403] On 14 December Chetwode laid out his plans for the next big push, but decided that ten days were needed to improve the roads yet further and let the logistical system catch up. In the meantime, only small, strictly limited actions were carried out to secure the existing lines.

While the army secured the area around Jerusalem, General Allenby made his official entry into the Holy City at noon on 11 December, and read the declaration placing it under Martial Law. The jubilation of 9 December had faded somewhat, although there can be no doubt that the city was glad to see the British arrive. Much is made in memoirs and the more populist of the post-war accounts about the delight of the people of Palestine at being freed from the 'tyranny' of the Ottoman Empire, without much, if any, qualification of what this actually meant. For the people of Jerusalem, and the rest of southern Palestine, the British occupation was a matter for celebration because it meant an end of the conscription of the younger men into the armed forces and the older ones into the hated 'labour' battalions. It also meant a new breath of economic life of the country. After years of having their produce requisitioned by the army, the arrival of the British meant not only an end to this state-sanctioned theft, but the sudden opening of considerable markets. Trade outside the country was reopened as the British blockade was lifted, although this took time to become fully re-established. More immediately, troops individually bought what food (oranges are frequently mentioned) and drink they could to make up for the deficiencies in their own supplies, while higher-level units also bulk-bought for the same reason. Soldiers bought whatever they could from both Arab and Jewish farms and villages, although frequent complaints were made that the prices were unreasonably high from both sources, albeit for different reasons that conformed to the common racial stereotyping of the time. Given the economic deprivations of recent years, though, none of the Palestinian farmers can really be blamed for making the most of this golden windfall while the opportunity lasted.

While XX Corps rested, and worked on their lines of communications, the offensive switched back to XXI Corps on the coastal plain. Here, the weather had had an equally heavy effect on the conditions faced by the army. The rain, amplified by run-off water from the mountains, left the ground boggy and made movement difficult. For the cavalry, with their horses to care for and try to keep warm as well as themselves, the burden was doubled. Sergeant Garry Clunie of the Wellington Mounted Rifles records the typical conditions faced through most of December:

> 8 December: Still raining cats and dogs. Mud everywhere about 6 inches deep except horse lines which are about 18 inches. Stand to this morning was great, we had to dig some of our gear out of the mud. Water and exercised horses this morning and afternoon. Heavy rifle fire last night. We will probably relieve our mates in trenches ... My bivvy is getting very wet inside with coming in with muddy boots. Shifted horse lines today.[404]

A few small attacks were made during the first half of the month to improve the line on the corps' right flank, in the foothills. However, it was the left flank that caused the most worry, as the Ottoman positions on the Nahr el Auja were still in place, meaning that their forces were still in artillery range of Jaffa. Plans were now made to push the front line further north, securing Jaffa. The corps commander, General Bulfin, decided to allocate this task to Major General Hill's 52nd (Lowland) Division, who were holding the left hand end of the line opposite the area to be attacked. Extensive preparations were made behind the lines, including bringing up the necessary engineering stores to make the right tools for an assault river crossing. Timber and canvas were stockpiled and supplemented by local foraging. Rafts (sometimes known as coracles) were made by stretching canvas over a wooden frame, large enough to carry fifteen men (plus two Royal Engineers to paddle the vessel) and also to be used as pontoons for making bridges.

Bulfin and Hills prepared a plan for a night crossing involving all three of the division's brigades. At the mouth of the river (where it opens out to some 36m (40yds) across) the 157th Brigade would cross at the ford. The commanding officer of the 6th HLI, Lieutenant Colonel Jason Anderson, and one of his officers, Lieutenant C.H. Hills, stripped off and swam around the ford on the night of 15 December to make sure that it was still passable, and to plot the Ottoman positions on the far side.*

Once across the ford, which was confirmed to be around 1m (3ft) deep, the brigade would advance directly up the coast. About 900m (1,000yds) inland, the 156th Brigade would cross initially by raft, until two pontoon bridges could be built behind them. They would then advance north and north-east, covering the 157th Brigade's flank and capture Slag Heap Farm and the village of Muwannis. On the right would be the 155th Brigade, which would cross in a bend in the river (which would protect their flanks) near Jerishe, about 3.2km (3,500yds) inland. Again using rafts until two pontoon bridges could be thrown across behind them, the brigade would advance east along the river to clear the Ottoman defensive positions around Hadra, and the destroyed bridge just south of it. To prepare for the operation Bulfin wanted to mount a twenty-four-hour barrage, but Hill demurred. Instead, he argued, a much smaller and shorter bombardment would help to maintain the element of surprise, particularly in the crucial period where the troops would need to gather on the exposed river banks, the perfect bunched targets for machine guns. Bulfin was persuaded, and a more limited

---

* For this, Anderson received a bar for his Distinguished Service Order, and Hills the Military Cross.

fire plan for a barrage of artillery and machine-gun fire was arranged. The same plan was executed for the few nights running up to the operation, so that the Ottoman forces would not be suspicious when the real attack started.

The 54th Division and the NZMR Brigade replaced the 52nd Division in the line on 18 December, and the troops (and the rafts and bridging materials) were positioned in orange groves near the river bank. At 8 p.m. on 20 December, the real bombardment began and the advance parties of the 156th Brigade began to cross the river. The main crossing was slated to start at 10.30 p.m., but was postponed half an hour after all of the Royal Engineer parties experienced difficulties in moving water-logged rafts over the deep mud of the river banks. Apart from that one delay, the rest of the plan went like clockwork. The Ottoman positions on the far side of the river were widely spaced, and many had been abandoned due to flooding. The eruption of bayonet-tipped Scotsmen from the night took most units by complete surprise, and by the morning all of the objectives had been taken. At a cost of around 100 casualties, the division had pushed the enemy back some 4km (2.5 miles) across a 4.8km (3-mile) front, killing over 100 enemy and capturing over 300 more.

During 21 December the division held fast, expecting heavy Ottoman counter-attacks and easily deflecting the small attacks that actually occurred. However, that night the offensive was renewed and further gains made, and 54th Division joined the attack on the right flank. Rapid advances were made, although 162nd Brigade encountered some heavy resistance around Bald Hill. After taking the hill, in the dark, Lance Corporal John Christie of the 1/11th London Regiment advanced alone into the dark with pockets full of hand grenades, entered the Ottoman trenches and single-handedly 'bombed' back two different counter-attacks while his comrades shored up the defences behind him. For his 'conspicuous gallantry' he received the Victoria Cross.[405]

On 22 December, the advance had gained so much ground that the 52nd Division artillery had to be brought forward (all except one howitzer that became badly bogged down). By the end of the day the Ottomans had been pushed back 11km (7 miles) from the Nahr el Auja, and 19km (12 miles) from Jaffa, which was now safely out of enemy artillery range.[406]

The line now solidified in its new position, and again a rough time was experienced by the front-line troops as the logistics system caught up, a task that was greatly exacerbated by the continuing bad weather, especially as part of the rail network was flooded.[407] Over the last week of December some units found themselves on quarter or half rations for days on end.[408] The shortages and the rain made for a grim Christmas, as Sergeant James Scott of the 2nd (London) Sanitary Company RAMC recalled:

> During our stay at the junction the wet weather set in just before Christmas and on Christmas Eve the wind was blowing very strong the rain coming down in torrents. The ground we camped on was at first so hard we could not drive the tent pegs in and now was a quagmire, pegs pulled out and tent ropes broke. Suddenly in the night our tent blew over leaving us entirely exposed to the elements. We raced to find shelter some in the cookhouse some in other tents. We had three tents blown over out of five. The cookhouse wasn't much shelter as the rain poured in at the roof.
>
> We were all glad when daylight came and the storm slackened a little. This was Christmas morning. Now the question arose what we were going to do for rations. Owing to the bad weather transport had been held up. For breakfast we had only four small tins of bully beef a few biscuits and tea without sugar and milk to divide between 25 of us, and we did not know when we would get the next [issue]. However later in the day we managed to get some more.[409]

Some units were slightly luckier; those that were positioned in or near villages often managed to buy extra food to ease through the shortages, and to celebrate Christmas.[410]

Christmas in the mountains was even more miserable for those clinging in isolated pockets to jagged mountainsides, although the scattered rocks provided an element of shelter. Private Henry Pope of the 2/15th London Regiment (2nd Civil Service Rifles) recorded in his diary:

> Christmas Eve!! Raining hard. Pack up and marched to hills in support as attack by Turks expected. Awful night, perishing cold and soaked through once more. Spent half the night carrying Lewis gun equipment from one place to another. Christmas Day – spent day in 'prehistoric stone cabin' or rather an alcove in some rocks with bivouac sheet for roof. Stay all day propped up on a stone because floor was a lake. Pouring with rain all day. Rations – 3oz of bully and about two biscuits. What a Christmas dinner! Half starved and shivering with cold.[411]

However, Christmas could have been worse. It had been Allenby's intention to restart the advance in the mountains on Christmas Eve, after carrying out a series of preliminary attacks on 23 December. As it was, although various small actions were fought in the week before Christmas, by 24 December the weather had deteriorated to such a point that the fighting had to be postponed. In fact, this postponement was not only fortunate for the troops. Intelligence now began to report, based on interviews with prisoners and deserters and on intercepted wireless messages, that von Falkenhayn was planning his own attack to attempt to retake Jerusalem with the 7th (OT) Army.[412] This was a fairly hopeless gesture; even with the arrival of the fresh 1st (OT) Infantry Division, von Falkenhayn could only muster at most 20,000 men to attack the 33,000 of Allenby's XX Corps, while the terrain where the main attack would fall was, in the words of the 60th Division's historian, 'the most difficult yet encountered'.[413] A series of steep ridges divided by deep, almost vertical ravines ran east–west across the area separating the northern British positions and the Ottoman attacking forces. Chetwode, with Allenby's support, decided to use the Ottomans' own plan against them. It seemed fairly certain that the main attacks would fall on the 60th Division, north of Jerusalem astride the road to Nablus, and on the 53rd Division to the east. Once the enemy attack against these points, expected around 27 December, were fully committed, the 74th and 10th Divisions to the left of the 60th would swing out and round, advancing east into the flank of the Ottoman attack. In one sweep, the army could roll up most of the remaining units in the 7th (OT) Army.

The expected attack came in the early hours of 27 December. To the east of Jerusalem the 53rd (OT) Infantry Division attacked the bulk of the 53rd (Welsh) Division, while the 26th (OT) Infantry Division attacked the right of the Welsh. To the north, the 19th (OT) Division came straight down the Nablus road against the 60th Division. Although the outposts of the 53rd (Welsh) Division were driven in, and hard fighting flared along their main line, the British positions east of Jerusalem did not face any serious danger throughout the day; indeed, some areas were barely engaged by the Ottoman attacks. The 60th Division, on the other hand, also had their piquets and outposts driven in, but then faced some serious and determined attacks along their whole front. Ottoman troops managed to penetrate into the British lines even if they failed to break through, and some vicious fighting occurred as counter-attacks were mounted to throw them back. The 2/16th London Regiment found itself in particular difficulties, and two platoons of the 2/15th mounted a local counter-attack to push the Ottomans back. Instead, they were themselves cut off, and faced a desperate fight for their own survival. Bernard Flynn recalled:

> The call in the morning for everybody out. The first enthusiastic close-quarters encounter with the Turks; my chagrin at missing a retreating Turk at 25 yards when firing from the standing position, surrounded and exposed to enemy

fire with men being killed and wounded around us. Barely
adequate cover behind an outcropping of rock ... [Corporal
James] 'Tiny' Warren ... being killed instantaneously on
raising his head to get a better sight to fire a rifle grenade.
[Second Lieutenant Roland] 'Bulldog' Harris a little to the
left behind some rocks, exuding confidence. A fatuous signal
to retreat from a runner up the hill – how the hell could we?
The Turks coming on again and a last desperate bayonet
charge led by 'Bulldog' and Charlie Jones. That was the last I
saw of Harris.[414]

The two platoons were almost wiped out, and the popular Second Lieutenant Harris was killed. Flynn himself was
wounded, but had to wait for several days before he was found
and taken for treatment.

In other areas the line held firm, and some troops even found
time for their first proper meal in days as a ration convoy made
it through. Sergeant William Mole was with the Machine
Gun Corps:

On Boxing night, the expected attack commenced; shells and
bullets were flying in all directions, and still it rained, and this
time, we had hail also, making things worse than ever. Once
the gun and myself were almost buried by the explosion of a
large shell which fell uncomfortably near us. All next day we
were worried by shells and bullets again flying in all directions.
After a time, we packed up and moved further away. The place
we came to next was a bit better, on account of being out of
range of most of the shells. On our arrival, we were greeted
by the arrival of the rations, including a bit of boxwood (dry).
The rain had stopped now and I managed to make some por-
ridge out of crushed biscuits and jam, and wonder of wonders,
we managed to make some hot cocoa (our first hot drink for
three days) and we fried some real good bacon.[415]

By 6 p.m. the attacks had ended, and the British line was still intact. The Ottoman position, however, was far from secure. At 5 a.m., once it was clear that the main Ottoman offensive had begun, the British had begun their own counter-stroke. To the left of the 60th Division, the other two divisions of XX Corps (the 74th Division on the right and the 10th Division on the left) had swung out of their positions and begun to advance into the open Ottoman flank. They had pivoted around to face east, moving along the tops of the precipitous ridgelines rather than having to struggle across them. With heavy artillery support, they made good progress even though they almost immediately ran into the 1st and 24th (OT) Infantry Divisions, which had been moving up to make their own attack, and the right flank of the 3rd (OT) Cavalry Division, which was holding the line to the west.

Through the day the two divisions made steady progress. By going with the grain of the landscape they had an easier route to follow, but the open ridgelines presented their own problems. Even as the bulk of the Ottoman forces fell back in confusion, small rearguards in isolated farms, villages or woods, or even just hidden among the jumbled piles of rocks, all took their toll. It took time to find sheltered paths to outflank and then attack each position, and in the meantime troops were often pinned down in the open. In one such ambush, Private James Duffy, a stretcher-bearer of the 6th Inniskilling Fusiliers received the Victoria Cross for repeatedly rescuing the wounded under heavy fire.[416] By dusk, all of the attacking division's objectives had been taken.

The following morning, 60th Division joined in the advance, and all three divisions turned north while the 53rd Division extended its left flank to maintain contact. With the grain of the landscape now against them, progress was slower, and although Herculean efforts had brought some artillery forward, the attackers were not nearly as well supported as the day before. Even so, progress continued to be made. On 29 December the

10th Division, slightly to the north of the others, halted while they caught up to the east. By 30 December the 74th was in line with the 10th, and they both held while the 60th Division made a small advance to come into line with them. With this achieved, Chetwode called a halt to all further operations.[417]

The counter-attack had worked. The Ottoman attack had been interrupted and thrown back on the western flank before it had had a chance to properly develop. The attacking divisions, including the newly arrived 1st (OT) Infantry Division, had all received bloody repulses, and been chased back beyond their original lines. The British had advanced across a 19km front, moving 4.8km (3 miles) north on the left and 9.5km (6 miles) north on the right, further securing Jerusalem. With the end of the operation, so ended the campaigns of 1917.

The Egyptian Expeditionary Force could look back at a job well done. The year had begun badly for the British, with the two defeats at Gaza, but had ended with a spectacular success. The Ottomans had held the Palestine line with 45,000–50,000 front-line troops, well dug-in (a skill the Ottomans excelled at) in most places, having had the best part of a year to create and reinforce their positions. Against them, the EEF had pitched around 75,000–80,000 infantry and 12,000 cavalry, falling well short of the usual military rule-of-thumb that an attacking force should outnumber the defender by three to one. During the following campaign, both sides had fought with determination and valour in the most difficult of conditions. The cost had been high for both sides; 28,000 Ottoman casualties and 21,000 British. Long marches, bad weather and huge supply problems had plagued both sides, but in the end the superior numbers, logistics and, it is probably fair to say, command of the British had won out. Not only had Allenby proven to be a steady commander supported by solid corps commanders, but the German/Ottoman command structure had proven to be disjointed, confused and at times unrealistic.

Now the armies both settled down to reorganise themselves and recoup their strength. British reinforcements began to arrive, and work continued apace on the inevitable restoration and expansion of the road and rail network. The Ottomans had fewer opportunities to either regain their strength or improve their communications and logistics. The only road worth the name between the 7th and 8th (OT) Armies was now over 48km (30 miles) to the north, at Nablus. Stark evidence of how bad the Ottoman supply situation had become for the average *Mehmetçik* was discovered by the 60th Division during their advance on 28 December. On retaking some of their outposts that had been over-run the day before, the bodies of the British dead were found to have been stripped. Later, Ottoman bodies were discovered wearing items of captured British uniform, having no chance of receiving new or warm clothing through their own supply system.[418] Given the conditions the Ottoman troops had faced, their level of resistance and resilience throughout the campaign had been extraordinary.

EPILOGUE

BY NEW YEAR'S Day, 1918, the Egyptian Expeditionary Force was exhausted. Men and equipment were worn out, units far below strength, and logistics increasingly tenuous. Allenby had been warned that he might lose some of his forces to France in the spring of 1918, and to limit his operations accordingly, but even without that restriction his forces were in dire need of time to rest, refit and reorganise. Even so, the rest did not last long.

In February 60th (London) and the AN&Z Mounted Division struck north-east into the Jordan Valley, taking Jericho and securing the northern end of the Dead Sea. Other smaller operations pushed the line north of Jerusalem into a more favourable position. In late March, a large-scale raid was mounted across the Jordan with the aim of capturing Amman, but unexpected Ottoman resistance by the 4th (OT) Army foiled the attack and forced a quick withdrawal. A second attempt was rapidly planned, although at this point the vague warning about needing troops in France resurged in spectacular style.

On 21 March 1918, as XX Corps had attacked across the Jordan, the Germans had launched their Spring Offensive on the Western Front, achieving dramatic and deep advances and pushing the British back in near disarray. Within weeks, the 52nd (Lowland) and 74th Divisions, with nine yeomanry regiments and nine infantry battalions, plus artillery and machine gun units, had been despatched to France. They were slowly replaced by Indian Army troops, but it was a lengthy process and most of the new units needed extensive training. Infantry and cavalry brigades across the army were mixed to include fresh Indian units alongside veteran British ones, but it still took many months to bring the army back up to full strength and fighting efficiency. Meanwhile, a second raid across the Jordan was launched in early April, with much the same results. After this failure, the army settled down to the defensive, training and reorganising. For large parts of the army this meant spending parts of the summer in the Jordan Valley, of which, the *Army Handbook on Palestine* declared: 'Nothing is known of the climate in summer time, since no civilised human being has yet been found to spend summer there.'

What the troops in the Jordan found was suffocating heat and lethal wildlife. Snakes and scorpions aside, the mosquitos that abounded in the valley (whose one redeeming feature was the plentiful supply of water) spread malaria that wreaked havoc among the ranks and created serious problems for the medical services. Skirmishing between patrols and piquets also created a smaller but steady trickle of casualties. Units had to be regularly rotated into the cooler hills or coastal plain to rest and recuperate from the climate alone. It was as unpleasant a situation for a soldier to find themselves in as any billet during the First World War, but for six months the army could do nothing but stand firm and endure it.

Opposite them the *Yildirim* made ineffectual attempts to heal its own wounds. In February 1918 von Falkenhayn was replaced by Liman von Sanders, who at least had more experience and understanding when it came to dealing with the Ottoman forces under his command. A few new formations arrived, but even when combined with the trickle of new conscripts sent as replacements, they came nowhere near to bringing the Ottoman forces back up to strength. After all, the *Yildirim* had been the Ottomans' last pool of reserve units, the results of scraping together every spare unit left in the empire, and they had been at least partially destroyed by Allenby. Morale among the 7th and 8th (OT) Armies remained low and the desertion rate high, although across the Jordan the 4th (OT) Army was buoyed by its successes against the British raids. By August, von Sanders had just twelve divisions to defend a 90km (56-mile) front, and most of them were at 15–20 per cent of their intended strength. Their own experiences in the Jordan Valley had been equally draining, or perhaps even more so as their own hopelessly inadequate medical services failed to cope.

After some hard times, 1918 would eventually see the ultimate and dramatic fruition of the Arab Revolt. Even after the fall of Aqaba and the establishment of direct contact with the British forces in Palestine, the campaign had remained highly peripheral, even if it did keep tens of thousands of Ottoman soldiers away from the main fighting fronts. The Arab contribution to the 3rd Battle of Gaza had not extended much beyond that achievement, despite Allenby and Lawrence agreeing on a more concrete contribution. They had agreed that the Arabs would blow up a railway bridge in the Yarmuk valley, to the east of the Sea of Galilee and far north of the main fighting fronts. This should not only add to the Ottomans' supply and communications problems, but also keep Ottoman troops tied down guarding such places rather than being redeployed to face the British. However, problems dogged this plan from the start. A cholera outbreak in Aqaba had severely limited communications and the flow of supplies into the port, and Lawrence was forced to make the raid with inadequate equipment, especially detonators and control cables. In the end, he left Aqaba with a fairly small force of tribesmen (including one strongly suspected of being, and later confirmed as, a traitor) and Indian machine-gunners on 24 October 1917. Efforts to raise much support from the tribes that they passed on the way north failed, and a week later, after establishing a base camp at Azraq, Lawrence led his small force after dark into the Yarmuk valley. However, as they approached the bridge, someone dropped his rifle and the clattering noise alerted the guards, who opened fire. The covering force of Indian machine-gunners returned fire, and in the confusion most of the explosives were dropped into the ravine under the bridge. Lawrence had no choice but to withdraw his men.

With only a small amount of explosives and some dubious detonators and cable left, Lawrence next tried to mine the railway and blow up a train. By now it was raining hard, soaking the equipment, but Lawrence persevered and placed a mine under a small bridge on the line between Amman and Dara on 10 November. However, the deficiencies in cable meant that the operator had to sit virtually totally exposed, behind a very small bush, just 55m (60yds) from the rails. Lawrence himself took the job, and watching with growing excitement as a double-engined and 'enormously long' train packed with troops pulled into view.[419] However, either the cable or the detonators failed, and no amount of effort on Lawrence's part could get the mine to blow. Instead he was forced to sit, helpless, in full view of the slowly passing troops. After a nerve-wracking few minutes, the train passed and Lawrence was able to scramble back to his waiting men. The following day a second attempt was made, after effecting repairs on the mine. This time it worked and a train was derailed, although, being so close to the explosion, Lawrence was himself stunned and injured by the blast. With some success salvaged from the previous failures, Lawrence and his party returned to Azraq.

Then followed one of the more controversial episodes in Lawrence's life: his reconnaissance to Dara. According to his later accounts he approached the town with a few Arab guides, and on 20 November entered with just one companion. He then claims to have been picked up by an Ottoman patrol and taken before the governor of the town. That night, he was badly beaten and sexually abused before managing to escape the following morning. This event has been hotly debated, based as it is only on Lawrence's own testimony, which exist in differing forms, all of which were written several years after the event. Either way, he arrived back at Aqaba on 26 November, an arduous journey to have made so quickly with the injuries he had suffered. On 11 December he was in Jerusalem for the grand entry by Allenby, standing in the crowd behind the general outside the Citadel looking scruffy in a borrowed uniform and grinning broadly.[420]

The Arabs took no more part in the 1917 campaign, but in January 1918 they advanced into the Dead Sea region. After defeating an Ottoman force in open battle at El Tafila, they swept down to the port of El Mezra where they captured part of the grain fleet that ran Ottoman supplies across the Dead Sea. Over the spring and summer the Arabs aggressively attacked the Ottoman rail network in the Trans-Jordan, drawing off troops and resources from the forces facing the British. During the final offensive of September and October 1918, they swept up the right flank of the British forces, rolling the shattered Ottoman forces out of northern Palestine and then Syria.

This final offensive began on 19 September 1918. The plan was superficially similar to that for the 3rd Battle of Gaza, albeit with the flanks reversed. This time, the cavalry smashed through the western end of the Ottoman line before turning northeast, and there were no water issues to hamper their subsequent advance. The cavalry divisions were let loose across the northern Palestine plains. Along with the aeroplanes of the Royal Air Force, who had been gaining and cementing their superiority in the air through the year, they rapidly destroyed the Ottoman command-and-control network and much of their logistics system too. Within days the 7th and 8th (OT) Armies were in full flight, and the columns of retreating men were mercilessly harried by cavalry and aircraft; tens of thousands surrendered as their forces disintegrated. On 21 September, the headquarters of the 8th (OT) Army was absorbed into von Sander's *Yildirim* headquarters, and that army effectively ceased to exist as an organised fighting formation.

Damascus fell on 1 October. True to his 1917 actions, Allenby then called a pause, despite political pressure from London, to allow his men to rest and his infantry and logistics to catch up. On 8 October Beirut was also captured, giving the British an important port close to their front lines. The offensive was renewed only when he was ready, and by mid October Homs and Tripoli had fallen and the advance on Aleppo, was underway. After the long ride of 355km (220 miles), Aleppo fell on 19 October, and von Sanders pulled his remaining forces back to Adana, across the border from Syria into Anatolia. Here his greatly depleted force was joined by the remains of the 7th (OT) Army under Mustapha Kemal, and they prepared to defend the Turkish homeland.

It never came to that. In the Balkans, Major General George Milne's British Salonika Force had broken out and had a clear path to advance on Constantinople, and now the southern armies were also defeated. Although, to the east, the Ottoman forces in the Caucasus were undefeated and had even been successful in their 1918 campaign, the empire was drained of reserves. The gathering and destruction of the *Yildirim* had left it an empty shell, and it was now unable to effectively defend itself. On 5 October the Ottoman government had decided to explore the possibility of an armistice, approaching the Spanish to ask the Americans (who had never declared war on the Ottoman Empire) to broker a deal. The effort failed, and instead Major General Charles Townsend, who had been captured with most of his army at Kut in Mesopotamia in 1916, was sent to speak directly to the British. After some negotiation, an armistice was signed on the deck of HMS *Agamemnon* on 30 October 1918.

The war was over, although considerable fighting remained, both actual and political. A revolt erupted in Egypt in 1919, diverting British troops who were preparing to go home for demobilisation, and the military was also still required for 'policing' across Syria, Palestine and the Trans-Jordan while civil authorities could be established. This took time as the European powers fought for their own claims and sought ways to avoid their commitments to each other and the Arabs. For the next few years the map of the Middle East was redrawn, inadvertently setting the stage for a further century of conflict across the region.

GLOSSARY

AFC: Australian Flying Corps

AIF: Australian Imperial Forces

ALH: Australian Light Horse

ANZAC: Australian and New Zealand Army Corps, also nickname for a soldier from those countries

A&NZ: Australian and New Zealand. Title of a mounted division in Egypt

AOC: Army Ordnance Corps

ASC: Army Service Corps

BIMBASHI: Egyptian Army Major

CCS: Casualty Clearing Station

CTC: Camel Transport Corps (part of Egyptian Labour Corps)

CORVÉE: Egyptian system for providing forced labour for government projects

DMC: Desert Mounted Corps

EEF: Egyptian Expeditionary Force

ELC: Egyptian Labour Corps

EMIR: Arab Governor

ESR: Egyptian State Railway

FA: *Flieger Abteilung*. German Air Force squadron

GENERAL SERVICE: Usually referred to items of equipment that were of the standard
Army pattern (i.e. GS wagons)

HAC: Honourable Artillery Company (a Territorial artillery unit)

HLI: Highland Light Infantry

ICC: Imperial Camel Corps

KHAMSIN/KHAMASEEN: The hot wind from central Africa that blows up through Egypt between March and May

KHEDIVE: Viceroy of Egypt

KOSB: King's Own Scottish Borderers

MEHMETÇIK: Literally 'Mehmet', nickname by Ottoman troops for themselves, equivalent of the British 'Tommy' or Australian 'Digger'

MONITOR: Shallow draft ship used as a floating gun platform

NAHR: River

NCO: Non-Commissioned Officer

NZMR: New Zealand Mounted Rifles

OT: Ottoman Turkish

PASHA: Senior Ottoman military or government official

QOWH: Queen's Own Worcestershire Hussars (Yeomanry)

RA: Royal Artillery

RAMC: Royal Army Medical Corps

RE: Royal Engineers

RFA: Royal Field Artillery

RFC: Royal Flying Corps

RGH: Royal Gloucestershire Hussars

RHA: Royal Horse Artillery

RN: Royal Navy

RNAS: Royal Naval Air Service

RNVR: Royal Navy Volunteer Reserve

RSF: Royal Scots Fusiliers

RWF: Royal Welch Fusiliers

TARBOOSH: A fez-like hat

WFF: Western Frontier Force

YILDIRIM: Thunderbolt

APPENDIX A:

ORDERS OF BATTLE, 1ST BATTLE OF GAZA

British and Imperial Forces

Eastern Force
General Officer Commanding:
Major General (temp. Lieutenant General) Sir Charles Dobell
 KCB CMG DSO

Force Troops
Imperial Camel Corps Brigade
Major (temp. Brigadier General) C.L. Smith VC MC
1st, 2nd and 3rd Battalions
Hong Kong and Singapore Camel Battery
Brigade Signal Section
Brigade Field Troop RE
Brigade Machine Gun Company
1/1st Scottish Horse Field Ambulance

229th Infantry Brigade (from 74th Division)
Colonel (temp. Brigadier General) R. Hoare

16th Devonshire Regiment, 12th Somerset Light Infantry,
    14th Royal Highlanders, 12th Royal Scots Fusiliers
4th Machine Gun Company

11th and 12th Light Armoured Car Batteries
4th Light Car Patrol
10th Heavy Battery RGA
91st Heavy Battery RGA

52nd (Lowland) Division
General Officer Commanding:
Colonel (temp. Major General) W.E.B. Smith CB CMG

155th Infantry Brigade
Lieutenant Colonel (temp. Brigadier General) J.B. Pollok-
    M'Call CMG
1/4th and 1/5th Royal Scots Fusiliers, 1/4th and 1/5th King's
    Own Scottish Borderers
155th Brigade Machine Gun Company

156th Infantry Brigade
Lieutenant Colonel (temp. Brigadier General) A.H. Leggett
    DSO
1/4th and 1/7th Royal Scots, 1/7th and 1/8th Scottish Rifles
156th Brigade Machine Gun Company

157th Infantry Brigade
Colonel (temp. Brigadier General) C.D.H. Moore DSO
1/5th, 1/6th and 1/7th Highland Light Infantry, 1/5th Argyll
    and Sutherland Highlanders
157th Brigade Machine Gun Company

Divisional Troops
Mounted Troops: HQ and 'C' Squadron, Royal Glasgow
    Yeomanry

Artillery: 261st, 262nd and 263rd Brigades, RFA
52nd Divisional Ammunition Column
Engineers: 2/1st, 2/2nd and 1/2nd Lowland Field Companies,
    RE
Signal Service: 52nd Divisional Signal Company
ASC: 52nd Divisional Train
Medical Units: 1/1st, 1/2nd, 1/3rd Lowland Field Ambulances

54th (East Anglian) Division
General Officer Commanding: Colonel (temp. Major General)
    S.W. Hare CB

161st Infantry Brigade
Lieutenant Colonel (temp. Brigadier General) W. Marriott-
    Dodington
1/4th, 1/5th, 1/6th and 1/7th Essex Regiment
161st Brigade Machine Gun Company

162nd Infantry Brigade
Lieutenant Colonel (temp. Brigadier General) A. Mudge
1/5th Bedford Regiment,1/4th Northampton Regiment,
    1/10th and 1/11th London Regiment
162nd Brigade Machine Gun Company

163rd Infantry Brigade
Major (Hon. Colonel, Temp. Brigadier General) T. Ward
1/4th and 1/5th Norfolk Regiment, 1/5th Suffolk Regiment,
    1/8th Hampshire Regiment
163rd Brigade Machine Gun Company

Divisional Troops
Mounted Troops: 1 Sqn 1/1st Hertfordshire Yeomanry (with
    HQ and Machine-Gun Section)
Artillery: 270th, 271st and 272nd Brigades, RFA
54th Divisional Ammunition Column

Engineers: 2/1st E. Anglian Field Company, RE
1/2nd E. Anglian Field Company, RE
1/1st Kent Field Company, RE
Signal Service: 54th Divisional Signal Company
ASC: 54th Divisional Train
Medical: 2/1st, 1/2nd and1/3rd E. Anglian Field Ambulances

Desert Column
General Officer Commanding:
Major General (temp. Lieutenant General) Sir P.W. Chetwode
    Bt CB DSO

Australian and New Zealand Mounted Division
General Officer Commanding:
Major General Sir H.G. Chauvel KCMG CB

1st Australian Light Horse Brigade detached

2nd Australian Light Horse Brigade
Colonel (temp. Brigadier General) G. de L Ryrie CMG
5th, 6th and 7th Regiments Australian Light Horse
2nd Australian Light Horse Signal Troop
2nd Australian Machine Gun Squadron

New Zealand Mounted Rifles Brigade
Colonel (temp. Brigadier General) E.W.C. Chaytor CB
Auckland, Canterbury and Wellington Mounted Rifles
    Regiments
New Zealand Mounted Rifles Signal Troop
New Zealand Machine Gun Squadron

22nd Mounted Brigade
Colonel (temp, Brigadier General) F.A.B. Fryer
1/1st Lincolnshire Yeomanry, 1/1st Staffordshire
    Yeomanry,1/1st East Riding Yeomanry

22nd Mounted Brigade Signal Troop
18th Machine Gun Squadron

Divisional Troops
Artillery: Leicester, Somerset, Inverness and Ayr Batteries
    RHA
Engineers: 1st Australian Field Squadron
Signal Service: 1st A. and NZ Signal Squadron
ASC: HQ Light Horse Divisional ASC
Mounted Divisional Ammunition Column
26 and 27 Australian Units of Supply
Medical: 1st and 2nd LH Field Ambulances
NZ Mounted Brigade Ambulance
1/1st North Midland Mounted Brigade Field Ambulance

Imperial Mounted Division
General Officer Commanding:
Colonel (temp. Major General) H.W. Hodgson CVO CB

3rd Australian Light Horse Brigade
Colonel (temp. Brigadier General) J.R. Royston CMG DSO
8th, 9th and 10th Regiments Australian Light Horse
3rd Australian Light Horse Signal Troop
3rd Australian Machine Gun Squadron

4th Australian Light Horse Brigade detached

5th Mounted Brigade
Colonel (temp. Brigadier General) E.A. Wiggin DSO
1/1st Warwick Yeomanry, 1/1st Gloucester Yeomanry,
    1/1st Worcester Yeomanry
5th Mounted Brigade Signal Troop
16th Machine Gun Squadron

6th Mounted Brigade
Lieutenant Colonel (temp. Brigadier General) T.M.S. Pitt
1/1st Buckinghamshire Yeomanry, 1/1st Berkshire Yeomanry,
    1/1st Dorsetshire Yeomanry
6th Mounted Brigade Signal Troop
17th Machine Gun Squadron

Divisional Troops
Artillery: 1/1st Berkshire and 1/1st Nottinghamshire Batteries
    RHA
'A' and 'B' Batteries HAC
Mounted Divisional Ammunition Column
Engineers: Imperial Mounted Division Field Squadron
Signal Service: Imperial Mounted Division Signal Squadron
Medical: 3rd and 4th LH Field Ambulances
1/1st South Midland Mounted and 1/2nd South Midland
    Mounted Brigades Field Ambulances

53rd (Welsh) Division
General Officer Commanding: Major General A.E. Dallas, CB
    CMG

158th Infantry Brigade
Major (temp. Brigadier General) S.F. Mott
1/5th, 1/6th and 1/7th Royal Welsh Fusiliers,
    1/1st Herefordshire Regiment
158th Brigade Machine Gun Company

159th Infantry Brigade
Colonel (temp. Brigadier General) J.H. du B. Travers CB
1/4th and 1/7th Cheshire Regiment, 1/4th and 1/5th Welsh
    Regiment
159th Brigade Machine Gun Company

160th Infantry Brigade
Colonel (temp. Brigadier General) W.J.C. Butler
1/4th Royal Sussex Regiment, 2/4th Royal West Surrey
    Regiment
2/10th Middlesex Regiment
160th Brigade Machine Gun Company

Divisional Troops
Mounted Troops: 1 Sqn 1/1st Hertfordshire Yeomanry
53rd Divisional Cyclist Company
Artillery: 1/1st Cheshire Brigade, RFA
265th, 266th and 267th Brigades, RFA
53rd Divisional Ammunition Column
Engineers: 1/1st and 2/1st Welsh Field Companies, RE
2/1st Cheshire Field Company, RE
Signal Service: 53rd Divisional Signal Company
ASC: 53rd Divisional Train
Medical: 1/1st, 1/2nd and 1/3rd Welsh Field Ambulances

Money's Detachment
Colonel N. Money
1/1st Royal Gloucestershire Hussars, 2/4th Royal West Kent
    Regiment
'A' Section 15th Heavy Battery RGA

Ottoman Forces

Fourth Army
General Officer Commanding: Djemal Pasha
Field Commander: Colonel Baron Kress von Kressenstein

Group Tiller
Commander: Major von Tiller (in Gaza)

Three battalions, 79th Infantry Regiment
Three battalions, 125th Infantry Regiment
2nd Battalion, 81st Infantry Regiment
Two batteries of Austrian heavy mountain howitzers

One battery of German 10cm field guns
Two batteries of Ottoman field guns
One company cavalry
One company camelry

3rd Infantry Division (at Jemmame)
31st Infantry Regiment
32nd Infantry Regiment

16th Infantry Division (at Tell el Sharia)
47th Infantry Regiment
48th Infantry Regiment

53rd Infantry Division (marching south from Jaffa)

3rd Cavalry Division (at Beersheba)
6th Cavalry Regiment
7th Cavalry Regiment
138th Infantry Regiment

NOTE ON THE STRUCTURE AND EQUIPMENT OF BRITISH AND IMPERIAL FORCES

The basic infantry unit of the British and imperial forces was the battalion (under a colonel or lieutenant colonel). For the British and ANZACs, this consisted of just over 1,000 officers and men, divided into four companies (under a major or captain) of just over 200 men, plus a battalion headquarters. Each company was divided into four platoons (under a lieutenant), each of which was divided into four sections (under a sergeant or corporal). Each battalion had small sections of specialist troops attached; medical staff, signallers (and, later, wireless operators), and from late 1915 members of the Machine Gun Corps with heavy machine guns (before then, they had been members of the battalion).

The basic infantry weapon was the .303in calibre Short Magazine Lee–Enfield (SMLE) rifle, which was rugged and accurate and came with a bayonet. Machine guns were also issued. The 'heavy' types, initially the Maxim but later the Vickers Machine Gun with a four-man crew, were used by battalion level units who could be moved around to where they were needed. Each platoon had its own 'light' machine guns with two-man crews, either Lewis guns or the French Hotchkiss gun. Both of these lighter types had magazines with open sections that easily became clogged and jammed in sandy conditions.

Battalions were usually numbered as part of a larger regiment, although this latter was a largely administrative designation. As a rule, the 1st and 2nd Battalions of a regiment were the regular troops, the 3rd and 4th Battalions the part-time soldiers of the Territorial Army, and the 5th and 6th Battalions the nominal formations of the Reserves (soldiers who had served as regulars, and bound to act as a reserve force for a set number of years). With the massive expansion of the army in 1914, many new battalions were established. The Territorial Army was meant only for home defence and not obliged to serve overseas, but the vast majority volunteered to do so anyway. As a result, a 'second line' of battalions was established to take their place. The original units, with a '1/' prefix, were despatched to the war, while battalions with a '2/' prefix were raised at home. Many of these units, once fully trained, were despatched to Egypt, and a 'third line' ('3/') were raised in their place. Many of these third-line units would be sent to the front later in the war, and a fourth line established at home. The Indian, Australian and New Zealand forces had a straightforward numerical system of units, and the above system should not be confused with the Gurkha system of having multi-battalion regiments. For example, the 2/7th Gurkha Rifles refers to the 2nd Battalion of the 7th Regiment.

On active service, the regiment was (for infantry) a largely irrelevant concept. Instead, three or four battalions were grouped together to form brigades. Above that, three or four brigades were grouped into divisions, and two to four divisions would make up a corps. Brigades, divisions and corps had additional support troops attached, ranging from artillery and cavalry to signals, medical and administrative units.

The artillery were split into several groups, each prefixed in the British service with the title 'Royal'. Horse artillery were the fast moving, lighter guns that would give close support to attacks. Field artillery were heavier guns for harder pounding, generally more sedentary and further back from the front lines. Garrison artillery were the big guns mostly used in static positions, such as coastal defences or fortresses, although they also operated some of the larger battlefield guns and mortars. The Indian forces also had mountain artillery, which were light guns (sometimes known as 'screw guns') that could be dismantled and carried to otherwise inaccessible areas on the backs of elephants, camels or mules. Artillery forces were usually organised into batteries of six field guns (or four for the Royal Horse Artillery) or four howitzers, which could be further split into sections.

Unlike the infantry, for the cavalry a regiment was a battlefield unit. As a note on terminology, technically the British, Australian and New Zealand cavalry were actually mounted rifles, who were to ride into battle and then fight on foot, although they would act like traditional cavalry when it came to scouting before and after battle, and even occasionally fight mounted.

In peacetime cavalry units did not have separate equivalents to battalions, although some formed second line units after the outbreak of the war. A regiment consisted of just over 500 officers and men, divided into three squadrons of 150 men plus a headquarters and a machine-gun section. Each squadron was sub-divided into four troops, and each troop into sections of four men. These men would ride four abreast on the march. As, in the vast majority of cases, the cavalry were supposed to only ride into action, and then fight on foot, one of those four would lead the horses of the other three to safety in battle. Obviously, this greatly weakened the fighting strength of the unit.

Cavalry could be grouped together in brigades and divisions, and would be in Egypt and Palestine, but could also be attached as individual regiments to infantry divisions or corps. Here, they would be on hand to act as scouts or messengers for the different headquarters, or as a highly mobile reserve, that could be despatched quickly to a point of danger or opportunity.

The Imperial Camel Corps were mounted infantry, in that they were mounted, but equipped and organised on the same company and battalion pattern as the infantry were. There were four battalions, any three of which served together as the Imperial Camel Corps Brigade, while the fourth was on detached garrison and patrol duties in Egypt. These battalions rotated that duty.

APPENDIX C:

ORDERS OF BATTLE, 1/5TH KING'S OWN SCOTTISH BORDERERS' RAID ON SEA POST, 11 JUNE 1917

First Wave: (OC Assault Lieutenant Turner)

Left Assault Party:
1 officer (2/Lieutenant MacKinnon), 15 riflemen (5 armed with hatchets)
2 x bombing parties: Each of 1 NCO, 2 throwers, 2 bayonet men, and 2 bomb carriers
2 sandbaggers (each with a shovel and 25 empty bags)
Followed by: 1 Royal Engineer and 3 other ranks with heavy axes
(All drawn from D Company)

Right Assault Party:
1 officer (Lieutenant McGeorge), 15 riflemen (5 armed with hatchets)
2 x bombing parties: Each of 1 NCO, 2 throwers, 2 bayonet men and 2 bomb carriers
2 sandbaggers (each with a shovel and 25 empty bags)
Followed by: 1 Royal Engineer and 3 other ranks with heavy axes
(1 bombing party from B Company, all others from C Company)

Second Wave: (OC Supports Captain Sir R.G.W. Grierson)

Reserve Assault Party:
1 officer (Lieutenant Muir), 15 riflemen (5 armed with hatchets)
2 x bombing parties: Each of 1 NCO, 2 throwers, 2 bayonet men and 2 bomb carriers
2 sandbaggers (each with a shovel and 25 empty bags)
(All from A Company)

Support Party:
1 officer (Capt. Penman) and 25 riflemen
Booty party: 10 other ranks (to collect enemy weapons, equipment or documents)
(All from C Company)

Others:
Battalion bombing officer (Lieutenant Burt, attached from 1/5th Argyll and Sutherland Highlanders)
5 Royal Engineers
2 axemen (from A Company)
6 bomb carriers
Support Signal Party: 1 NCO, 1 telephone operator and 1 linesman, plus 8 runners
4 stretcher-bearers (2 stretchers) (from A Company)

Third Wave:

Bombing reserve: 1 officer and 5 bomb carriers
Reserve signal party: 1 NCO, 2 telephone operators and 2 linesmen, plus runners
2 x demolition parties: Each of 4 Royal Engineers (3 with heavy axes, 1 with a mine)
Medical party: 4 stretcher-bearers (2 stretchers)

Reserve:

2 officers (Capt. Gibson (OC Reserve) and Capt. Johnstone),
    60 other ranks (from A Company)
2 x bombing parties: Each of 1 NCO, 2 throwers, 2 bayonet
    men and 2 bomb carriers (attached from 1/4th KOSB)

1 Lewis gun (from A Company)
12 bomb carriers (from C Company)
2 Royal Engineer parties: Each of 3 Royal Engineers
12 stretcher-bearers (6 stretchers) (from B, C and D Companies)

Beach Party:

1 officer (Lieutenant McEwan), 25 other ranks (from
    C Company)
1 Lewis gun (from C Company)
1 bombing party: 1 NCO, 2 throwers, 2 bayonet men and
    2 bomb carriers (attached from 1/4th KOSB)

Beach Party Reserve:

1 officer (Capt. Scott Elliot), 15 other ranks (from C Company)
1 bombing party: 1 NCO, 2 throwers, 2 bayonet men and
    2 bomb carriers (attached from 1/4th KOSB)
3 bomb carriers (from C Company)
4 stretcher-bearers (2 stretchers) (supplied by 1/4th KOSB)

Regimental Aid Post:

3rd Lowland Field Ambulance
10 stretcher-bearers (5 stretchers) each from 1/4th KOSB and
    1/5th Royal Scots Fusiliers

Artillery Support:

A, B and C Batteries, 261st Brigade, Royal Field Artillery
A, B and C Batteries, 262nd Brigade, Royal Field Artillery
A and B Batteries, 267th Brigade, Royal Field Artillery

Total from 1/5th KOSB:
11 officers and 361 NCOs and other ranks
(Not including troops providing supporting fire from
    1/4th King's Own Scottish Borderers, 1/5th Royal Scots
    Fusiliers, 1/6th and 1/5th Highland Light Infantry,
    1/5th Argyll and Sutherland Highlands, 155th Brigade
    Machine Gun Company, and Royal Field Artillery)

APPENDIX D:

NOTE ON THE STRUCTURE AND EQUIPMENT OF OTTOMAN FORCES

The Ottoman Army had undergone massive reorganisation just before the First World War, as a result of their defeats in the Balkans Wars. These wars had cost the Ottomans some 250,000 men and seen forty-three divisions wiped from their order of battle. They had also led to the loss of much of the empire's European lands, and with them a significant proportion of their population and their industrial base, both of which losses would lead to considerable problems during the First World War.

The Ottoman Army raised their divisions based on set geographical recruiting areas, and so the loss of the Balkans meant that these had to be redrawn. The army also radically changed its structure in that all reserve units were abolished. Instead of having (as Britain had) specifically reservist battalions, brigades and divisions, all Ottoman front-line units were instead held at a peace-time strength of around 40 per cent. In time of war, reservists were channelled into regular formations to make up their numbers. In this way, all of their units had a solid core of professional soldiers, although equally it meant that each contained a majority of older troops whose training and experience was probably out of date. Despite this, again due to the Balkans Wars, the Ottoman Army had the most experienced army of any of the Great Powers in 1914.

An Ottoman infantry division was built around three infantry regiments. Each division also had an artillery regiment, a cavalry squadron, a pioneers (engineers) company and a sanitation company, to give a full strength of 10,000–12,000 men. An infantry regiment consisted of three battalions, numbered as the 1st, 2nd and 3rd battalions of that particular regiment. Each battalion had four companies, each of four officers and 260 non-commissioned officers and men, as well as a small battalion headquarters and a machine-gun company.

Three divisions would be grouped together to make a corps. These would also have their own artillery regiment and a cavalry regiment attached.

A cavalry regiment consisted of four front-line squadrons of 130 officers and men, plus a regimental headquarters of thirty officers and men. Each regiment also had a fifth squadron that acted as a depot, who trained and provided reinforcements and remounts. The cavalry were armed with carbines and swords, and a few units carried lances.

An artillery regiment, as attached to an infantry division, had either two or three battalions, each of three batteries of four field guns. Those regiments attached to a corps were different, with two mountain-gun battalions (each of three batteries of four guns) and a heavy battalion, of three batteries of six either heavy artillery pieces or howitzers.

All of the above strengths were theoretical, paper-strengths. During the war, few units reached full strength, and by 1917 most were lucky to be at 50 per cent. The Ottomans were perpetually short of officers (who often commanded much higher formations than their British equivalents would, with colonels commanding regiments (equivalent to a brigade) or even divisions) and experienced NCOs, as well as men to fill the ranks. Heavy weaponry was also in extremely short supply, especially artillery and machine guns, many of which had to be supplied by Germany or Austria. Even then, many units were greatly under strength.

At the start of the war, the average Ottoman soldier was well equipped. Their khaki uniform was not unlike British uniforms, and was topped by a 'kabalak'. This type of hat had been designed by Enver Pasha (and so was also known as an 'enveriye') and consisted of a frame around which two long strips of fabric were wound to make the cover. Each man carried a rifle – most commonly an 1893 or 1903 pattern bolt-action, magazine-feed 7.65mm Mauser. For this they carried 130 rounds of ammunition and a bayonet. The quality of uniforms, equipment and boots declined rapidly soon after the start of the war, as the expansion of the army and shortages of raw materials (cotton imports from Egypt were immediately stopped, for example) were felt.

Other supporting services for the front-line troops were also often lacking. Medical services were frequently poorly supplied and under strength, leading to serious health problems and high rates of sickness and disease. The poor food provided for soldiers further exacerbated this. Ottoman soldiers could, indeed had to, survive on rations that their opponents could scarcely believe sustained life. The official rations were meagre, and even these were seldom met in the field, leading to (among other problems) widespread scurvy and dysentery. Pay, which could have been used to buy extra food, was low and usually far in arrears. The ability of the average *mehmetçik* to endure the harshest of conditions for months on end and still maintain the ability to fight with skill and determination is staggering.

APPENDIX E:

ORDERS OF BATTLE, EGYPTIAN EXPEDITIONARY FORCE, 3RD BATTLE OF GAZA

General Headquarters

Commander-in-Chief: General Sir Edmund H.H. Allenby, KCB
Chief of the General Staff: Major General L.J. Bols, CB DSO
Brigadier General, General Staff: Brigadier General G. Dawnay, DSO MVO
Deputy Adjutant General: Major General J. Adye, CB
Deputy Quartermaster General: Major General Sir Walter Campbell, KCMG CB DSO
Major General, Royal Artillery: Major General S.C.U. Smith, CB
Engineer-in-Chief: Major General H.B.H. Wright, CB CMG

Desert Mounted Corps
GOC: Lieutenant General Sir H.G. Chauvel, KCMG CB
General Staff: Brigadier General R.G.H. Howard-Vyse, DSO
Deputy Adjutant and Quartermaster General: Brigadier General E.F. Trew, DSO
GOC Royal Artillery: Brigadier General A.D'A. King, CB DSO

Australian and New Zealand Mounted Division
GOC: Major General E.W.C. Chaytor, CB CMG

1st Australian Light Horse Brigade: Brigadier General C.F. Cox, CB
1st Regt ALH, 2nd Regt ALH, 3rd Regt ALH

2nd Australian Light Horse Brigade: Brigadier General G. de L. Ryrie, CMG
5th Regt ALH, 6th Regt ALH, 7th Regt ALH

New Zealand Mounted Rifles Brigade: Brigadier General W. Meldrum, CB DSO
Auckland M.R. Regt, Canterbury M.R. Regt, Wellington M.R. Regt

Artillery: XVIII Brigade RHA (Inverness, Ayr, and Somerset Btys)
Engineers: A. and NZ Field Sqn

Australian Mounted Division
GOC: Major General H.W. Hodgson, CB CVO

3rd Australian Light Horse Brigade: Brigadier General L.C. Wilson, CMG
8th Regt ALH, 9th Regt ALH, 10th Regt ALH

4th Australian Light Horse Brigade: Brigadier General W. Grant, DSO
4th Regt ALH, 11th Regt ALH, 12th Regt ALH

5th Mounted Brigade: Brigadier General P.D. Fitzgerald, DSO
1/1st Warwick Yeo., 1/1st Gloucester Yeo., 1/1st Worcester Yeo.

Artillery: XIX Brigade RHA (Notts. Bty RHA, 'A' and 'B' Btys HAC)
Engineers: Australian Mounted Division Field Sqn

Yeomanry Mounted Division
General Officer Commanding (GOC): Major General G. de S. Barrow, CB

6th Mounted Brigade: Brigadier General C.A.C. Godwin
1/1st Bucks Yeo., 1/1st Berks Yeo., 1/1st Dorset Yeo.

8th Mounted Brigade: Brigadier General C.S. Rome
1/1st City of London Yeo., 1/1st County of London (Middlesex) Yeo., 1/3rd County of London Yeo.

22nd Mounted Brigade: Brigadier General F.A.B. Fryer
1/1st Lincs. Yeo., 1/1st Staffs. Yeo., 1/1st E. Riding Yeo.

Artillery: XX Brigade RHA (Berks, Hants, and Leicester Btys)
Engineers: No. 6 Field Sqn RE

Corps Troops
Machine Gun Corps: Nos 2, 3, 11, and 12 Light Armoured Motor Btys
Nos 1 and 7 Light Car Patrols

Attached
7th Mounted Brigade: Brigadier General J.T. Wigan, DSO
1/1st Sherwood Rangers, 1/1st S. Notts. Hussars
Attached: Essex Bty RHA
Imperial Camel Corps Brigade: Brigadier General C.L. Smith, VC MC
2nd (Imperial) Bn, 3rd (A and NZ) Bn, 4th (A and NZ) Bn
Attached: Hong Kong and Singapore Mountain Bty

XX Corps
GOC: Lieutenant General Sir P.W. Chetwode, Bt. KCMG CB
  DSO
General Staff: Brigadier General W.H. Bartholomew, CMG
Deputy Adjutant and Quartermaster General: Brigadier
  General E. Evans, DSO
GOC Royal Artillery: Brigadier General A.H. Short, CB
Chief Engineer: Brigadier General R.L. Wailer

53rd (Welsh) Division
GOC: Major General S.F. Mott

158th Brigade: Brigadier General H.A. Vernon, DSO
1/5th R. Welsh Fusiliers, 1/6th R. Welsh Fusiliers, 1/7th
  R. Welsh Fusiliers, 1/1st Herefordshire Regt

159th Brigade: Brigadier General N.E. Money, DSO
1/4th Cheshire Regt, 1/7th Cheshire Regt, 1/4th Welsh Regt,
  1/5th Welsh Regt

160th Brigade: Brigadier General V.L.N. Pearson
1/4th R. Sussex Regt, 2/4th R. West Surrey Regt, 2/4th
  R. West Kent Regt, 2/10th Middlesex Regt

Artillery: 265th Brigade RFA ('A' and 'C' Btys)
266th Brigade RFA ('A' and 'C' Btys)
267th Brigade RFA ('A' and 'B' Btys)
Engineers: 436th, 437th, and 439th Field Coys RE

60th (2/2nd London) Division
GOC: Major General J.S.M. Shea, CB DSO

179th Brigade: Brigadier General Fitzj. M. Edwards, CMG
  DSO

2/13th London Regt, 2/14th London Regt, 2/15th London
   Regt, 2/16th London Regt

180th Brigade: Brigadier General C.F. Watson, CMG DSO
2/17th London Regt, 2/18th London Regt, 2/19th London
   Regt, 2/20th London Regt
181st Brigade: Brigadier General E.C. Da Costa
2/21st London Regt, 2/22nd London Regt, 2/23rd London
   Regt, 2/24th London Regt

Artillery: 301st Brigade RFA ('A', 'B' and 'C' Btys)
302nd Brigade RFA ('A' 413th and 'C' Btys)
303rd Brigade RFA ('A', 'B' and 'C' Btys)
Engineers: 519th, 521st, and 522nd Field Coys RE
Pioneers: 1/12th Loyal N. Lancashire Regt

74th (Yeomanry) Division
GOC: Major General E.S. Girdwood

229th Brigade: Brigadier General R. Hoare
16/Devonshire Regt, 12/Somerset LI, 14/R. Highlanders.,
   12/R. Scots Fusiliers

230th Brigade: Brigadier General A.J. O'Neill
10/E. Kent Regt, 16/R. Sussex Regt, 15/Suffolk Regt,
   12/Norfolk Regt

231st Brigade: Brigadier General C.E. Heathcote, DSO
10/Shropshire LI, 24/R. Welsh Fusiliers, 25/R. Welsh Fusiliers,
   24/Welsh Regt

Artillery: XLIV Brigade RFA (340th and 382nd Btys)
117th Brigade RFA ('A', 'B' and 'C' Btys)
268th Brigade RFA ('A' 366th, and 'C' Btys)

Engineers: 5th (R. Monmouth) and 5th (R. Anglesey) Field
  Coys RE

Corps Troops
Mounted Troops: 1/2nd County of London Yeo.
Artillery: XCVI Heavy Artillery Group (15th, 91st, and
  181st Heavy Btys; 378th, 383rd, and 440th Siege Btys)

10th (Irish) Division
GOC: Major General J.R. Longley, CB

29th Brigade: Brigadier General R.S. Vandeleur, CMG
6/R. Irish Rifles, 5/Connaught Rangers, 1/Leinster Regt,
  6/Leinster Regt

30th Brigade: Brigadier General F.A. Greer, DSO
1/R. Irish Regt, 6/R. Munster Fusiliers, 6/R. Dublin Fusiliers,
  7/R. Dublin Fusiliers
31st Brigade: Brigadier General E.M. Morris.
5/R. Inniskilling Fusiliers, 6/R. Inniskilling Fusiliers, 2/R Irish
  Fusiliers, 5/R. Irish Fusiliers

Artillery: LXVII Brigade RFA ('A', 'B' and 'C' Btys)
LXVIII Brigade RFA ('A', 'B' and 'C' Btys)
263rd Brigade RFA (75th and 'C' Btys)
Engineers: 65th, 66th, and 85th Field Coys RE
Pioneers: 5/R. Irish Regt

XXI Corps
GOC: Lieutenant General E.S. Bulfin, CB CVO
Brigadier General, General Staff: Brigadier General
  E.T. Humphreys, DSO
Deputy Adjutant and Quartermaster General: Brigadier
  General St. G.B. Armstrong

GOC Royal Artillery: Brigadier General H.A.D. Simpson Baikie, CB

Chief Engineer: Brigadier General R.P.T. Hawksley

52nd (Lowland) Division
GOC: Major General J. Hill, DSO

155th Brigade: Brigadier General J.B. Pollok-McCall, CMG
1/4th R. Scots Fusiliers, 1/5th R. Scots Fusiliers, 1/4th KOSB, 1/5th KOSB

156th Brigade: Brigadier General A.H. Leggett, DSO
1/4th R. Scots, 1/7th R. Scots, 1/7th Scottish Rifles, 1/8th Scottish Rifles

157th Brigade: Brigadier General C.D.H. Moore, DSO
1/5th HLI, 1/6th HLI, 1/7th HLI, 1/5th Argyll and Sutherland Highlanders

Artillery: 261st Brigade RFA ('A', 'B' and 'C' Btys)
262nd Brigade RFA ('A' and 'B' Btys)
264th Brigade RFA ('A' and 'C' Btys)
Engineers: 410th, 412th, and 413th Field Coys RE

54th (East Anglian) Division
GOC: Major General S.W. Hare, CB

161st Brigade: Brigadier General W. Marriott-Dodington
1/4th Essex Regt, 1/5th Essex Regt, 1/6th Essex Regt, 1/7th Essex Regt

162nd Brigade: Brigadier General A. Mudge
1/5th Bedfordshire Regt, 1/4th Northamptonshire Regt, 1/10th London Regt, 1/11th London Regt

163rd Brigade: Brigadier General T. Ward, CMG
1/4th Norfolk Regt, 1/5th Norfolk Regt, 1/5th Suffolk Regt,
 1/8th Hampshire Regt

Artillery: 270th Brigade RFA ('A', 'B' and 'C' Btys)
271st Brigade RFA ('A' and 'B' Btys)
272nd Brigade RFA ('B' and 'C' Btys)
Engineers: 484th and 486th Field Coys RE

75th Division
GOC: Major General P.C. Palin, CB

232nd Brigade: Brigadier General H.J. Huddleston, DSO MC
1/5th Devonshire Regt, 2/5th Hampshire Regt, 2/4th Somerset
 LI, 2/3rd Gurkhas

233rd Brigade: Brigadier General the Hon. E.M. Colston, DSO
1/5th Somerset LI, 1/4th Wiltshire Regt, 2/4th Hampshire
 Regt, 3/3rd Gurkhas

234th Brigade: Brigadier General F.G. Anley, CB CMG
1/4th Duke of Cornwall's LI, 2/4th Dorset Regt,
 123rd Outram's Rifles, 58th Vaughan's Rifles (Frontier
 Force)

Artillery: XXXVII Brigade RFA (389th, 390th, and
 405th Btys)
172nd Brigade RFA (391st, 392nd, and 406th Btys)
1st S. African FA Brigade ('A' and 'B' Btys)
Engineers: 495th and 496th Field Coys RE

Corps Troops
Mounted Troops: Composite Regt (1 Sqn R. Glasgow Yeo.,
 1 Sqn Duke of Lancs Yeo., 1 Sqn 1/1st Herts. Yeo.)

Artillery: XCVII Heavy Artillery Group (189th and
  195th Heavy Btys; 201st, 205th, 300th, and 380th Siege Btys)
C Heavy Artillery Group (10th Heavy Bty; 43rd, 134th, 379th,
  422nd, and 423rd Siege Btys)
102nd Heavy Artillery Group (202nd Heavy Bty; 209th,
  292nd, 420th, 421st, and 424th Siege Btys)
Machine Gun Corps: 'E' Company, Tank Corps 211th Machine
  Gun Coy

General Headquarters Troops

Royal Flying Corps Middle East
GOC: Brigadier General W.S. Brancker (Replaced Brigadier
  General W.G.H. Salmond on 5 November 1917)

Palestine Brigade, RFC: Lieutenant Colonel A.E. Borton, DSO
5th (Corps Artillery) Wing: Nos 14 and 113 Sqns RFC
40th (Army) Wing: No. 67 Sqn Australian F.C., No. 11 Sqn
  RFC
No. 21 Balloon Coy
Artillery: VIII Mountain Brigade RGA (10th and 11th Btys)
IX Mountain Brigade RGA ('A', 'B' and 12th Btys)

SELECT BIBLIOGRAPHY

For reasons of space, this is only a select bibliography, based on those documents and books quoted or cited in the text, or others that are particularly illuminating or useful.

Primary Sources

Australian War Memorial
PR01376 Sgt Charles Doherty

I have also extensively consulted: AWM4 War Diaries from the First World War, which are very helpfully available on the AWM's website.

Imperial War Museum
10403 Major General G.P. Dawnay
10414 Field Marshal Lord Chetwode
12702 Lieutenant Colonel F.H.A. Wollaston DSO
12705 C.R. Hennessey
1292 C.C.M. Millis
13560 Corporal Charles Henry Livingstone DCM
13595 J.W. Gough
15153 Sergeant William Mole
2792 Thomas Brookes Minshall
4684 Lieutenant Colonel Sir Randolf Baker DSO
5743 Sergeant James Eneas Scott

6873 W.N. Hendry
7818 T.G. Edgerton
90/1/1 Sir Arthur Lynden-Bell

Museum of the Queen's Own Worcestershire Hussars (Yeomanry)

Armstrong, Lieutenant Colonel, *Some EEF Reminiscences, 1917–1918*
Bell, Major W., *War Diary*
Dabbs, Corporal A.G., *The Land of Promises*
Hampton, Major the Lord, *The Chronicle of a Yeomanry Squadron in Palestine*,
     Jordan and Syria
Holyoake, Lieutenant A.V., *My War*
Pritchard Collection (various correspondence with First World War veterans)

National Archives of Australia

AWM255/7 'Yilderim' Translation by Captain G.O. De R. Channer of
     Publication No. 1 of the Turkish General Staff by Lieutenant Colonel
     Hussein Husni Amir Bey

The National Archives

AIR 1/2031/204/326/26 Notes on the RFC/RAF in Egypt and
     Palestine, November 1915–September 1918
CAB 1/44 Documents collected for the information of the special mission
     appointed to enquire into the situation in Egypt, 1920
CAB 44/14 Relations between Great Britain, Italy and the Senussi, 1912–1924
CAB Various minutes and reports among the Cabinet papers, as referenced
FO 141/448/6 Senussi establishments and brethren in Tripolitania, an histori-
     cal account of the Senussi movement and biographical notes on the living
     members of the Senussi family, 1918–1928
FO 141/464/7 Arab Movement in Egypt, Pan-Islamic & -Arab propaganda,
     1915–1928
FO 141/468/1 Activities of Sayyid Mustafa Idrisi, intermediary between the
     British Residency at Aden and the Idrisi, 1915–1929
FO 141/469/2 Egyptians executed, deported, interned or imprisoned or
     invited to leave Egypt on political grounds, 1915–1917
FO 141/472/5 Senussi prisoners of war (British and Italian), 1915–1919
FO 141/473/2 Intelligence on the Turkish expedition against Egypt, 1915–1918
FO 141/484/1 The Political and Constitutional situation in Egypt, 1884–1927
FO 141/629/4 Ministerial and political situation in Egypt, 1914–1922
FO 141/651/1 Italian position in Cyrenaica and negotiations of the Anglo-
     Italian Mission for an agreement with Idris Senoussi, 1916–1917
FO 141/734/1 Correspondence on the development of British policy on Arab
     independence and resistance to Turkish domination during the First World
     War, 1915–1918

FO 141/735/2 Policy memoranda and intelligence reports on military operations against Turkey, 1914–1919

FO 141/736/1 Intelligence reports from the Arab Bureau on the Arab revolt against Turkish rule in Hedjaz and elsewhere, 1916–1917

FO 141/825/2 The conduct of British Troops and their relations with the indigenous population, 1915–1929

FO141/469 Egypt's involvement in the First World War

FO633/101 Report on the great invasion of locusts in Egypt in 1915

FO882/4 Garland's Report

FO882/6 Miscellaneous Correspondence

FO882/7 Miscellaneous Correspondence

WO 158/624 Arab Forces: Historical documents: Summary, 1914–1916

WO 158/625 Arab Forces: Supply of arms and ammunition etc to the Sherif of Mecca, 1916–1917

WO106/716 EEF: Report on Operations, March–July 1917

WO32/3116 Report of the Committee of the Lessons of the Great War

WO33/946/26 Telegrams, European War: Egypt

I have also extensively consulted the War Diaries available in AIR 1 and WO95, and the correspondence in WO158. These files are too many to list, and are easily found through the catalogue on TNA's website.

Published Sources

British Official Histories and Publications

Allenby, General Sir E.H.H. (1919) *A Brief Record of the Advance of the Egyptian Expeditionary Force*, HMSO. London

Badcock, Lieutenant Colonel G.E. (1925) *A History of the Transport Services of the Egyptian Expeditionary Force, 1916–1917–1918*, High Rees Limited. London

Butler, Colonel A.G. DSO (1930) *The Australian Army Medical Services in the War of 1914–1918*: Vol. 1, Australian War Memorial, Melbourne

Cutlack, F.M. (1923) *Official History of Australia in the War of 1914–1918: Vol. 8: The Australian Flying Corps*, Angus and Robertson Ltd, Sydney

Falls, Captain C. (1930) *Military Operations: Egypt and Palestine Vol. 2*, HMSO

General Staff (1916) *Handbook of the Turkish Army*, HMSO, London

Gullett, H.S. (1923) *Official History of Australia in the War of 1914–1918: Vol. 7: The AIF in Sinai and Palestine, 1914–1918*, Angus and Robertson Ltd, Sydney

Jones, Captain H.A. (1935) *The War in the Air Vol. 5*, Oxford University Press, Oxford

MacMunn, Lieutenant General Sir G. KCB KCSI DSO, & Captain C. Falls (1928) *Military Operations: Egypt and Palestine Vol. 1*, HMSO, London

Murray, General Sir A. (1920) *Sir Archibald Murray's Despatches*, HMSO, London

Divisional/Corps histories
Dalbiac, Colonel P.H. (1927) *History of the 60th Division (2/2nd London Division)*, George Allen & Unwin Ltd, London
Dudley Ward, Major C.H. DSO MC (1922) *The 74th (Yeomanry) Division in Syria and France*, John Murray, London
Dudley Ward, Major C.H. DSO MC (1927) *History of the 53rd (Welsh) Division (T.F) 1914–1918*, Western Mail Limited, Cardiff
Preston, Lieutenant Colonel The Hon. R.M.P. DSO (1921) *The Desert Mounted Corps: An Account of the Cavalry Operations in Palestine and Syria, 1917–1918*, Constable and Company Ltd, London
Thompson, Lieutenant Colonel R.R. (1923) *The Fifty-Second Lowland Division 1914–1918*, Maclehose, Jackson & Co., Glasgow

Regimental/Battalion/Squadron histories
Anon. (1921) *The Fifth Battalion Highland Light Infantry in the war, 1914–1918*, MacLehose, Jackson & Co., Glasgow
Baly, L. (2004) *Horseman, Pass By: The Australian Light Horse in World War I*, Spellmount, Staplehurst
Blick, Lt G. (1933) *The 1/4th Battalion The Wiltshire Regiment 1914–1919*, Batler and Tanner Limited, London
Bourne, Lieutenant Colonel G.H. (1926) *History of the 2nd Light Horse Regiment AIF*, Northern Daily Leader, Tamworth
Brownlie, Major W.S. (1964) *The Proud Trooper: The History of the Ayrshire (Earl of Carrick's Own) Yeomanry*, Wm. Collins, Sons & Co., London
Burrows, J.W. (1931) *The Essex Regiment: Essex Territorial Infantry Brigade (4th, 5th, 6th and 7th Battalions)*, Essex Territorial Army Association, Southend-on-Sea
'C' (1926) *The Yeomanry Cavalry of Worcestershire, 1914–1922*, Mark & Moody Ltd, Stourbridge
Clifford, R. (1991) *The Royal Gloucestershire Hussars*, Alan Sutton Publishing Co., Stroud
Dudley Ward, Major C.H. DSO MC (1921) *Regimental Records of the Royal Welch Fusiliers Vol. IV: Turkey – Bulgaria – Austria*, Foster Groom & Co. Ltd
Eames, Major F.W. (1930) *The Second Nineteenth: Being the History of the 2/19th London Regiment*, Waterlow and Sons Ltd, London
Elliot, Captain W.R. MC (1920) *The Second Twentieth: Being the History of the 2/20th Bn. London Regiment*, Gale & Polden Ltd, Aldershot
Ewing, Major J. MC (1925) The Royal Scots 1914–1919, Oliver and Boyd, Edinburgh
Fuller, Colonel J.F. DSO (1920) *Tanks in the Great War*, John Murray, London

Gibbons, Lieutenant Colonel T. DSO (1921) *With the 1/5th Essex in the East*, Benham and Company Limited, Colchester

Gillon, Captain S. (1930) *The KOSB in the Great War*, Thomas Nelson and Sons, Ltd, London

Hamilton, A.S. MM (1936) *The City of London Yeomanry (Roughriders)*, The Hamilton Press Ltd, London

Hounslow, E.J. (2013) *Fighting for the Bucks: The History of the Royal Bucks Hussars, 1914–1918*, The History Press, Stroud

Knight, J. (2005) *The Civil Service Rifles in the Great War: 'All Bloody Gentlemen'*, Pen and Sword Military, Barnsley

Lloyd, M. (2001) *The London Scottish in the Great War*, Leo Cooper, Barnsley

Mollo, B. (1969) *The Sharpshooters: 3rd County of London Yeomanry, 1900–1961, Kent and County of London Yeomanry, 1961–1970*, Historical Research Unit, London

Nicol, Sergeant C.G. (1921) *The Story of Two Campaigns: Official War History of the Auckland Mounted Rifles Regiment, 1914–1919*, Wilson & Horton, Auckland

Orange, Dr V. & Stapleton, AVM D.C. (1996) *Winged Promises: a History of No. 14 Squadron RAF, 1915–45*, RAF Benevolent Find Enterprises, Fairford

Powles, Colonel C.G. CMG DSO (ed.) (1928) *The History of the Canterbury Mounted Rifles, 1914–1919*, Whitcombe & Tombs Ltd, Auckland

Scott Elliot, Captain G.F. (1928) *War History of the 5th Battalion King's Own Scottish Borderers*, Robert Dinwiddle, Dumfries

Wilkie, Major A.J. (1924) *The Official War History of the Wellington Mounted Rifles Regiment 1914–1919*, Whitcombe and Tombs Limited, Auckland

Wilson, Brigadier General L.C. (1919) *Narrative of Operations of the Third Light Horse Brigade from 27 October 1917 to 11 July 1919*, L.C Wilson, Egypt

Wyrall, E. (1926) *The Die-Hards in the Great War: A History of the Duke of Cambridge's Own (Middlesex Regiment) 1914–1917*, Harrison & Sons, London

Wyrall, E. (1933) *The History of the Somerset Light Infantry (Prince Albert's) 1914–1919*, Methuen & Co. Ltd, London

Campaign histories

Anglesey, Marques (1994) *A History of the British Cavalry 1816–1919*, Vol. 5: Egypt, Palestine and Syria 1914 to 1919, Leo Cooper, London

Bruce, A. (2002) *The Last Crusade: The Palestine Campaign in the First World War*, John Murray Ltd, London

Daley, P. (2009) *Beersheba: A Journey Through Australia's Forgotten War*, Melbourne University Press

Erickson, Lieutenant Colonel E.J. (Retired) (2008) *Gallipoli & the Middle East, 1914–1918*, Amber Books Ltd, London

Ford, R. (2010) *Eden to Armageddon: World War I in the Middle East*, Phoenix, London

Grainger, J.D. (2006) *The Battle for Palestine 1917*, The Boydell Press, Woodbridge

Kearsey, Lieutenant Colonel A. (1931) *A Summary of the Strategy and Tactics of the Egypt and Palestine Campaigns, with Details of the 1917–1918 Operations Illustrating the Principles of War*, Gale & Polden, London

Sheffy, Y. (1998) *British Military Intelligence in the Palestine Campaign, 1914–1918*, Frank Cass, London

Wakefield, A. & Moody, S. (2004) *Under the Devil's Eye: Britain's Forgotten Army at Salonika, 1915–1918*, Sutton Publishing, Stroud

Wavell, Colonel A.P. (1928) *The Palestine Campaign*, Constable and Co. Ltd, London

Woodward, D.R. (2007) *Forgotten Soldiers of the First World War*, Tempus Publishing Ltd, Stroud

British Empire memoirs/biographies

Bluett, A. (2007) *A Gunner's Crusade*, Leonaur Ltd, Driffield

Bostock, H.P. (1982) *The Great Ride*, Artlook Books, Perth

Clunie, K. & Austin, R. (ed.) (2009) *From Gallipoli to Palestine: The War Writings of Sergeant G. T. Clunie of the Wellington Mounted Rifles, 1914–1919*, Slouch Hat Publications, McCrae, Australia

Conner, J. (2011) *ANZAC and Empire: George Foster Pearce and the Foundations of Australian Defence*, Cambridge University Press

Fowler, J.E. (1979) *Looking Backward*, Roebuck Society Publications, Canberra

Gardner, B. (1965) *Allenby*, Cassell & Company Ltd, London

Garfield, B. (2007) *The Meinertzhagen Mystery: The Life and Legend of a Colossal Fraud*, Potomac Books Inc., Washington D.C.

Godrich, V. (2011) *Mountains of Moab: The Diary of a Cavalryman with the Queen's Own Worcestershire Hussars, 1908–1919*, The Genge Press, Minehead

Hamilton, P.M. OBE (1995) *Riders of Destiny: The 4th Australian Light Horse Field Ambulance 1917–18*, Mostly Unsung Military History, Gardenvale

Hatton, S.F. (1930) *The Yarn of a Yeoman*, Naval & Military Press Ltd, Uckfield

Hogue, O. (2008) *The Cameliers*, Leonaur Ltd

Hughes, M. (ed.) (2004) *Allenby in Palestine: The Middle East Correspondence of Field Marshal Viscount Allenby, June 1917–October 1919*, Army Records Society, Sutton Publishing Limited, Stroud

Hynes, J.P. (2010) *Lawrence of Arabia's Secret Air Force*, Pen & Sword Aviation, Barnsley

Inchbald, G. (2005) *With the Imperial Camel Corps in the Great War*, Leonaur, Driffield

Livermore, B. (1974) *Long 'Un: A Damn Bad Soldier*, Harry Hayes, West Yorkshire

Mackie, J.H.F. (ed.) (2002) *Answering the Call: Letters from the Somerset Light Infantry, 1914–1919*, Raby Books, Eggleston

Meinertzhagen, Colonel R. CBE DSO (1960) *Army Diary*, Oliver & Boyd, Edinburgh

Moore, Lieutenant A.B. (1920) *The Mounted Rifleman in Sinai and Palestine*, Whitcombe & Tombs Ltd, Auckland

Robertson, J. (1938) *With the Cameliers in Palestine*, Reed Publishing, Dunedin

Rolls, S.C. (2005) *Steel Chariots in the Desert*, Leonaur Ltd, Driffield

Seward, D. (2009) *Wings Over the Desert: In Action with an RFC pilot in Palestine, 1916–18*, Haynes Publishing, Yeovil

Slater, G. (ed.) (1973) *My Warrior Sons: The Borton Family Diary, 1914–1918*, Peter Davies, London

Sutherland, L.W. (1936) *Aces and Kings*, John Hamilton, London

Teichman, Captain O. DSO MC (1921) *The Diary of a Yeomanry M.O.T.*, Fisher Unwin Ltd, London

Wilson, R. (1987) *Palestine 1917*, D.J. Costello (Publishers) Ltd, Tunbridge Wells

Egypt

Ahmed, M. (ed.) (2003) *Egypt in the 20th Century*, MegaZette Press, Middlesex

Elgood, Lieutenant Colonel P.G. CMG (1924) *Egypt and the Army*, Oxford University Press, Oxford

McGuirk, R. (2007) *The Sanusi's Little War*, Arabian Publishing, London

Richmond, J.C.B. (1977) *Egypt 1798–1952*, Methuen & Co. Ltd, London

Storrs, R. (1943) *Orientations*, Nicholson & Watson, London

Vatikiotis, P.J. (1991) *The History of Modern Egypt*, Weidenfeld & Nicolson, London

Arab Revolt

Asher, M. (1999) *Lawrence: The Uncrowned King of Arabia*, Penguin Books Ltd, London

Barr, J. (2006) *Setting the Desert on Fire: T.E. Lawrence and Britain's Secret War in Arabia, 1916–1918*, Bloomsbury, London

Barr, J. (2011) *A Line in the Sand: Britain, France and the Struggle that Shaped the Middle East*, Simon & Schuster UK Ltd, London

Knightly, P. & Simpson, C. (1969) *The Secret Lives of Lawrence of Arabia*, Thomas Nelson & Sons Ltd, London

Lawrence, T.E. (1979) *Seven Pillars of Wisdom*, Penguin Books Ltd, London

Ottoman memoirs

Aaronsohn, A. (1916) *With the Turks in Palestine*, Atlantic Monthly

Al-Askari, J. (2003) *A Soldier's Story: From Ottoman Rule to Independent Iraq*, Arabian Publishing, London

Djemal Pasha (1922) *Memories of a Turkish Statesman: 1913–1919*, Hutchinson & Co., London

Nogales General R.D. (1926) *Four Years Beneath the Crescent*, Charles Schribner's Sons, London

Nogales, General R.D. (1932) *Memoirs of a Soldier of Fortune*, Wright & Brown, London

Sanders, General L. von (1928) *Five Years in Turkey*, US Naval Institute, Annapolis

S. Tamari & I. Nassar (eds) (2014) *The Storyteller of Jerusalem: The Life and Times of Wasif Jawhariyyeh, 1904–1948*, Olive Branch Press, Massachusetts

Tamari, S. (2011) *Year of the Locust: A Soldier's Diary and the Erasure of Palestine's Ottoman Past*, University of California Press, Berkeley

Ottoman Army/Empire

Erickson, Lieutenant Colonel E.J. (Retired) (2001) *Ordered to Die: A History of the Ottoman Army in the First World War*, Greenwood Press, London

Erickson, Lieutenant Colonel E.J. (Retired) (2007) *Ottoman Army Effectiveness in World War I: A Comparative Study*, Routledge, Abingdon

Finkel, C. (2005) *Osman's Dream: The Story of the Ottoman Empire 1300–1923*, John Murray, London

McMeekin, S. (2011) *The Berlin–Baghdad Express: The Ottoman Empire and Germany's Bid for World Power, 1898–1918*, Penguin Books, London

Palestine and Syria

Gilbert, M. (2008) *Israel: A History*, Black Swan, London

Kedar, B.Z. (1999) *The Changing Land Between the Jordan and the Sea: Aerial Photographs from 1917 to the Present*, Yad Izhak Ben-Zvo Press & Ministry of Defence, Israel

Montifiore, S.S. (2011) *Jerusalem: The Biography*, Phoenix, London

Rose, R. (2009) *'A Senseless Squalid War': Voices from Palestine 1890s–1948*, Pimlico, London

General

Bowyer, C. (2002) *For Valour: The Air VCs*, The Caxton Publishing Group, London

Gliddon, G. (2005) *VCs of the First World War: The Sideshows*, Sutton Publishing, Stroud

Hooton, E.R. (2010) *War Over the Trenches*, Midland Publishing, Surrey

Horner, D.M. (ed.) (1984) *The Commanders: Australian Military Leadership in the Twentieth Century*, Allen & Unwin Pty. Ltd, Sydney

Mason, P. (1974) *A matter of Honour: An Account of the Indian Army, its Officers and Men*, Jonathon Cape Ltd, London

Articles & papers

Askakal, M. '"Holy War made in Germany"? Ottoman origins of the 1914 Jihad' in *War in History*, No. 18 Vol. 2 2011

Fahmy, Z. 'Media Capitalism: Colloquial Mass Culture and Nationalism in Egypt 1908–1918' in *International Journal of Middle East Studies*, Vol. 42 No. 1 2010

Flanagan, Dr B P. (ed.) 'The History of the Ottoman Air Force in the Great War' in *Cross and Cockade Journal*, Vol. 11 No. 2 Summer 1970, Vol. 11 No. 3 Autumn 1970, Vol. 11 No. 4 Winter 1970 & Vol. 13 No. 2 Summer 1972

Gröschel, D.H.M. & Ladek, J. 'Wings over Sinai and Palestine: The adventures of Flieger Abteilung 300 "Pascha" in the fight against the Egyptian Expeditionary Corps, from April 1916 until the Third Battle of Gaza in November 1917' in *Over the Front*, Vol. 13 No. 1 Spring 1998

Kitchen, J.E. '"Khaki Crusaders": Crusading rhetoric and the British Imperial soldier during the Egypt and Palestine campaigns, 1916–1918' in *First World War Studies*, Vol. 1 No. 2 2010

Kress von Kressenstein, Colonel Baron 'The campaign in Palestine from the enemy's side' in *Journal of the Royal United Services Institution*, Vol. 62 1922

Sheffy, Y. 'Origins of the British breakthrough into south Palestine: The ANZAC raid on the Ottoman railway 1917' in *Journal of Strategic Studies*, Vol. 22 No. 1 2008

Sheffy, Y. 'British intelligence and the Middle East, 1900–1918: How much do we know?' in *Intelligence and National Security*, Vol. 17 No. 1 2002

Sheffy, Y. 'The spy who never was: An intelligence myth in Palestine, 1914–1918' in *Intelligence and National Security*, No. 14 Vol. 3 1999

Sheffy, Y. 'Chemical Warfare and the Palestine Campaign, 1916–1918' in *The Journal of Military History*, Vol. 73 No. 3 2009

Uyar, M. 'Ottoman Arab Officers between Nationalism and Loyalty during the First World War' in *War in History*, No. 20 Vol. 4 2013

Varnava, A. 'British Military Intelligence in Cyprus during the Great War' in *War in History*, No. 19 Vol. 3 2012

Websites

There are regrettably few websites dedicated to the campaigns in Egypt and Palestine during the First World War. However, I can recommend the excellent and comprehensive Australian Light Horse Studies Centre (alh-research. tripod.com), and the Australian War Memorial. The latter includes online PDF copies of the Australian Official Histories.

There are many general First World War forums that include areas on Egypt and Palestine, such as: Desert Column (desert-column.phpbb3now. com), for all Australian military 1899–1920; The Great War Forum (1914–1918.invasionzone.com); and New Zealand Mounted Rifles Forum (www. nzmr.org).

END NOTES

Prologue

1   Dalbiac p. 166
2   Tamari & Nassar (eds) p. 103
3   Tamari & Nassar (eds) p. 199
4   Slater p. 110
5   For Robertson's suggestion see: WO33/946/26, and for Allenby's expla-
    nation see his letter to his wife of 14 December 1917 quoted in Hughes
6   Falls Vol. 2 p. 261
7   A fascinating discussion of this area can be found in Kitchen, 'Khaki
    Crusaders'
8   Edgerton IWM 7818

1. To the Borders of Palestine, 1882–1916

9   Elgood p. 47
10 Clunie p. 112
11 5th HLI p. 129
12 5th HLI p. 126
13 Godrich p. 88
14 5th HLI p. 136
15 5th HLI p. 132
16 Dawnay IWM 10403 Letter to wife, 8 March 1917
17 Dawnay IWM 10403 Letter to wife, 10 March 1917

2. First Battle of Gaza: Opening Moves

18   Murray to Robertson 10 December 1916. Murray called Palestine by the technically correct name of 'southern Syria'. Reproduced in MacMunn & Falls Vol. 1 p. 259
19   See correspondence in MacMunn & Falls Vol. 1 pp. 258–61
20   MacMunn & Falls Vol. 1 pp. 272–3
21   Dudley Ward *74th Yeomanry Division*
22   Conner p. 104
23   MacMunn & Falls Vol. 1 p. 279
24   Nogales *Four Years* p. 255
25   MacMunn & Falls Vol. 1 pp. 276–7
26   Bowyer pp. 84–8
27   MacMunn & Falls Vol. 1 p. 287
28   Sheffy *British Military Intelligence* pp. 208–14; Dawnay IWM 10403 Letter to wife, 8 March 1917
29   Anglesey p. 93
30   53rd Division Report
31   MacMunn & Falls Vol. 1 p. 287
32   MacMunn & Falls Vol. 1 p. 284
33   Dudley Ward *53rd Division* p. 77
34   Dudley Ward *53rd Division* pp. 77–9
35   Desert Column Report, WO95/4471
36   Desert Column Report, WO95/4471
37   Dudley Ward *53rd Division*, pp. 83–5
38   Livingstone IWM 13560
39   A reference to 'The Battle of Lungtungpen', in which British troops strip naked to cross a river and attack the enemy. 'C' QOWH p. 88
40   Eastern Force Report
41   MacMunn & Falls Vol. 1 pp. 295–6.
42   War Diary of 1/5th RWF, quoted in Dudley *RWF* p. 126
43   MacMunn & Falls Vol. 1 pp. 295–6
44   Dudley Ward *53rd Division* pp. 88–9
45   Nogales *Four Years* pp. 246–7
46   MacMunn & Falls Vol. 1 p. 321
47   'C' p. 89
48   MacMunn & Falls Vol. 1 p. 278

3. First Battle of Gaza: Disaster

49   MacMunn & Falls Vol. 1 p. 300; Gullett Vol. VII p. 300
50   Gullett Vol. VII p. 280
51   Quoted in Anglesey p. 98

52   Clunie p. 136
53   MacMunn & Falls Vol. 1 p. 300
54   MacMunn & Falls Vol. 1 p. 307
55   MacMunn & Falls Vol. 1 p. 307
56   MacMunn & Falls Vol. 1 p. 308; Gullett Vol. VII p. 284
57   MacMunn & Falls Vol. 1 p. 308
58   MacMunn & Falls Vol. 1 p. 307
59   Desert Column Report
60   MacMunn & Falls Vol. 1 p. 309
61   MacMunn & Falls Vol. 1 p. 311
62   MacMunn & Falls Vol. 1 p. 310
63   Sheffy *British Military Intelligence* p. 231
64   MacMunn & Falls Vol. 1 p. 310
65   Dudley Ward *53rd Division* p. 94; 53rd Division Report
66   MacMunn & Falls Vol. 1 p. 311
67   MacMunn & Falls Vol. 1 pp. 312–13; Dudley *53rd Division* p. 95
68   MacMunn & Falls Vol. 1 p. 313
69   Dudley Ward 53*rd Division* p. 95
70   53rd Division Report
71   MacMunn & Falls Vol. 1 pp. 315 & 321
72   MacMunn & Falls Vol. 1 p. 289
73   MacMunn & Falls Vol. 1 p. 294
74   TNA WO32/3116 Report of the Committee of the Lessons of the Great
     War, App. IV p. 64

4. *Second Battle of Gaza*

75   Text reproduced in MacMunn & Falls Vol. 1 p. 322
76   TNA CAB23/40/5
77   TNA CAB23/2/28; Text of signals reproduced in MacMunn & Falls Vol.
     1 p. 322
78   MacMunn & Falls Vol. 1 p. 328
79   MacMunn & Falls Vol. 1 p. 335
80   Murray's Despatch of 28 June 1917, paragraph 9
81   MacMunn & Falls Vol. 1 p. 329, and Eastern Force Order No. 40 on pp.
     421–4
82   Dawnay IWM 10403 Eastern Force General Instructions – Artillery,
     9 April 1917, in folder 'Palestine 1917'
83   Chetwode IWM 10414 Letter to Dawnay 6 February 1917
84   Dawnay IWM 10403 Eastern Force General Instructions 12 April 1917, in
     folder 'Palestine 1917'
85   Dawnay IWM 10403 Eastern Force General Instructions 14 April 1917, in
     folder 'Palestine 1917'

86   Gröschel & Ladek, 'Wings over Sinai and Palestine'
87   TNA CAB24/9/78
88   Hooton pp. 129, 131 & 140
89   Jones Vol. 5 pp. 209–216; Gröschel & Ladek, 'Wings over Sinai and Palestine'
90   Sheffy, 'Chemical Warfare and the Palestine Campaign, 1916–1918'
91   Fuller Chapter 11
92   Dawnay IWM 10403 Special Instructions – Tanks, in folder 'Palestine 1917'
93   Dawnay IWM 10403 Eastern Force Instructions 4 & 10 April 1917, in folder 'Palestine 1917'
94   MacMunn & Falls Vol. 1 p. 349
95   Nogales *Four Years* p. 277
96   5th HLI pp. 146–7
97   MacMunn & Falls Vol. 1 p. 333; Fuller p. 100
98   'C' p. 96
99   Sheffy *British Military Intelligence* pp. 232–3
100 Gröschel & Ladek 'Wings over Sinai and Palestine'
101 Wavell p. 88
102 Sheffy 'Chemical Warfare and the Palestine Campaign, 1916–1918'
103 Bailey IWM 85/4/1
104 Minshall IWM 2792
105 MacMunn & Falls Vol. 1 pp. 336–7
106 MacMunn & Falls Vol. 1 p. 343; Fuller p. 101; Dudley Ward *53rd Division* pp. 106–8
107 MacMunn & Falls Vol. 1 pp. 340-341; Gillon pp. 265–6
108 Wollaston IWM 12702
109 MacMunn & Falls Vol. 1 p. 338
110 MacMunn & Falls Vol. 1 pp. 340–1
111 MacMunn & Falls Vol. 1 pp. 344–5
112 Nogales *Four Years* p. 281
113 Nogales *Four Years* p. 282
114 MacMunn & Falls Vol. 1 pp. 345–6
115 Sheffy *British Military Intelligence* pp. 233–4
116 Murray's Despatch of 28 June 1917, paragraph 11
117 MacMunn & Falls Vol. 1 pp. 347–8
118 MacMunn & Falls Vol. 1 pp. 348 & 350; Dudley Ward *53rd Division* p. 108
119 TNA CAB45/78/D Dawnay to Director, Historical Section, 4 December 1924

5. Ottoman Palestine

120 Rose p. 7
121 Gilbert p. 30
122 Gilbert p. 28
123 Tamari pp. 86–7 Note: the reference 'Tamari' denotes information from the editor, 'Tamari/Turjman' denotes information from the diary.
124 Djemal Pasha p. 191 & p. 201
125 Montefiore p. 396
126 Montefiore p. 397
127 Tamari pp. 10–11 & pp. 58–9
128 Tamari/Turjman p. 94
129 Tamari/Turjman pp. 130–1
130 Montefiore p. 397
131 Gilbert pp. 30–3
132 Montefiore pp. 398–400, p. 416
133 Nogales *Four Years* p. 312
134 Tamari/Turjman p. 97
135 Quoted in Tamari p. 45
136 Uyar *Ottoman Arab Officers*
137 Tamari/Turjman p. 133
138 Sheffy *British Intelligence* p. 77, pp. 82–3, pp. 160–7
139 Djemal Pasha p. 202
140 Tamari & Nassar (eds) p. 93
141 Tamari/Turjman pp. 92–3
142 Aaronsohn Chapter 4
143 Tamari/Turjman p. 94
144 Tamari/Turjman p. 95
145 Tamari/Turjman pp. 154–5
146 Tamari/Turjman p. 141
147 Tamari/Turjman p. 142
148 Aaronsohn Chapter 7
149 Tamari/Turjman pp. 93–4
150 TNA FO633/101
151 Aaronsohn Chapter 7
152 Tamari/Turjman p. 103
153 Tamari/Turjman p. 107
154 Tamari/Turjman pp. 102–3
155 Tamari/Turjman p. 108 & p. 118
156 Tamari/Turjman p. 114
157 Tamari/Turjman pp. 109–10
158 Tamari/Turjman pp. 111–12
159 Totah and Barghouti *The History of Palestine* (1920) pp. 253–4, quoted in Tamari pp. 10–11

6. Egypt 1917

160 Richmond p. 172
161 Vatikiotis pp. 254–5
162 Elgood p. 300
163 Vatikiotis p. 255
164 Elgood pp. 320–1
165 Richmond p. 174; Vatikiotis p. 255
166 Elgood p. 324
167 See Woodward, pp. 52–63, for a very good summation of the uses and treatment of the CTC
168 Murray's Despatch of 28 June 1917, Appendix F
169 Fahmy 'Media Capitalism: Colloquial mass culture and nationalism in Egypt 1908–1918'
170 TNA FO141/469
171 Inchbald p. 73
172 MacMunn & Falls Vol. 1 p. 142
173 McGuirk p. 264
174 Rolls p. 110
175 Rolls p. 112 & p. 115
176 Rolls pp. 116–17
177 Rolls p. 118
178 MacMunn & Falls Vol. 1 pp. 143–4; McGuirk pp. 264–71
179 MacMunn & Falls Vol. 1 pp. 141–4

7. Arab Revolt

180 TNA FO882/4 Garland's Report
181 Barr *Desert* pp. 68–70
182 Falls Vol. 2 p. 398
183 Barr *Desert* pp. 95–6
184 Barr *Desert* p. 107
185 Lawrence *Seven Pillars*, Chapter 34 (There are so many different editions of *Seven Pillars* that chapters are given rather than page numbers, to aid finding the quote in any copy.)
186 Barr *Desert* p. 106
187 Barr *Desert* pp. 226–7
188 TNA FO882/6
189 Lawrence *Seven Pillars*, Chapter 42
190 Lawrence *Seven Pillars*, Chapter 43
191 Lawrence *Seven Pillars*, Chapter 43
192 Some have questioned whether this patrol ever took place. See Asher p. 246

193   Falls Vol. 2 p. 398
194   Barr *Desert* pp. 144–5
195   TNA FO882/7
196   Ja'far al-Askari, p. 130
197   Rolls pp. 141–2
198   Rolls pp. 130–1
199   Ja'far al-Askari, pp. 255–6
200   Falls Vol. 2 pp. 397–8
201   Barr *Desert* p. 154

8. Trench Warfare

202   Hatton p. 141
203   MacMunn and Falls Vol. 1 p. 361
204   Bostock pp. 80–1
205   Sheffy 'Origins of the British breakthrough'
206   Chetwode IWM 10414
207   MacMunn & Falls Vol. 1 p. 363
208   Robertson pp. 98–103
209   Sheffy 'Origins of the British breakthrough'
210   Nogales *Four Years* pp. 291–2
211   Dawnay IWM 10403 'Battle of Philistia' file
212   Thompson p. 340
213   Thompson p. 337
214   Gillon pp. 267–8; Thompson pp. 342–5; Scott Elliot pp. 148–152;
       Divisional, Brigade, battalion, battery and MG company reports in TNA
       WO95/4608, WO95/4607, and WO95/4597
215   Minshall IWM 2792 25 April 1917
216   Mackie p. 293
217   Godrich p. 108
218   Godrich p. 108
219   MacMunn & Falls Vol. 1 pp. 355–8
220   TNA WO95/4368, EEF War Diary September 1917
221   Quoted in Lloyd p. 194
222   MacMunn & Falls Vol. 1 pp. 358–62
223   TNA WO106/716 Lynden-Bell to Maurice 26 May 1917

9. Allenby

224   TNA CAB24/11/33
225   TNA CAB23/44B/1 and CAB23/13/24
226   TNA CAB23/2/42 and CAB23/2/44
227   TNA CAB23/2/52 and CAB23/13/4
228   TNA CAB23/3/2

229 Armstrong p. 219
230 Badcock *Transport Services* p. 316
231 Inchbald pp. 140–1
232 Inchbald pp. 140–1
233 Godrich p. 107
234 Bluett pp. 152–3
235 Livermore p. 89
236 TNA WO158/611
237 TNA WO158/611
238 Sutherland pp. 160–1
239 Jones Vol. V p. 230
240 Jones Vol. V pp. 231–3
241 See TNA CAB23/2/41
242 Jones Vol. V p. 227 & p. 231
243 Jones Vol. V p. 227
244 Jones Vol. V p. 229
245 TNA WO106/716 Lynden-Bell to Maurice 26 May 1917

10. Plans

246 Erickson *Ottoman Army Efficiency* p. 105
247 Erickson *Ordered to Die* p. 169
248 Erickson *Ordered to Die* p. 169
249 Flanagan 'The Reports of Major Serno Part 3'
250 Von Sanders pp. 175–9
251 Djemal pp. 185–9
252 Erickson *Ottoman Army Efficiency* p. 107
253 Von Sanders p. 184
254 Flanagan 'The Reports of Major Serno Part 3'
255 Djemal pp. 189–92
256 Erickson *Ordered to Die* p. 171; Djemal pp. 192–3
257 Erickson *Ottoman Army Efficiency* p. 115
258 Erickson *Ottoman Army Efficiency* pp. 103–4
259 Erickson *Ottoman Army Efficiency* p. 117
260 Erickson *Ottoman Army Efficiency* pp. 115–17; Erickson *Ordered to Die* pp. 171–2
261 Falls Vol. 2 p. 35
262 TNA WO158/611/65
263 Falls Vol. 2 p. 35
264 TNA WO95/4368 EEF War Diary September 1917 Enc. 8
265 TNA WO95/4368 EEF War Diary September 1917 Enc. 58
266 TNA WO95/4368 EEF War Diary September 1917 Enc. 84
267 TNA WO95/4368 EEF War Diary September 1917 Enc. 1

268 TNA WO95/4368 EEF War Diary September 1917 Enc. 1
269 TNA WO106/725
270 See: Garfield *The Meinertzhagen Mystery*, for a full and fascinating discussion of this 'ruse'
271 Husnu p. 100
272 Dalbiac p. 117
273 Falls Vol. 2 pp. 20–2
274 QOWH(Y)M Hampton p. 4

11. Beersheba

275 Dalbiac p. 118; Falls Vol. 2 p. 47
276 Dalbiac p. 118
277 Allenby p. 98
278 Falls Vol. 2 pp. 20–2
279 Hüsnü p. 102
280 Gliddon pp. 145–9; Falls Vol. 2 pp. 38–9
281 Hüsnü p. 102
282 Quoted in Kedar p. 49
283 Hüsnü p. 106
284 Hüsnü p. 113
285 Hennessey IWM 12705
286 Quoted in Dudley Ward *RWF* p. 151
287 Hennessey IWM 12705
288 Gough IWM 13595
289 Borton p. 130
290 Dalbiac p. 120; Falls Vol. 2 p. 48
291 Hendry IWM 6873
292 Gliddon pp. 150–3
293 Dalbiac pp. 120–2; Falls Vol. 2 pp. 48–50
294 Moore p. 83
295 Falls Vol. 2 pp. 54–5 & 82–3
296 Nicol Chapter 25
297 Moore p. 87
298 WO95/4472 Operations of A&NZ Mounted Division 21 October – 7 December 1917
299 Wavell p. 123
300 Doherty AWM PR01376
301 Fowler pp. 21–7
302 Hüsnü p. 112
303 Falls Vol. 2 pp. 58–9
304 Hüsnü p. 112

305 WO95/4472 Operations of Desert Mounted Corps 22 October –
18 November 1917
306 Hamilton pp. 67–8
307 Dalbiac p. 122

12. *Breakthrough*

308 Falls Vol. 2 pp. 64–5
309 Unidentified sailor, IWM 10448
310 Falls Vol. 2 pp. 65 & 77; Hüsnü Part 3 Chapter II
311 Falls Vol. 2 p. 68
312 Sgt W.M. Town IWM 15018 (all quotations by Town from this source)
313 Allenby's Despatch
314 For Ottoman intentions, see Dudley Ward *53rd Division* p. 126, for a
conversation a divisional staff officer had with Kress von Kressenstein in
1920
315 Hüsnü pp. 143–4
316 Wavell p. 106
317 Dudley Ward *53rd Division* p. 128
318 Dudley Ward *53rd Division* p. 136
319 Verner IWM 12581
320 Dalbiac pp. 126–7
321 Verner IWM 12581
322 Hüsnü pp. 150–1
323 Borton pp. 136–7
324 Hendry IWM 6873
325 Gough IWM 13595
326 Verner IWM 12581
327 Falls Vol. 2 pp. 108–9
328 Falls Vol. 2 p. 75
329 Milson IWM 5826
330 Hüsnü p. 182
331 Hüsnü pp. 155 & 167

13. *Pursuit*

332 Wavell pp. 142–5
333 Thompson Chapter 21
334 Dalbiac pp. 132–3
335 Falls Vol. 2 pp. 117–124
336 Crombie QOWH(Y)M (Pritchard Collection)
337 Teichman p. 184
338 Mercer quoted in Falls Vol. 2 p. 123

339 Haydon QOWH(Y)M (Pritchard Collection)
340 Gibbons p. 105
341 Elliot p. 123
342 Scott IWM 5743
343 Allenby p. 104; Dalbiac pp. 136–40
344 Allenby p. 96
345 Allenby p. 101
346 Allenby pp. 101 & 102
347 Thompson pp. 401–2
348 Dudley Ward *74th Division* p. 106
349 Dalbiac pp. 130–1
350 Preston p. 97
351 Ewing p. 524
352 Thompson pp. 406–8; Ewing pp. 522–5
353 Teichman gives an excellent description of this in his diary for
     11 November 1917
354 Falls Vol. 2 pp. 146–54 & 174
355 Falls Vol. 2 pp. 156–8
356 Falls Vol. 2 pp. 158–62
357 Quoted in Hounslow p. 119
358 Thompson p. 420; Gillon pp. 274–7
359 Falls Vol. 2 p. 170
360 Falls Vol. 2 pp. 170–1
361 Falls Vol. 2 pp. 162–3
362 Falls Vol. 2 pp. 162–3

14. Into the Judean Mountains

363 See for example Robertson's messages on 13 and 16 November 1917,
     quoted in Hughes, pp. 84 & 85–7
364 Hüsnü p. 179
365 Preston p. 104
366 Mackie pp. 305–6
367 Gibbons p. 108
368 Wavell pp. 158–9
369 Hatton pp. 174–5
370 Gibbons p. 107
371 5th HLI p. 177
372 Falls Vol. 2 pp. 194–6; Wavell pp. 160–1
373 QOWH(Y)M Hampton
374 Hatton pp. 185–7
375 Falls Vol. 2 p. 198
376 Falls Vol. 2 pp. 202–4; Thompson pp. 441–4

377 Falls Vol. 2 pp. 205–6
378 Falls Vol. 2 pp. 208–11
379 Falls Vol. 2 pp. 213–16; Wilkie Chapter 22; Nicol Chapter 27; Powles & Wilkie Chapter 6
380 Preston p. 112
381 Falls Vol. 2 pp. 220–5; Preston pp. 112–14
382 Thompson p. 471
383 Falls Vol. 2 pp. 221 & 234–6; Gliddon pp. 165–7; Thompson pp. 458–74
384 Falls Vol. 2 pp. 321–34; Dudley Ward *RWF* pp. 162–4
385 Quoted in Kedar p. 110
386 Lieutenant Colonel A.C. Temperley quoted in Elliot p. 130
387 Lieutenant Colonel A.C. Temperley quoted in Elliot p. 132
388 Dalbiac pp. 149-51; Eames pp. 87–92
389 Falls Vol. 2 pp. 228 & 235–6

15. Jerusalem

390 TNA WO95/4472 Report of Operations of two cars of No. 7 Light Car Patrol under the command of Lieutenant McKenzie on 30 November and 1 & 2 December
391 Millis IWM 1292
392 Dudley Ward *53rd Division* pp. 141–51
393 See, for example, 5th HLI p. 186
394 Falls Vol. 2 pp. 244–5; Dalbiac pp. 156–8
395 Gliddon pp. 170–6; Dalbiac p. 157
396 Falls Vol. 2 p. 247; Dalbiac pp. 158–60
397 Falls Vol. 2 p. 248; Dudley Ward *74th Division* pp. 130–2
398 Falls Vol. 2 p. 250; Dudley Ward *53rd Division* p. 157
399 Falls Vol. 2 pp. 243–4
400 TNA WO95/4663
401 Quoted in Kedar p. 140
402 Falls Vol. 2 pp. 256–8; Dalbiac pp. 161–2; Dudley Ward *74th Division* pp. 134–6
403 Falls Vol. 2 pp. 258–9
404 Clunie p. 176
405 Gliddon pp. 177–80
406 Falls Vol. 2 pp 265–9; Thompson pp. 482–500
407 5th HLI p. 194
408 Clunie p. 178
409 Scott IWM 5743
410 Gibbons pp. 119–20
411 Quoted in Knight p. 194
412 Sheffy *British Military Intelligence* pp. 242–3

413 Falls Vol. 2 pp. 277–8 & 291; Dalbiac p. 186
414 Quoted in Knight p. 195
415 Mole IWM 15153
416 Gliddon pp. 181–5
417 Falls Vol. 2 pp. 279–89; Dalbiac pp. 182–8; Dudley Ward *53rd Division* pp. 141–51
418 Dalbiac p. 180

Epilogue

419 Lawrence *Seven Pillars* Chapter 77
420 Lawrence *Seven Pillars* Chapters 73–81; Barr *Desert* pp. 183–200; Asher pp. 273–98

INDEX